Contemporary Literary Theory

A CHRISTIAN APPRAISAL

Edited by

Clarence Walhout *and* Leland Ryken

WILLIAM B. EERDMANS PUBLISHING COMPANY
GRAND RAPIDS, MICHIGAN

Copyright © 1991 by Wm. B. Eerdmans Publishing Co.
255 Jefferson Ave. S.E., Grand Rapids, Mich. 49503

Printed in the United States of America

Library of Congress Cataloging-in-Publication Data

Contemporary literary theory: a Christian appraisal / edited by
  Clarence Walhout and Leland Ryken.
      p.   cm.
  Includes bibliographical references.
  ISBN 0-8028-0479-9 (paper)
  1. Criticism. 2. Christianity and literature. I. Walhout, Clarence,
1934-   . II. Ryken, Leland.
  PN98.R44C66 1991
  801'.95'09045 — dc2091-36869
CIP

Susan Van Zanten Gallagher's essay, "Feminist Literary Criticism: A
Chorus of Ethical Voices," originally appeared in a slightly different form
under the title "Feminist Literary Criticism: An Ethical Approach to
Literature" in *Christian Scholar's Review*, 17 Mar. 1988, pp. 254-271.

CONTENTS

INTRODUCTION

Clarence Walhout

Among the many voices that have been clamoring for the attention of literary theorists and teachers during the last several decades, one of the weakest, or most ignored, has been that of Christianity. If a person were to look for evidence that ours is a post-Christian age, he or she might well turn to the field of literary theory. The sparsity of persuasive Christian theory, however, does not indicate a lack of Christian teachers and critics. Church-related colleges in the United States are still numerous, and many are staffed by professors who are committed to Christian beliefs. Many of these professors would welcome a Christian approach to literary study rather than a Freudian or Marxist or poststructuralist or purely formalist approach. Yet there is nothing that can be called "Christian literary theory" to stand on equal terms with these others. Christian professors are for the most part eclectic and imitative, skimming off what they can from their secular colleagues and deploring whatever seems to be hostile to their religious beliefs.

Why is there such a dearth of Christian theorizing in the field of literary study? Three reasons seem to predominate. First, Christians as well as non-Christians often perceive Christianity as a matter of private religious belief that is distinct from the public matters of learning and research within academic disciplines. Second, the view that Christianity is anachronistic and that Christian scholars are out of step with the modern world has intimidated Christians into silence and isolationism. And third, Christians often view religious experience as narrowly religious rather than broadly cultural; that is, they conceive of religion as a kind of experience that exists alongside of but separate from other kinds of experience, such as political or economic or aesthetic experience. They see religion as important in both its private and its public manifestations but as separate from and even injurious to one's participation in other cultural activities.

Whatever the reasons, there seems to be little reason to look to Christianity for an entree into the contemporary arena of literary theorizing. Too often Christians seem content to dismiss some movements in literary theory as inherently misguided because of their secular assumptions and to view other movements as religiously neutral and therefore as compatible with Christian belief.

Neither of these practices, however, is acceptable. To ignore or dismiss secular theories because they are alien to Christian belief is historically simplistic. Whether Christian or non-Christian, ideas and theories and intellectual traditions are never *sui generis*. They always grow out of the historical interaction of a multiplicity of conflicting or counterbalancing claims. The effort to separate Christianity from the mainstream of intellectual and cultural movements is not only futile; it is self-destructive. On the other hand, to regard theories as religiously neutral and available for eclectic appropriation is also unjustified. No theory of any significant comprehensiveness comes without philosophical assumptions or presuppositions. The presuppositions which lie behind comprehensive theories are of no little import for anyone assessing the theory. Whatever is of value in any particular theory needs to be rethought and reshaped if it is to be employed in the context of different presuppositions. Comprehensive theories are not philosophically or religiously neutral.

It is a necessary if imposing task, therefore, for philosophically serious Christians to assess and rethink the principles and implications of the secular theories they confront. The resources for such rethinking are present in our society. What has been lacking is the recognition that Christians must participate fully and actively and self-consciously in the debates over literary theory that have been going on for a quarter of a century and will, no doubt, go on until some temporary consensus is achieved. Christianity is likely to have no significant influence on these debates if they go on as they have been going on in our day. Christians seem to function at best as cheerleaders for certain teams and at worst as disappointed spectators demoralized by the victories of their rivals. But cheerleaders and spectators have little effect on the real outcome of the games. What is needed is a full participation in the contests — not a clearing of the decks, not a cantankerous sultanism, not an obsequious self-abnegation, not a disillusioned retreat, but a serious, thoughtful, sensitive, and at times even jocular engagement with one's fellow players, both Christian and non-Christian.

This volume attempts to encourage participation in the debates over contemporary literary theory. It aims to assess in a constructive way the dominant movements in literary theory that contemporary teachers of literature will inevitably encounter. It does not offer a normative guide or a fully developed alternative theory; rather, it presents a series of critical reflections from a Christian point of view. Although no attempt has been made to impose uniformity of judgment, the authors share a commitment to what may be characterized as traditional or orthodox Christian belief. Within Christianity there exists a variety of viewpoints and attitudes, and readers of these essays may detect some of that variety. Some authors are more sympathetic to secular movements than are others; some are appreciative, others more judgmental. All agree, however, that Christian theory needs to develop in the context of engagement rather than isolation. If there is a viable Christian alternative to existing theories, it must begin with a full awareness of the issues and controversies that concern all theorists.

This book is written primarily for teachers and students who are interested in but somewhat baffled or intimidated by the complexity of contemporary criticism. Accordingly, it is a kind of introduction to the field. But it also attempts to go beyond introduction to assessment and to analysis of what is important in Christian literary theory. In assessing the variety of current theories, it takes a step in the direction of what might become a Christian contribution to literary understanding. Its aim, in sum, is to provide a springboard for thoughtful interaction with contemporary movements in literary criticism.

FORMALIST AND ARCHETYPAL CRITICISM

Leland Ryken

DESPITE CHANGING WINDS IN CURRENT LITERARY THEORY, the formalist criticism of the New Critics continues to be at the center of the academic study of literature. In one form or another, its methods still set the agenda for what goes on in the literature classroom. No matter what else teachers of literature do, they interact with literary texts in terms of the categories bequeathed by formalist criticism. Moreover, recent trends must be understood partly in terms of their common reaction to formalist criticism.

While never enjoying the prominence that characterized New Criticism, the archetypal approach to literature likewise continues to exert a pedagogical influence that is concealed by its obscurity on the current theoretic scene. Not only does its vocabulary routinely enter critical essays; it is also the organizing principle for numerous anthologies of literature. A recent subject index of the annual *MLA International Bibliography* lists nine columns of entries under the related topics of archetype and myth (Hardin 42).

For purposes of this essay, archetypal criticism will be considered as a close relative of formalism. In addition to sharing important theoretic assumptions, the two movements are joined chronologically. Archetypal criticism shared the critical spotlight with formalist criticism during the 1950s and may have overshadowed it during the subsequent decade.

In the description and assessment of formalist and archetypal criticism that follow, I do not mean to imply that the traits I ascribe to these approaches are unique to them. In keeping with the aims of other essays in this volume, my concern is to delineate accurately the main tenets of the movements I discuss.

FORMALIST CRITICISM

The most common type of formalism in America, known as New Criticism, established itself as the dominant way of viewing literature during the 1940s and then remained prominent for two more decades. The theorists who established the major tenets of the movement were Cleanth Brooks, John Crowe Ransom, Allen Tate, Robert Penn Warren, and William K. Wimsatt. Its practitioners included virtually all college teachers of literature during the middle of the century. The differences between the theorists and the practitioners are often huge, and many of the charges made against the movement in recent years are true of the practitioners but not of the original theorists.

The roots of the movement can be traced back philosophically to Kant and aesthetically to the English Romantic poets. These early spokesmen were preoccupied with differentiating literature from other forms of knowledge and discourse. This concern coincided with a moment in history when knowledge was becoming specialized and fragmented. In particular, the rise of science (broadly defined to include not only the physical sciences but all of the cognitive or "thought" disciplines that use a predominantly conceptual vocabulary) produced a climate in which Kant and the Romanticists found it easy to view the realm of knowledge in terms of a grand dichotomy between reason and imagination, between the abstract and the concrete.

Formalist theory can be called ontological in the sense that it seeks to define the distinctive knowledge that literature and the arts express. This is worthy of emphasis, inasmuch as the movement is often (and, as regards its theorists, incorrectly) charged with being unconcerned with meaning. "The function of criticism," writes Allen Tate, is "to maintain and demonstrate the special, unique, and complete knowledge which the great forms of literature afford us. And I mean quite simply *knowledge*, not historical documentation and information" (8). John Crowe Ransom, in his essay entitled "Wanted: An Ontological Critic," argues that poetry "intends to recover" the world of human experience and thereby express "a kind of knowledge which is radically or ontologically distinct" from the world that scientific discourse gives us (*The New Criticism* 281). In the best analysis of the subject, William C. Handy comments in his book entitled *Kant and the Southern New Critics* that "the ontological critics are concerned . . . with knowledge entities — artistic as distinct from scientific, and equally as significant" (30).

What, then, constitutes the distinctive form of knowledge that literature and the arts contribute to the human race? Formalist theory poses the answer in terms of a series of contrasts: concrete rather than abstract language, image rather than concept, imagination rather than intellect. Kant stated the essential principle when he wrote, "We have a faculty of mere aesthetical Judgment by which we judge forms without the aid of concepts" (179). According to Kant, it is the function of the imagination to express an intuitive truth "for which an adequate concept can never be found" (236). Romantic poets articulated variations on the theme. Shelley, for example, opens his *Defence of Poetry* by contrasting reason and imagination, declaring that poetry is "the expression of the imagination" (355). What the imagination gives us is a concrete presentation of human experience — "the very image of life expressed in its eternal truth" (360).

Shelley's word *image* foreshadows a key idea in twentieth-century formalist criticism. Convinced that literature gives us a distinctive form of knowledge, formalist critics turn their attention to the language of literature. Their typical strategy is to compare literary and nonliterary types of writing and to analyze what gets left out of the latter. Their general conclusion: literature does not primarily convey ideas or scientific facts but instead embodies the very quality of human experience. Literature does not tell us *about* reality but re-creates it by various techniques of concretion (which is what I mean by "image" in the present discussion). As C. S. Lewis states in "The Language of Religion," the best brief introduction to the subject, "the most remarkable of the powers of Poetic language" is "to convey to us the quality of experiences" (133). In a similar vein is Sartre's definition of literature as "an image-making consciousness of the world in its totality" (60).

The tendency to view literature in terms of a distinctive subject matter embodied in concrete language is so basic to formalist theory that it forms the content of the opening chapter in most of the introduction-to-literature books that are a hallmark of the movement. The usual strategy is to begin by defining literary discourse in contrast to expository or "scientific" discourse. The summary near the end of the opening chapter of *An Approach to Literature* by Cleanth Brooks, John Purser, and Robert Penn Warren is prototypical:

> Literature gives us a picture of life — not the picture that science gives and not a picture that is actually (historically) true, but a picture that has its own kind of truth — a "truth" that includes important elements that science, from its very nature, is forced to leave out. The "truth" of literature takes the form, not of abstract statement, but of a concrete and dramatic presentation, which may allow us to experience imaginatively the "lived" meanings of a piece of life. (8)

If we come to such a passage fresh from contemporary charges that formalist criticism removes literature from the realm of meaning, we cannot help being surprised by the emphasis on truth, meaning, and human experience we find here. To counter the recent caricature, we might profitably add the opening lines of the preface to *Understanding Poetry* by Cleanth Brooks and Robert Penn Warren:

> Poetry gives us knowledge. It is a knowledge of ourselves in relation to the world of experience, and to that world considered, not statistically, but in terms of human purposes and values. . . . It embodies the human effort to arrive — through conflict — at meaning. . . . Poetry — like all the arts — involves this kind of experiential knowledge. (xiii)

For all their antagonism toward the Aristotelian theory of literature as an imitation of life, the *theorists* of the movement never relinquished their conviction that the subject of literature is human experience. The notion that literature is a presentational form (it presents human experience) became commonplace. In the words of Cleanth Brooks, "The poem . . . is a simulacrum of reality . . . by *being* an experience rather than any mere statement about experience" (*The Well Wrought Urn* 213). Formalist *critics*, in contrast to formalist theorists, have often treated technique as self-rewarding and conducted minute analyses of the aesthetic properties of literary works divorced from any interest in the experiential content of those works.

In view of what I have said about the formalists' preoccupation with the linguistic structures that enable literature to express a distinctive form of knowledge, we can understand Cleanth Brooks oft-quoted assertions that "form and content cannot be separated" and "form is meaning" ("The Formalist Critic" 72). The concept of form must be construed very broadly here: in fact, it means the entire medium by which meaning is communicated. The "form" of a story is setting, character, and action. The form of poetry is primarily imagery and figures of speech, though it also encompasses such nuances as meter and rhythm. The formalist movement is not interested in form for its own sake, nor does it divorce form from content or meaning. Formalist theory champions the view that the form of literature exists to embody human experience. As Brooks, Purser, and Warren put it near the end of their introduction, "A piece of literature exists in its form. We shall be constantly concerned with the implications of this fact. We shall be concerned not only because questions of form are in themselves important, but because without an understanding of, and feeling for, form, we can never grasp the human significance of literature" (8).

The same emphasis appears in Mark Schorer's frequently reprinted essay entitled "Technique as Discovery." In the opening two paragraphs, Schorer makes these assertions:

> It is only when we speak of the *achieved* content, the form, the work of art as a work of art, that we speak as critics. . . . When we speak of technique, we speak of nearly everything. For technique is the means by which the writer's experience, which is his subject matter, compels him to attend to it; technique is the only means he has of discovering, exploring, developing his subject, of conveying its meaning, and, finally, of evaluating it. (70)

The principle that literary meaning is embodied in literary form produces two important corollaries. One is suggested by the phrase that became the motto and cliché of the movement — "the work itself." Formalist criticism makes the literary text the entire focus of literary analysis. The movement bequeathed the concepts of "the intentional fallacy," the fallacy of basing literary interpretation on what we know about the author, and "the affective fallacy," the fallacy of basing interpretation on a reader's response to a literary work (Wimsatt and Beardsley). "Literary criticism," writes Cleanth Brooks, "is a description and an evaluation of its object," the implication being that the object is the work of literature itself, not something beyond it ("The Formalist Critic" 72).

A second corollary that follows from the assumption that meaning is embodied in a distinctly literary form is a relentless resistance of any attempt to reduce the meaning of a literary work to its paraphrasable content. A landmark essay of the twentieth century was Brooks' essay entitled "The Heresy of Paraphrase," in which Brooks argued that the full meaning of a literary text can never be adequately translated from its given form into a paraphrase of its propositional content. "The whole story is the meaning," writes Flannery O'Connor in orthodox formalist manner, "because it is an experience, not an abstraction" (73).

Current theories generally reject the formalist belief that the language used in literature and the knowledge gained from it are distinctive from other types of discourse and knowledge. But this distinctiveness is at least partly confirmed by recent brain research. That research has found that the two sides of the human brain respond differently to different types of stimuli (Corballis and Beale; Segalowitz; Springer and Deutsch). The left hemisphere's forte is analysis, reason, and logic. The right hemisphere is dominant in visual and other sensory processes, as well as in emotion and humor.

Although language processes tend to activate the left hemisphere, differentiation exists on the basis of the type of language involved, lending credibility to the formalist theory that literary and nonliterary language communicate differently. The ability to grasp metaphor depends on the right hemisphere. Conceptual and emotionally neutral words activate the left hemisphere, while words that name images and are emotionally laden activate the right hemisphere.

What this suggests is that we assimilate concrete and conceptual language differently, which is what formalist theory asserts. I am not, of course, identifying literature totally with the right hemisphere. But if we picture language as existing on a continuum from the abstract to the concrete, there is no doubt that literature tends toward the concrete, whereas scientific and discursive language tends toward the abstract. In some sense, therefore, the two types of writing appeal to different parts of the human mind and affect people differently.

I have taken this excursion into recent brain research partly to suggest the continuing validity of principles articulated by formalist theory. There is a current tendency to think that once we have identified the context of a movement, we have put an end to its continuing relevance. It is indeed possible to see formalist theory as part of a two-hundred-year-long attempt to assert the limitations of scientific and cognitive knowledge and to show that literature and the arts complement that knowledge with another, equally important type of knowledge. That assertion is, if anything, even more relevant in a computer-dominated and statistical culture than it was when formalist criticism was in the ascendancy. There are timeless principles at the core of formalist theory, a view confirmed by Austin Wright's recent book entitled *The Formal Principle in the Novel,* which asserts the formalist case with no less forcefulness and validity than like writings did in the days when New Criticism was the latest fashion.

Nor should we forget that on the academic scene, formalist criticism arose as a reaction against the tendency to talk about everything *except* works of literature. It would be wrong to dismiss this response and its original occasion as a past chapter in literary study. In fact, the syndrome of the disappearing text has recently asserted itself with alarming strength as teachers of literature abandon the text in favor of biographical, historical, cultural, ideological, and theoretical considerations.

ARCHETYPAL CRITICISM

Although archetypal criticism developed in the twentieth century independently of formalist criticism, and although it did not consciously grow out of formalism, the perspective of time shows that the two approaches share essential principles. The word *archetype* means literally "first molded"; Webster's Dictionary defines it as "the original pattern or model of which all things of the same type are representations or copies." According to Northrop Frye, modern archetypal theory can be traced back to the work of psychologist Carl Jung and beyond that to "pre-literary categories such as ritual, myth and folktale" ("The Archetypes of Literature" 554), though as a literary movement it has long since been emancipated from its psychological and anthropological roots. Jung theorized that the human race shares psychic responses to certain universal human images and patterns. In fact, these images "make up the groundwork of the human psyche. It is only possible to live the fullest life when we are in harmony with these symbols; wisdom is a return to them" (47).

Building on this premise, archetypal criticism has been interested in identifying and exploring the recurrent images, character types, and plot motifs that make up the world of the literary imagination. Whereas formalist criticism makes the individual work of literature the context within which to interact with that work, archetypal criticism places a work of literature into the context of the total canon of imaginative literature. The theory underlying such criticism is succinctly stated in two landmark essays — Northrop Frye's "Archetypes of Literature" and T. S. Eliot's "Tradition and the Individual Talent." Frye speaks of "the total structure of literature itself" (*Structure* 88), while Eliot's famous term "tradition" is used to denote the same thing — "poetry as a living whole of all the poetry that has ever been written" (478). Despite their differences in interactive context, the tendency of both formalist and archetypal criticism is to view literature as a more or less self-contained imaginative world, instead of relating it to extra-literary contexts.

Although archetypal theorists do not belabor the point as formalists do, they too assume that literature speaks a language all its own. It is a language broadly defined to include plot motifs and character types as well as images and symbols. (We might note in passing that formalist critics have generally been interested in other, more specialized aspects of literary discourse, especially metaphor, irony, paradox, and ambiguity.) This emphasis on images insures a degree of "right-brain" assimilation of literature — another link between archetypal and formalist criticism.

Yet another thing that the formalist and archetypal approaches share is a preference for what is universal in a work of literature. Both approaches, for example, in effect exorcise from the act of interpretation the author and the specific situation that produced a work. Whereas the Romantic tradition had made literature little more than the personal expression of the writer, Eliot disparages the Romantic "prejudice" that values the writer's originality, believing instead that "the best . . . parts of his work may be those in which the dead poets, his ancestors, assert their immortality most vigorously" ("Tradition and the Individual Talent" 476). The poet, writes Eliot, "has, not a 'personality' to express, but a particular medium" (480). Frye agrees: "The true father or shaping spirit of the poem is the form of the poem itself, and this form is a manifestation of the universal spirit of poetry, the 'onlie begetter' of Shakespeare's sonnets who was not Shakespeare himself" (*Anatomy of Criticism* 98). At the level of literary content, both formalist and archetypal theorists are interested in the aspects of a work that are true for all people at all times.

It is no surprise, therefore, that for both formalist and archetypal theorists, literature is essentially nonchronological and ahistorical. The "self-contained literary universe" of which Frye speaks (*Anatomy of Criticism* 118) is timeless in the sense that it is permanent and universally applicable (though not, as is sometimes charged, therefore unrelated to human life in this world). For Eliot, similarly, all literature "has a simultaneous existence and composes a simultaneous order" ("Tradition and the Individual Talent" 476). This simultaneity effectively obliterates chronology as the organizing principle for literature. We should note, however, that anthologies based on archetypes tend to organize works chronologically within a given archetypal category, and Frye himself recognizes the history of literary genres as cultural and chronological developments of archetypal universals. More recently, an archetypal theorist has advanced the notion of "historical archetypes," showing that it is possible to view archetypes as developing throughout the history of literature (Fisch).

ASSESSMENTS

As we examine some assessments of these influential twentieth-century movements, it is important that we avoid what C. S. Lewis called the chronological fallacy — the belief that because something is not currently fashionable, it cannot be true. Our own distance from these earlier movements allows us to see weaknesses in them that were much less apparent two decades ago, but reactions such as we have recently witnessed against these movements produce their own blind spots. René Wellek argues that some of the recent accusations "can be so convincingly refuted by an appeal to the texts that I wonder whether current commentators have ever actually read the writings of the New Critics" (144).

We must also remember that formalism itself arose as an attempt to combat certain tendencies in the existing academic and social culture. Such reactions are typically overstated, or in any case make complete sense only when we take into account what critics are speaking against.

The greatest strength of the formalist and archetypal approaches is pedagogical. They have given twentieth-century teachers and critics tools with which to talk about literature. It is as simple as that. The history of the academic study of literature before the 1940s is strewn with anecdotes about teachers who, though they may have valued literature for aesthetic reasons, lacked the tools with which to discuss the literary qualities of texts. As a result, they talked about a host of substitutes — the historical context, the writer's life, linguistic minutiae, and general appreciative comments of the pleasant-hours-in-the-library variety. The New Critics of the mid-century approached literary works with the confidence and precision of chefs preparing a banquet.

But of course the precision of the formalist and archetypal approaches exacts a price. The "close reading" of texts that formalism bequeathed to literary study frequently involves technical vocabulary and a rather narrow focus. Formalist criticism specializes in the lyric poem and is less effective with narrative; the reverse is true of archetypal criticism. For all their focus on the work itself, both approaches leave uncovered much that is important in a literary text, such as its ideas, morality, and worldview, as well as authorial presence and reader response. This said, we must recognize that this charge of incompleteness can be leveled against any critical approach.

Formalist and archetypal approaches each have their distinctive pedagogical strengths. The distinctive strength of formalist criticism is its clarity of focus. Because of the formalists' preoccupation with what René Wellek and Austin Warren in *Theory of Literature* labeled "the mode of existence" of a literary work, critics in this tradition know what they are studying — namely, a presentation of human experience in an artistic form. With the object of study thus defined, critics and teachers conduct the *explication de texte* for which the movement is famous.

The genius of archetypal criticism, on the other hand, is its organizing and integrating ability. It is able to show that beneath the surface complexity of a literary text we can find simple patterns that organize the details. Furthermore, because, as Frye asserts, "all themes and characters and stories that you encounter in literature belong to one big interlocking family" (*The Educated Imagination* 48), archetypal criticism is able to unify a reader's total literary experience. Equally important, it enables a teacher to begin with the literature (no matter how unsophisticated) that a student already knows and then open the door to similar literature. As a pedagogical device, archetypal criticism works wonders, which no doubt explains why so many anthologies have adopted archetypes as an organizing principle.

Another major contribution of formalist and archetypal approaches is that they establish literature as a discipline in its own right and as an art form. They rescue literature from the stigma of being a stepchild of other disciplines, including philosophy, sociology, ethics, theology, and psychology. It was formalist criticism that allowed people in our century to regard literature on its own terms, "not defined in terms of something else," to quote Eliot (*The Use of Poetry* 147). In particular, the formalist and archetypal movements have vindicated literature as a form of knowledge that cannot be adequately communicated by other forms of discourse. As Frye puts it, "The constructs of the imagination tell us things about human life that we don't get in any other way" (*The Educated Imagination* 124-25). Lately the charge has too often been made that these movements are guilty of making literary discourse "privileged." It must be remembered that the discourse of *every* academic discipline is privileged in the sense that it does certain things better than any other discipline. If the Romantic tradition deified the poetic imagination, that deification should not be used to discredit the more modest claims of formalist and archetypal critics that the literary imagination gives us a unique and necessary form of knowledge.

The Christian tradition has long held that truth comes to us in the image as well as the concept. The confidence with which it has made this assertion rests on three foundations. One is the Incarnation, which has been a convenient model for what a work of art is — the embodiment of truth in concrete rather than abstract form. The Christian sacraments have also been adduced in Christian aesthetics to assert the same position, for the sacraments too use concrete, sensory objects to embody and express spiritual realities.

Of all the modern critical approaches, the formalist and archetypal approaches are perhaps the most consonant with the incarnational and sacramental biases of Christian aesthetics, and it should come as no surprise that in our century Christian critics have found these approaches congenial. It is the theologian H. Richard Niebuhr, not a formalist critic, who wrote the following: "We are far more image-making and image-using creatures than we usually think ourselves to be. . . . Man . . . is a being who grasps and shapes reality . . . with the aid of great images, metaphors, and analogies" (151, 161). A formalist critic could not have said it better.

The third Christian foundation for believing that truth comes to us through the image as well as the abstraction is the example of the Bible. The Protestant tradition in particular has recognized that when the Bible expresses truth, it appeals to a range of human capacities. The Puritan William Ames, for example, noted that "in form of expression, Scripture does not explain the will of God by universal and scientific rules" but rather by such forms as stories and examples (187). Other Puritans noted regarding the Bible that "imagination hath use while the soul is joined to the body" (quoted in Lewalski 167), and that "examples are of greater force than precepts" (quoted in Kaufmann 70). Similarly, Sir Philip Sidney argues that although Christ could have stated the truth of the parables in the form of "moral commonplaces," he instead embodied the truth in a form so concrete that "meseems I see before my eyes" the details of the parables (120). Barbara Lewalski has documented at length a Reformation tradition governed by the assumption that "the poetic language of scripture in itself . . . is a vehicle of truth" (83).

I have deliberately used quotations predating the nineteenth century because they help to dispel a recent misconception that when Christian critics appeal to the truth of the imagination, their thinking has been adulterated by ideas from the Romantic or the formalist tradition. I have read several recent attacks on Dorothy Sayers' view of the creative imagination that charge her with having gotten her ideas from the Romantics rather than from Christian sources. She may indeed have been influenced by modern aesthetics, but all the available evidence suggests that this is not the case. Her theoretic writings are filled with references to the creeds of Christendom but are devoid of references to the Romantics. Theorists who argue along Sayers' lines can reach their conclusions on the basis of Christian traditions that predate the Romantic movement. Sir Philip Sidney's *Apology for Poetry*, for example, appeals to Christian doctrine and the example of the Bible to assert such aesthetic principles as the imaging of truth, the creativeness of the author, and the existence of a world of the imagination beyond the world of nature.

As noted, formalist and archetypal theories of the imagination as a vehicle of truth have parallels in the Christian tradition, and it is misleading to regard modern Christian theorists who speak in these terms as having been somehow tainted by formalist and archetypal theories. The congruence is instead a matter of the deep structure of thought that underlies the respective movements.

This is equally true of the formalists' endorsement of artistic form and beauty. Formalist criticism provided a new foundation for regarding human creativity and artistic craftsmanship as things worthy of human pursuit and enjoyment. I should note, however, that this possibility did not excite the enthusiasm of formalist theorists, who were so preoccupied with establishing literature as a form of knowledge that their defense of literature is actually rather utilitarian and didactic. Contrary to some recent charges, we will look in vain for a "hedonistic" defense of literature among formalist theorists.

The potential for such a defense is nevertheless present in their theory, and many practitioners have shown a high regard for the purely artistic side of literature. Here too we find a concurrence between formalist criticism and a Christian view of literature and the arts. Artistry is one of God's gifts to the human race. According to the biblical account, when God created the perfect human environment, it satisfied a dual criterion, both aesthetic and utilitarian: "The Lord God made to grow every tree that is pleasant to the sight and good for food" (Gen. 2:9). The Bible rings with celebration of beauty, both natural and cultural. If we ask what recent critical traditions have done justice to this Christian endorsement of artistic beauty, the most obvious answer is the formalist tradition (which, of course, lacks a specifically Christian orientation).

It is possible to find a similar congruence in the formalist elevation of the unique gifts of the writer. I am not now speaking of the Romantic deification of the writer as superior moral being, but of the more modest claim that the writer, as orator of the imagination (to use the phrase of Wallace Stevens), has special gifts that most people lack. The best biblical support of this notion is not, as is usually assumed, the Genesis account of a creative God's making people in his image but rather the Exodus account of the inspiration of the artists who beautified the tabernacle. We read, for example, that God "called," "inspired," and "filled . . . with ability . . . and with all craftsmanship" those who devised "artistic designs" for the tabernacle (Exod. 35:30-35). An analysis of the entire passage will show that this version of the artist's inspiration says nothing about the process of creativity but focuses instead on the artist's talent and ability to produce something artistic. This is obviously a far cry from Romantic versions of inspiration, but it is close to formalist criticism, which has a high regard for the talents and products of the artist but steers clear of the mysteries of literary composition.

The Christian doctrine of creation carries with it a respect for the integrity of created things. Things have inherent value because they are part of the created order. A tree has value as a tree because that is what God created it to be. Its value depends on its fulfilling its created purpose. Christianity, therefore, has no objection per se to the formalist and archetypal emphasis on the world of the literary imagination having value in and of itself. Literature first of all removes us from life and takes us to a world that is ontologically different from the tangible world in which we live. It is a world that exists only in our imagination and is made out of something as intangible as words. I can recall how, as an undergraduate, I had an impoverished understanding of literature in the absence of any understanding that literature is first of all a world of its own, having its own conventions and integrity.

But the world of literature also has links to the real world in which we live, a correspondence that formalist and (to a lesser degree) archetypal theories have obscured or even denied. When these movements were in the ascendancy, it was an axiom that literature was nonreferential — that "a poem should not mean but be." Eliseo Vivas popularized the notion that the aesthetic experience is "an experience of intransitive attention" (153), while John Crowe Ransom asserted that "over every poem which looks like a poem is a sign which reads: This road does not go through to action" (*The World's Body* 131).

We might notice in this an odd contradiction within formalist criticism. Formalist theorists were generally obsessed with literature as something that gives us knowledge of human experience. If pursued, this notion would have led to a body of criticism that explored the correspondence between the world of the literary imagination and the world of lived reality. In fact, such criticism is a rarity in the movement, where practitioners have been much more interested in matters of technique for their own sake. In the very essay in which Cleanth Brooks asserts that a poem is "at some level a simulacrum of the world of reality" and "a portion of reality as viewed and valued by a human being," he argues that his theory of literature "shifts the emphasis from truth of correspondence to truth of coherence," and that "the critic finds himself talking less about the correspondence of the poem to reality than about the coherence among the parts of the poem" ("Implications" 68, 64).

This sealing off of the world of literature from other concerns is objectionable, partly on Christian grounds. In particular, critics in these movements generally exempt literature from the intellectual scrutiny that we apply to truth claims. I. A. Richards went so far as to claim that "we need no beliefs, and indeed we must have none, if we are to read *King Lear*" (72). There is an incipient anti-intellectualism in the statements that formalist and archetypal critics make about the limitations of propositional discourse, as well as in their vague claims about the imagination giving us a "higher truth." The Christian faith is, among other things, a claim to intellectual or cognitive truth (as well as other forms of truth). Equally objectionable is the way in which formalist and archetypal critics remove literature from ethical considerations. For the most part, critics in these traditions consider irrelevant both ethical issues in works of literature and the moral influence of literature on its readers. For Christian readers, these concerns are always relevant.

My assessment of the formalist and archetypal approaches has emerged as mingled praise and blame, and the same ambivalence exists when we turn to their views of the centrality of language in the literary enterprise.

Formalist theory in particular has a high regard for the ability of literary language to communicate meaning. It is a word-based aesthetic. What critics in the movement do best is explore the nuances of literary language (even though the theory underlying the movement would enable practitioners to do more and different things with literary texts than they typically do). The care that these critics lavish on written texts shows a humility before the written text that is often lacking in more recent critical approaches.

This reverence before a literary text strikes a responsive chord in Christians, who accept the Bible as an authoritative repository of truth and are therefore committed to the principle that language can be trusted to convey understandable meaning. Christianity is a religion in which the word has a special sanctity. Openness to receive what the Bible has to say instead of imposing one's own meanings on it has been at least the theoretic aim of many segments of Christianity through the centuries. Again, therefore, we should not be surprised that many Christian critics have found the approach of formalist criticism congenial. The two share a basic orientation toward written texts and a conviction about the ability of language to communicate meaning.

This is not to say that the centripetal focus of formalist criticism on "the text itself" is without limitations. Chief among them is the inability of such criticism to enrich our experience of a work by bringing in material from outside the work. And by severing the link between the work and the reader, it has isolated the experience of reading from other aspects of a person's life.

Before leaving my assessment of the formalist and archetypal approaches, I need to defend them against an additional charge. I am not convinced that critics in these camps are actually anti-historical. It is certainly true that they are not primarily interested in the historical and biographical context of literary works, and this too ranks as a limitation of the formalist and archetypal approaches — an index to their incompleteness in themselves.

But there is nothing inherently wrong with being interested in universal human experience, nor is it more Christian to talk about historical context than the universal elements in a work of literature. Formalist criticism has been interested in the recognizable human experience in literature, while archetypal criticism is by definition devoted to the universal dimension of literature as it pursues the recurrent patterns found there. To understand the universal human condition is something that Christians owe to themselves and to the human race, and it is an obligation imposed on them by the Christian faith itself. The Bible, we might note, is a universal, elemental book that speaks to all people in all times and places. It is therefore no accident that the current interest in a literary approach to the Bible has been, more than anything else, a blend of formalist and archetypal practices. Formalist and archetypal approaches view literature not so much as timeless but as always timely and therefore relevant to the human condition at every point in history.

While we can now see that literary criticism is never as objective as formalist and archetypal critics long contended that it is, it is nonetheless true that the formalist and archetypal approaches are more objective than many others are. I can recall a time when the study of literature on pluralistic campuses was a great bonding agent — an enterprise in which people of varied persuasions could meet on common ground and find a shared human bond. In losing this, we have lost much of what literature as a human institution has to offer society. Christians have every reason to lament its passing, partly because they face the prospect of being banished from mainstream academic criticism, where adherence to such prevailing ideologies as Marxism and feminism is the prerequisite for acceptance.

Viewed from a Christian perspective, formalist and archetypal approaches turn out to be both friend and foe. Because of their ostensible lack of theological orientation, it has seemed surprising and occasionally infuriating to some that Christian critics have adopted them as critical procedures. But we should not be surprised. It is no accident that recent criticisms of the formalist and archetypal approaches have seen in them an incipient Christian orientation (see, for example, Wellek 156, Shusterman 4, Culler 79).

Christianity shares with the formalist and archetypal approaches a conviction that truth is expressed by image as well as abstraction, an appreciation for human creativity and artistry, a high regard for the ability of language to communicate meaning, and a desire to understand elemental human experience. At these points, Christian critics will continue to find formalist and archetypal approaches attractive, not so much in spite of their differences from much that is currently fashionable but because of them.

FURTHER READING

(Titles with an asterisk are recommended as introductions.)

Primary Sources

Brooks, Cleanth. *The Well Wrought Urn*. New York: Harcourt, Brace, & World, 1947.

Frye, Northrop. *Anatomy of Criticism*. Princeton: Princeton University Press, 1957.

Wimsatt, William K. *The Verbal Icon.* Lexington: University of Kentucky Press, 1954.

Secondary Sources

*Handy, William J. *Kant and the Southern New Critics.* Austin: University of Texas Press, 1963.

Jefferson, Ann, and David Robey. *Modern Literary Theory: A Comparative Introduction* (chapters 1 and 3). Totowa, N.J.: Barnes & Noble, 1982.

Patnaik, J. N. *The Aesthetics of the New Criticism.* New Delhi: Intellectual Publishing House, 1982.

Wellek, René. *The First Half of the Twentieth Century: American Criticism, 1900–1950.* Vol. 6 of *A History of Modern Criticism: 1750–1950.* New Haven: Yale University Press, 1986.

Young, Thomas Daniel, ed. *The New Criticism and After.* Charlottesville: University of Virginia, 1976.

Works Cited

Ames, William. *The Marrow of Theology.* Ed. John D. Eusden. Boston: Pilgrim, 1968.

Brooks, Cleanth. "The Formalist Critic." *Kenyon Review* 13 (1951): 72-81.

———. "Implications of an Organic Theory of Poetry." In *Literature and Belief,* ed. M. H. Abrams, 53-79. New York: Columbia University Press, 1958.

———. *The Well Wrought Urn: Studies in the Structure of Poetry.* New York: Harcourt, Brace & World, 1947.

*Brooks, Cleanth, John T. Purser, and Robert Penn Warren. *An Approach to Literature.* 4th ed. New York: Appleton-Century-Crofts, 1964.

Brooks, Cleanth, and Robert Penn Warren. *Understanding Poetry.* 3rd ed. New York: Holt, Rinehart & Winston, 1960.

Corballis, Michael C., and Ivan L. Beale. *The Ambivalent Mind: The Neuropsychology of Left and Right.* Chicago: Nelson-Hall, 1983.

Culler, Jonathan. *Framing the Sign: Criticism and Its Institutions.* Norman: University of Oklahoma Press, 1988.

*Eliot, T. S. "Tradition and the Individual Talent." In *Selected Essays, 1917-1932,* 3-11. New York: Harcourt, Brace, 1932. Rpt. in

Criticism: The Major Statements, ed. Charles Kaplan, 475-82. New York: St. Martin's Press, 1975.

————. *The Use of Poetry and the Use of Criticism*. Cambridge: Harvard University Press, 1933.

Fisch, Harold. *A Remembered Future: A Study in Literary Mythology*. Bloomington: Indiana University Press, 1984.

Frye, Northrop. *Anatomy of Criticism: Four Essays*. Princeton: Princeton University Press, 1957.

*————. "The Archetypes of Literature." *Kenyon Review* 13 (1951): 92-110. Rpt. in *Criticism: The Major Statements*, ed. Charles Kaplan, 548-61. New York: St. Martin's Press, 1975.

————. *The Educated Imagination*. Bloomington: Indiana University Press, 1964.

————. *The Stubborn Structure: Essays on Criticism and Society*. Ithaca: Cornell University Press, 1970.

Handy, William C. *Kant and the Southern New Critics*. Austin: University of Texas, 1963.

Hardin, Richard F. "Archetypal Criticism." In *Contemporary Literary Theory*, ed. G. Douglas Atkins and Laura Morrow, 42-59. Amherst: University of Massachusetts Press, 1989.

Jung, Carl. *Psychological Reflections*. Ed. Jolande Jacobi. Princeton: Princeton University Press, 1953.

Kant, Immanuel. *Kant's Kritik of Judgment*. Trans. J. H. Bernard. London: Macmillan, 1892.

Kaufmann, U. Milo. *The Pilgrim's Progress and Traditions in Puritan Meditation*. New Haven: Yale University Press, 1966.

Lewalski, Barbara K. *Protestant Poetics and the Seventeenth-Century Religious Lyric*. Princeton: Princeton University Press, 1979.

*Lewis, C. S. "The Language of Religion." In *Christian Reflections*, ed. Walter Hooper, 129-41. Grand Rapids: William B. Eerdmans, 1967.

Niebuhr, H. Richard. *The Responsible Self*. New York: Harper & Row, 1963.

O'Connor, Flannery. *Mystery and Manners*. Ed. Sally and Robert Fitzgerald. New York: Farrar, Straus & Giroux, 1961.

Ransom, John Crowe. *The New Criticism*. Norfolk, Conn.: New Directions, 1941.

————. *The World's Body*. New York: Charles Scribner's Sons, 1938.

Richards, I. A. *Science and Poetry.* New York: W. W. Norton, 1926.

Sartre, Jean-Paul. *What Is Literature?* Trans. Bernard Frechtman. New York: Philosophical Library, 1949.

Schorer, Mark. "Technique as Discovery." In *The Modern Critical Spectrum,* ed. Gerald and Nancy Goldberg, 70-83. Englewood Cliffs, N.J.: Prentice-Hall, 1962.

Segalowitz, Sid J. *Two Sides of the Brain.* Englewood Cliffs, N.J.: Prentice-Hall, 1983.

Shelley, Percy B. *Defence of Poetry.* In *Criticism: The Major Statements,* ed. Charles Kaplan, 355-80. New York: St. Martin's Press, 1975.

Shusterman, Richard. *T. S. Eliot and the Philosophy of Literary Criticism.* New York: Columbia University Press, 1988.

Sidney, Sir Philip. *An Apology for Poetry.* In *Criticism: The Major Statements,* ed. Charles Kaplan, 109-47. New York: St. Martin's Press, 1975.

Springer, Sally P., and Georg Deutsch. *Left Brain, Right Brain.* Rev. ed. New York: W. H. Freeman, 1985.

Tate, Allen. *Collected Essays.* Denver: Alan Swallow, 1959.

Vivas, Eliseo. *Creation and Discovery: Essays in Criticism and Aesthetics.* Chicago: Henry Regnery, 1955.

Wellek, René. *The First Half of the Twentieth Century: American Criticism, 1900-1950.* Vol. 6 of *A History of Modern Criticism, 1750-1950.* New Haven: Yale University Press, 1986.

Wellek, René, and Austin Warren. "The Mode of Existence of a Literary Work of Art." In *Theory of Literature,* 3rd ed., 142-57. New York: Harcourt, Brace & World, 1956.

Wimsatt, William K., and Monroe C. Beardsley. "The Intentional Fallacy" and "The Affective Fallacy," in *The Verbal Icon: Studies in the Meaning of Poetry,* 2-39. Lexington: University of Kentucky Press, 1954.

Wright, Austin M. *The Formal Principle in the Novel.* Ithaca: Cornell University Press, 1982.

MORAL CRITICISM:
PROMISES AND PROSPECTS

James Vanden Bosch

INTRODUCTION

IT IS REASONABLE TO HAVE A NUMBER OF MISGIVINGS ABOUT writing an essay on moral criticism. I am aware, for instance, of conflicting bits of evidence which suggest that, for a variety of reasons, such a task is not really necessary. An assessment of the prospects of moral criticism would be unnecessary if moral criticism were as close to death as the recent *Guide to Literary Criticism and Research* suggests: "Certainly, the approach that Babbitt, More, and Fuller epitomize has become less popular and influential during the last decades. Whether this decline is attributable to the excesses of the critics or to the deficiencies of the approach itself — or, perhaps, to the moral laxness of other critics — is a matter for debate" (Stevens and Stewart 65). It may be true that one kind of traditional moral criticism, usually associated with conservative politics and conservative theology, is in decline. When the demise of moral criticism is noted or mourned, it is almost always this variety of moral criticism which is referred to.

It is also possible that an assessment of the prospects of moral criticism is unnecessary for a quite different reason — namely, because of the special status which Jonathan Culler claims that religion, especially Christianity, has within the literary establishment in England and America. His reading of the present situation in the literary community will surprise many critics, Christian and otherwise. According to Culler, it is the habit of "professional academic criticism" to interpret literary works "in the terms of a general aesthetic ideology: a marriage of Eliot and Frye, in which the meaning of a work is a symbolic structure related to a typology heavily informed by Christian doctrine." Culler decries "the unreflective acceptance of Christianity that makes attacks on it seem odd and tedious behavior"; he scolds a literary establishment that has allowed "Christianizing aestheticism" to get "out of hand"; he claims that "our most famous critics — Northrop Frye, Wayne Booth, Geoffrey Hartman, Hugh Kenner, Harold Bloom — are promoters of religion. They do not, as is often claimed, make literature a substitute for religion. Rather, they make religion a substitute for literature" ("A Critic against the Christians" 1328). If Christianity and religious concerns really do have this privileged status within the literary establishment, then it may be superfluous to make a case for moral criticism, a species of criticism often assumed to be a natural outgrowth or result of religious approaches to literary works.

But I have other, more realistic reasons for hesitating. First, moral criticism, whether identified with Irving Babbitt and Paul Elmer More or (indirectly) with the entire academic literary establishment, is not a new approach, nor is it an unusual one. In fact, it may be one of the most commonly practiced forms of contemporary criticism. Regardless of its present low ideological or theoretical status, moral criticism continues to find its adherents and its practitioners; sooner or later, even the purest of critics lapse into moral criticism. Second, this critical approach may *not* be one that Christian critics should give much of their attention to. Especially because moral criticism seems to come so easily to some Christian critics, it is an approach that perhaps needs to be resisted, not encouraged. Third, traditional moral criticism is readily perceived as, or can deteriorate into, something very similar to censorship, an approach to literary studies that is notoriously unproductive of good. Fourth, the label suggests a stereotype, a caricature, the work of a person whose approach to literature is stale and gray, stodgily correct, unimaginative, committed to the heavy-handed enforcement of doctrinaire morality. Fifth, for all of its apparent simplicity and commonness, moral criticism turns out to be remarkably difficult to describe accurately and even more difficult to *do* well.

DEFINITIONS OF MORAL CRITICISM

The vagueness of the term "moral criticism" is well illustrated by the explanations and definitions provided by the standard glossaries of literary terminology. One such handbook describes moral criticism as the practice of judging literature "according to the ethical principles that, in a given critic's opinion, should govern human life" (Holman and Harmon 313). Another handbook describes moral criticism as being based on the belief "that literature has an effect upon the way people lead their lives" and that "one of the legitimate concerns of criticism is an appropriate response to that belief" (Frye, Baker, and Perkins 131). A third such source describes moral criticism as a response to the peculiar nature of literature, which it describes as "draw[ing] much of its value out of a serious and complex relevance to the rest of experience"; a full evaluation of literature, then, would need "to consider what that relevance is, how far it goes, and what light there may be in it" (*Princeton Encyclopedia* 172-73). Each of these definitions or descriptions is based on a different aspect of moral criticism: the moral standard employed, the effects of literature upon an audience, and the nature of literature. Although these may be trivial examples, they are evidence of the imprecision and vagueness that accompany many discussions of moral criticism. And when the label is simply attached to a body of criticism without considerable explanation, the term fails almost entirely in specifying the particular features of the work it is intended to describe.

M. H. Abrams helps to clarify part of the problem when he includes moral criticism within the larger category of pragmatic criticism, criticism that "views the work as something which is constructed in order to achieve certain effects on the audience (effects such as aesthetic pleasure, instruction, or kinds of emotion), and tends to judge the value of the work according to its success in achieving that aim" (Abrams, *Glossary of Literary Terms* 39). But as liberating as it may be to notice that judgments concerning the ability of a work of art to achieve aesthetic pleasure and to achieve moral instruction are similar in kind, Abrams' definition does not begin to describe the large territory typically claimed by the term "moral criticism."

And the territory is large. The term can include a great variety of ways of bringing together the activities of moral judgment and literary evaluation. The moral critic could, for instance, use moral standards to judge the artist or to judge the culture that produced a particular artist or art form; the moral critic could also apply moral standards to the art work itself, to the audience of the art work, or to the effect (actual, intended, or supposed) of that art work on its audience. The particular varieties of moral criticism I've just sketched are based on the assumption that the moral standards employed are extrinsic to the work of art. But the practice of moral criticism does not demand such an assumption. A work of art can be examined in order to discover and make explicit the moral sensibility which informs that work. Or the morality embodied in a work of art can be emphasized in order to call attention to the limitations or the general rightness of conventional ways of thinking about or responding to moral issues. Nor does the label help us to discriminate among the many potential sources of moral values that could be and are employed in the practice of criticism. Christianity and secularism, radical and conservative ideologies, humanism and existentialism — even a brief listing makes it evident that moral criticism springs from many sources, that moral criticism may have many ends in view. Finally, the term, especially when it is used dismissively to describe an "outmoded" or "impure" variety of criticism, does not indicate that moral criticism allows for gradations of achievement, that it can be done poorly or well. It can be heavy-handed and unimaginative, but it can also be creative and intelligent.

The preceding is a brief look at several complications related to a study of moral criticism: its present disputed status, the difficulty of defining or describing it adequately, and, related to this difficulty, the numerous and potentially conflicting varieties of practice that "moral criticism" seems to entail. Let me add one more complication to this list. It is true that moral criticism of the traditional sort has low theoretical status at the present moment. To the extent that criticism has been dominated by formalist theories or by the newer "new criticisms," there has been little room for moral criticism of the traditional variety. By at least some of the standards of yesterday and today, moral criticism is impure or outmoded, based upon illusory assumptions about the possibility of moral consensus, about the effects of literature upon the audience, and about the relationship of moral judgments to aesthetic judgments. Yet there are regular and persistent calls for certain kinds of moral criticism, and today we hear many voices call for one kind of moral criticism or another. These various calls, of course, arise from various readings of the contemporary situation, and they are not in agreement about the kind of moral criticism that should be practiced. Some call for a continued form of moral criticism, others for a revitalized form, still others for a new form. And those who call for moral criticism seem willing to take the risk of engaging in one pathetic fallacy after another — the affective fallacy, the genetic fallacy, the intentional fallacy, the heresy of paraphrase — in order to get at an important fact about literature.

Ethnic studies, feminist criticism, and Marxist criticism,

for example, remind us of the role of literature and literary study in exposing and possibly correcting the ills or evils of a culture or society. Because of the nature of literature and the critic's commitments, at least one feminist critic — Josephine Donovan — believes that feminist criticism *must* be moral criticism if it is to remain a positive and powerful force (45, 52). A similar case can be made for political criticism and for ethnic studies. For Jonathan Culler, one of the prime glories of comparative literature is that its "broad, supranational perspective . . . enables it to transcend and situate the pieties of nations and parties" ("Comparative Literature and the Pieties" 32). Culler, too, wants criticism to be moral criticism, although his criticism would serve to liberate readers from all regional and parochial moralities.

What is clear is that all such critical approaches take seriously the critical task of judging the extent to which a literary work or a literary tradition maintains or subverts conventional ways of understanding ideas, or women, or politics, or economics, or nationalism, or race. Such critics then base the value of that work or tradition, at least in part, on the extent to which it allows specific versions of wholeness, truth, or justice to thrive.

VARIETIES OF MORAL CRITICISM

The contemporary discussion related to the large subject of morality and criticism is extensive and diverse. One measure of this diversity is the fact that the present status of moral criticism itself is often dramatically disputed. As I have already noted, the recently published *Guide to Literary Criticism and Research* states that moral criticism — defined as the kind of criticism practiced by Irving Babbitt, Paul More, and Edmund Fuller — "has become less popular and influential during the last decades" (Stevens and Stewart 65). Many critics and commentators have echoed some form of this judgment, often in the context of arguing for the importance of moral criticism. In 1977, in *On Moral Fiction*, John Gardner argued for a return to a more vigorous moral criticism. In 1981, Wayne Booth claimed that ethical criticism is one kind of criticism urgently needed today ("Criticulture" 162-76). In 1986, in *The Moral Imagination*, Christopher Clausen made the case for trying to bring "an undogmatic moral criticism back to life," even if "discussions of literature and ethics make most contemporary critics squirm in their chairs" (xi, 1). And in 1987, in *The Culture of Criticism and the Criticism of Culture*, Giles Gunn charged that "critics have developed one or another argument for the necessity of banishing such discussions from criticism altogether" (21).

But, regardless of these assessments, it is clear to many other observers that many kinds of moral criticism are being practiced today. By 1988, Wayne Booth admitted that what was most striking about moral criticism was the "contrast between theoretical abstinence and practical indulgence" ("Why Ethical Criticism Fell on Hard Times" 281). And in his recent book-length study of moral criticism, Booth agreed with Fredric Jameson's assessment that "the predominant form of literary and cultural criticism today . . . is what we call *ethical* criticism," although Jameson sees this as a problem to be solved, not a situation to be celebrated (*The Political Unconscious* 59-60). Further, Murray Krieger has argued recently that all critics are part of "the moral gang" of criticism, that moral criticism in one form or another is almost impossible to avoid ("In the Wake of Morality" 133).

Such disagreement and vacillation about moral criticism are due partly to contemporary disagreements about literary criticism in general. Meaningful agreement on basic assumptions is hard to achieve, as is evident in the various relocations of critical interest related to structuralism, deconstructionism, hermeneutical studies, feminism, and New Historicism. The entire range of supposedly "traditional" critical concepts is contestable; there is little apparent consensus on such matters as the canon, the notion of textuality, "determinable meaning," the role of the critic, and the relative status of various interpretive communities. In this climate, the subject of moral criticism will naturally elicit deep suspicions and strong feelings, so that such questions as "Whose morality?" and "Which view of the good?" must be answered before further talk of moral criticism can proceed with profit.

In *The Ethics of Criticism*, Tobin Siebers has noted that if there is a contemporary crisis in criticism, it is accounted for and dated very differently by different observers. He has suggested that the crisis in criticism "is defined around the nature of criticism itself": "Modern theory seems too aware of the [etymological] relation between 'criticism' and 'cutting.' . . . Critical distinctions appear too arbitrary for modern tastes, and we have learned to suspect that arbitrariness conceals self-interest and aggressive willfulness" (15).

It is not necessary, however, to argue that literary criticism is in a state of crisis in order to note that there is substantial interest in moral criticism today. Yet even a brief survey of the contemporary debate concerning moral criticism makes it clear that there are many kinds of moral criticism, each with its own history (often explicit), each with its own protagonists and vocabulary. Although it is not in the scope of this study to examine and catalog every variety of moral criticism currently practiced or proposed, a brief analysis of a few representative statements purporting to describe the present situation will expose the basic features of an important part of the current discussion of moral criticism.

Most of these statements share at least a few rhetorical strategies. The authors typically assert that there is at present a crisis in criticism and then go on to identify and account for the crisis; they often claim to belong to a discernible tradition in criticism that needs to be reappropriated or refurbished; and they employ particular metaphors and terminology that help to focus the work of criticism.

Moral Criticism and the Present Situation

Of course, not all critics engaged in this discussion assert that
there is a present crisis in criticism. Take James Boyd White,
for instance. In *When Words Lose Their Meaning,* he proposes a
"way of reading" that facilitates moral discourse about literature,
but he does so without entering into explicit debate with other
critics or other ways of reading (3-23). And Denis Donoghue
has recently asserted that talk of such a crisis is "implausible,
given the ease with which events lose their eventfulness and
settle down in the narrative that equably observes them" (1399).
Nevertheless, many critics, especially those who call for moral
criticism, posit the existence of "a crisis in criticism," a crisis
that leads to various claims concerning why a specific kind of
criticism is needed now. Such explanations of the current critical
situation have been offered by critics and commentators vastly
different from one another in critical orientation.[1] Of course,
not all of these critics call for what they themselves would refer
to as moral or ethical criticism. But all of them do note a

1. Various explanations of the current critical scene are offered by the
following: M. H. Abrams in a series of essays written over the last decade;
John Gardner in *On Moral Fiction* (1978); Gerald Graff in *Poetic Statement
and Critical Dogma* (1970) and *Literature against Itself* (1979); Russell Kirk
in *Enemies of the Permanent Things: Observations of Abnormality in Literature
and Politics* (1969, 1984); Murray Krieger in "In the Wake of Morality: The
Thematic Underside of Recent Theory" (1983); Giles Gunn in *The Culture
of Criticism and the Criticism of Culture* (1987); Christopher Clausen in *The
Moral Imagination: Essays on Literature and Ethics* (1986); Jim Merod in *The
Political Responsibility of the Critic* (1987); Tobin Siebers in *The Ethics of
Criticism* (1988); Michael Walzer in *The Company of Critics* (1988); Terry
Eagleton in *The Function of Criticism* (1984); Josephine Donovan in "Beyond
the Net: Feminist Criticism as a Moral Criticism" (1983); Alexander Bloom
in *Prodigal Sons: The New York Intellectuals and Their World* (1986); Alan Wald
in *The New York Intellectuals* (1987); William Barrett in *The Truants: Adven-
tures among the Intellectuals* (1982); Paul Bové in *Intellectuals in Power: A
Genealogy of Critical Humanism* (1986); Russell Jacoby in *The Last Intellectuals*
(1987); and Wayne Booth in *The Company We Keep: An Ethics of Fiction*
(1988).

problem in criticism, and they typically go on to call for something very much like moral criticism (a form of criticism attentive to the social and political implications of literature), or for criticism committed to specific social and political concerns.

A brief analysis of five of these critics will reveal how different each kind of advocacy is. M. H. Abrams, John Gardner, Terry Eagleton, Josephine Donovan, and Wayne Booth represent various traditions of criticism and thus provide different accounts not only of the state of contemporary criticism but also of the evolution of that state.

M. H. Abrams

For more than fifteen years, Meyer Abrams has been fighting battles on two critical fronts in order to make his case for "the traditional or humanistic paradigm of the writing and reading of literature" ("How to Do Things with Texts" 566). On one front, he has fought against an over-reliance on the objective theory of art. Abrams has taken on this task to make room for an "alternative language of criticism," a language of criticism that will "account for the way [works of art] engage our total consciousness and call insistently upon our sympathies and antipathies, our range of knowledge, our common humanity, our sense of what life and the world are really like and how people really act, our deep moral convictions and even religious beliefs (or lack of them)" ("What's the Use of Theorizing About the Arts?" 48).

On another front, Abrams has debated critical theorists such as Morse Peckham and J. Hillis Miller in order to achieve the same end — to maintain "access to the inexhaustible variety of literature as determinably meaningful texts by, for, and about human beings, as well as access to the enlightening things that have been written about such texts by the humanists and critics who were our precursors" ("How to Do Things with Texts" 588).

Abrams claims that both the objective theory of art and

certain forms of critical theory make humanistic criticism marginal. In the two essays just cited and others,[2] Abrams has argued that the traditional humanities approach to literature — which deals with questions that "typically involve normative and evaluative elements" ("What's the Use of Theorizing About the Arts?" 51) — may be imprecise and inconclusive, but "its great exponents" have shown "how well and profitably the game can in fact be played" (54).

John Gardner

In *On Moral Fiction,* John Gardner attributes the decline of criticism to the laziness and evasiveness of literary critics. Critics who should answer the hard critical questions — Is the work of art true, life-giving, and moral? — have taken the easy way out: "What the bad critic needs is some handy formula; and for most of this century the central question for both popular and scholarly critics has therefore been: What is the simplest formula I can hope to get away with?" (129). Gardner's list of formulaic evasions includes New Criticism, Marxist criticism, generic criticism, structuralism, "destructionist criticism, and the safest, easiest approach of all, 'hermaneutics [sic],' or opinion, bastard grandson of the eighteenth century's rule of taste" (129). Gardner's claim that "true art treats ideals, affirming and clarifying the Good, the True, and the Beautiful" (133) has clear implications for moral criticism: "its ultimate concern is with ends" (133) — that is, with determining to what extent a work of art has supported those ideals. For Gardner, the present need is relatively simple, in concept if not in practice.

2. See also "A Note on Wittgenstein and Literary Criticism," "The Deconstructive Angel," "Behaviorism and Deconstruction: A Comment on Morse Peckham's 'The Infinitude of Pluralism,'" "Kant and the Theology of Art," and "From Addison to Kant: Modern Aesthetics and the Exemplary Art."

Terry Eagleton

Terry Eagleton describes his *Function of Criticism* as "a drastically selective history of the institution of criticism in England since the early eighteenth century" (7). According to Eagleton, "modern criticism was born of a struggle against the absolutist state" (107); today, by contrast, criticism "engages at no significant point with any substantive social interest, and as a form of discourse is almost entirely self-validating and self-perpetuating" (108). Eagleton sees two reasons for this radical diminishment of criticism. The first cause is the virtual disappearance of the "public sphere" that had thrived in eighteenth-century England. Eagleton defines the public sphere as that political and cultural possibility "in which private individuals [can] assemble for the free, equal interchange of reasonable discourse, thus welding themselves into a relatively cohesive body whose deliberations may assume the form of a powerful political force" (9). The second cause is "inscribed within [criticism] from the outset": "the contradiction . . . between an inchoate amateurism and a socially marginal professionalism" (69).

Taken together, these two explanations would seem to allow Eagleton very little hope for the future of criticism. But, he says, the seemingly chaotic interests of current criticism ("semiotics, psychoanalysis, film studies, cultural theory, the representation of gender, popular writing, and of course the conventionally valued writing of the past") have at least this much unity — "a concern with the symbolic processes of social life, and the social production of forms of subjectivity":

> It is possible to argue that such an enquiry might contribute in a modest way to our very survival. For it is surely becoming apparent that without a more profound understanding of such symbolic processes, through which political power is deployed, reinforced, resisted, at times subverted, we shall be incapable of unlocking the most lethal power-struggles now confronting us. (124)

Josephine Donovan

For Josephine Donovan, feminist criticism (at least in what she refers to as the "images of women" approach) is moral criticism, "based on the assumption that literature affects us, that it changes our attitudes and our behavior" (51). The problem with this tradition in criticism, however, is that "the morality expressed has been for the most part sexist. Feminist criticism is a moral criticism which attempts to redress the balance" (51). Donovan attempts to "set down a theoretical moral basis" for such criticism, and she finds Iris Murdoch to be a rich source for critical reflection. Murdoch contributes a helpful view of the function of art: "it promotes moral growth by helping us to *see* beyond the usual illusions and facile stereotypes by which we habitually organize the chaos of 'reality'" (54). Specifically, literature "can foster the growth of moral attention to contingent realities beyond the self and beyond self-promoting fantasies" (56). For Donovan, this orientation not only provides a way of explaining the value of literature in general; it also provides a basis for the judgment that male authors in the Western tradition have written works that are "morally insufficient, for they do not attend to the independent reality of women" (57).

Wayne Booth

A few years ago Wayne Booth wrote an essay entitled "Why Ethical Criticism Fell on Hard Times," a subject on which he has commented extensively. (The essay, originally published in the journal *Ethics*, was subsequently revised to become Chapter Two of *The Company We Keep*.) Booth calls ethical criticism "the most important of all forms of criticism" ("Why Ethical Criticism Fell on Hard Times" 293) and "the most important, and also the most difficult, of all human achievements except the creating of significant art works themselves" ("Criticulture" 168). What Booth hopes to achieve in his work he states simply: the "restoration of a criticism that grants literary works their true importance to souls and societies by appraising their distinctive powers for good or ill" ("Criticulture" 168).

Booth attempts to account for the decline of this kind of criticism, even though he knows that a "full history of the decline of a theoretically coherent and confident ethical criticism of narratives, from the time of Samuel Johnson through Coleridge and Arnold to high modernism, would require almost as many volumes as have been devoted to other, better-known cultural revolutions" ("Why Ethical Criticism Fell on Hard Times" 281). Without attempting a full history, Booth suggests that "four dogmas of our cultural climate" make the practice of moral criticism very difficult today.

The first of these is "the theoretical rejection of inquiry into values." According to Booth, the "notion that one can obtain knowledge only about facts, never about values" does not allow evaluative criticism any real status as knowledge, since it can never be more than an expression of personal preference. The second dogma is that "thought proceeds by probing the world's convictions critically to discover which of them cannot be doubted"; the burden of proof, then, falls on the critic who affirms the value of a work of art and must be able to prove that that value cannot be doubted. The third dogma is "the increasing awareness of immense variability" ("Why Ethical Criticism Fell on Hard Times" 286), or "the belief that conflicting values cancel each other out" (*The Company We Keep* 34). This belief is based on the observation that there is very little agreement on the value of particular authors and texts; "and if that is true of *all* value judgments, it must be true a fortiori of ethical judgments, the most complex and difficult kind" ("Why Ethical Criticism Fell on Hard Times" 287). The fourth dogma is related to those theories of art "that elevated abstract form to the top of every aesthetic pyramid" (288). Here Booth rehearses very briefly what Abrams has argued at length: the tendency of such theories of art to make ethical criticism of artistic content largely irrelevant to the proper interests of criticism.

Booth argues that critics too often accept these dogmas uncritically. He cites philosophers who have published "proof upon proof that moral decisions and moral argument can be rational after all and that utter relativism and subjectivism is irrational" ("Why Ethical Criticism Fell on Hard Times" 289). The majority of Booth's *The Company We Keep* is devoted to showing that discussions of the moral judgments involved in responding to a narrative can be not only rational and respectable but also rewarding.

*   *   *

The five "stories" I have summarized in the preceding pages hold very little in common except the shared view that contemporary criticism must make room for criticism that addresses the social, political, and moral implications of literature. But these critics see at least part of the current situation in quite different ways. Other critics add to the diversity of interpretations I have already noted. Gerald Graff provides an account that is slightly different from the five preceding; so do Giles Gunn, Russell Kirk, Michael Walzer, and Tobin Siebers. Graff, Booth, and Abrams do seem to be in essential agreement on the causes of the current situation, primarily because of the number of commitments, literary and otherwise, they share. But where the shared commitments are few, the narratives become very different; the case for moral criticism varies according to assumptions about literature, morality, and the role of criticism. This variety or lack of convergence becomes even more apparent when one examines the traditions and vocabularies that mark these critics' approaches to criticism.

Exemplars and Traditions

Because Booth is interested primarily in demonstrating what a responsible ethical criticism would look like for current practice, he does not devote much of his attention to a list of critics who belong in a tradition he wishes to affirm. He mentions Plato, Samuel Johnson, Coleridge, Matthew Arnold, Tolstoy, and F. R. Leavis as key figures in any complete history of the fortunes of ethical criticism, but he does not go on to flesh out a tradition of which they are a part. Gerald Graff is similarly brief. In *Literature against Itself* he lists Erich Auerbach, Wayne Booth, Georg Lukacs, Yvor Winters, Edmund Wilson, Irving Howe, and E. D. Hirsch among "critics who, in diverse ways, have challenged prevailing vanguard dogmas" (4). In *The Culture of Criticism and the Criticism of Culture*, Giles Gunn examines and affirms the kind of moral criticism practiced by Edmund Wilson, Lionel Trilling, and Kenneth Burke (23). Michael Walzer's *The Company of Critics* studies the example of eleven critics committed to the kind of criticism he prefers. Because "the everyday world is a moral world," Walzer says, critics "would do better to study its internal rules, maxims, conventions, and ideals, rather than to detach [themselves] from it in search of a universal and transcendent standpoint" (ix). The critics who best illustrate what such an effort looks like include Antonio Gramsci, Ignazio Silone, George Orwell, Albert Camus, Simone de Beauvoir, and Michel Foucault. In contrast, Terry Eagleton and Paul Bové cite critics who constitute a largely negative tradition. In *The Function of Criticism* Eagleton discusses the contradictions or limitations inherent in the work of Joseph Addison and Richard Steele, Johnson, Arnold, and Leavis. Bové's book, *Intellectuals in Power: A Genealogy of Critical Humanism*, is meant to be an exposé of the inevitable failure of critical humanism as a tool for "oppositional intellectual practice" (xi). Bové's imperfect critics are represented by I. A. Richards and Erich Auerbach. The various studies of the New York Intellectuals (by William Barrett, Irving Howe, Alfred Kazin, Harold Bloom, Alan Wald, and Russell Jacoby, for instance) construct similar groupings of good, fallen, or failed critics.

It is not surprising that different critics should claim such widely different figures for inclusion in their positive or negative traditions. Such variety makes it clear that arguments about the nature and place of moral criticism are based on very different histories and models. But critics who have committed themselves to revitalizing moral criticism differ in more than their sense of tradition. Their vocabularies are similarly heterogeneous.

Terminologies

The terms *moral, morality, ethical,* and *ethics* are used in confusing and sometimes arbitrary ways in the discussion I have been describing. Some part of this confusion may be related to the peculiar ambiguities of such words as *moral* and *ethical,* ambiguities that allow such phrases as "moral holiday" and "ethical deliberation" to be understood in ways very different from the intended meaning. At times this natural ambiguity allows critics to write about "moral criticism" as if it were a counter to immoral criticism, or "ethical criticism" as criticism that exhibits specific virtues.

Sometimes *ethical* and *moral* are distinguished from one another in order to meet a particular need. For instance, Wayne Booth decided to refer to his subject as "ethical criticism" because that formulation seems to him to be more inclusive than "moral criticism" (*The Company We Keep* 8). For Booth, "moral criticism" suggests a narrow interest in "moral" judgments and the "quite limited moral standards" of honesty, decency, or tolerance (8). He intends the word *ethical* to "cover all qualities in the character, or ethos, of authors and readers, whether these are judged to be good or bad." Ethical criticism, says Booth, "attempts to describe the encounters of a storyteller's ethos with that of the reader or listener" (8). However, something very much like this kind of broad criticism is what other critics also have in mind when they use the term "moral criticism." Booth's choice of phrase is not wrong or improper, but it does demonstrate that these decisions are often made unilaterally.

Other discussions of literature and morality seem to maintain the traditional philosophical distinction between morality and ethics. This traditional understanding defines morality as a personal or social standard of conduct, and ethics as moral philosophy, the branch of philosophy that involves "philosophical thinking about morality, moral problems, and moral judgments" (Frankena, *Ethics* 3). Here *moral* is used in the same way in which it was used in "Literature and/as Moral Philosophy," a special section of a 1983 issue of *New Literary History*. That issue featured an article by D. D. Raphael entitled "Can Literature Be Moral Philosophy?" in which he argued that it can be, has been, and is (4-5, 8-10).

Very often, however, the words *moral* and *ethical* are used as if they were synonymous. The words are often used interchangeably in the contemporary discussion of moral criticism. For example, a recent issue of *Novel* (1988) brought together several essays on "the novel as ethical paradigm," focusing on a discussion of how readers respond to the moral patterns established or challenged by works of fiction. But even when these words are used interchangeably, it is not always clear just what the words mean or refer to from one essay to the next.

The same problem arises with related words and phrases. Lionel Trilling made extensive use of the phrase "the moral imagination," a phrase he apparently borrowed from Edmund Burke (92-93), but Trilling's use of it is quite different from Burke's, and both are different from the uses to which the phrase is put by Christopher Clausen in *The Moral Imagination*, Gertrude Himmelfarb in *Marriage and Morals among the Victorians* (xii-xiii), and Russell Kirk in *Enemies of the Permanent Things* (16, 20). The same is true of "moral realism," another phrase important to Trilling in the 1940s. Trilling's use makes one kind of sense in the context of the development of political and theological realism in the forties; but "moral imagination" and "moral realism" take on quite a different meaning in the context of moral philosophy — as used, for instance, by Sabina Lovibond in her *Realism and Imagination in Ethics* (11, 195).

The Languages of Morality

All of these disagreements — a lack of consensus on the vocabulary appropriate to the work of moral criticism, the different arguments concerning the present status of moral criticism, and the varied critics who make up the several traditions of moral criticism — point to a situation that could be described as a crisis, not in criticism first of all but in ethics. This is the picture drawn by Alasdair MacIntyre in *After Virtue: A Study in Moral Theory*. According to MacIntyre,

> The language of morality is in . . . [a] state of grave disorder. . . . What we possess . . . are the fragments of a conceptual scheme, parts of which now lack those contexts from which their significance derived. We possess indeed simulacra of morality, we continue to use many of the key expressions. But we have — very largely, if not entirely — lost our comprehension, both theoretical and practical, of morality. (2)

MacIntyre's assessment of "the nature of moral disagreement today" has broad relevance to what I have noted about the peculiarities of moral criticism. MacIntyre has noted three characteristics of contemporary moral utterance. First, the arguments are conceptually incommensurable — that is, "the rival premises are such that we possess no rational way of weighing the claims of one as against another." "From our rival conclusions we can argue back to our rival premises," MacIntyre points out; "but when we do arrive at our premises argument ceases and the invocation of one premise against another becomes a matter of pure assertion and counter-assertion." Second, these arguments "none the less purport to be *impersonal* rational arguments"; such an appeal "presupposes the existence of *impersonal* criteria — the existence, independently of the prefer-ences or attitudes of speaker and hearer, of standards of justice or generosity or duty." Third, the many sources of morality we have inherited have become "an unharmonious melange of ill-assorted fragments": "all those various concepts which inform our moral discourse were originally at home in larger totalities of theory and practice in which they enjoyed a role and function supplied by contexts of which they have now been deprived" (*After Virtue* 8-10).

MacIntyre's sense of the current situation develops into a thesis — namely, that the Enlightenment project to find a rational basis for morality has failed, and that, for the sake of moral clarity, ethics must reappropriate a teleological tradition of morality. His provocative thesis has engendered a very productive debate, and although it is not necessary to trace out the details of this ongoing conversation, several of its features have some bearing on the subject of moral criticism.

After Virtue and its sequel, *Whose Justice? Which Rationality?* have prompted a large response from scholars within the field of ethics and from adjoining fields.[3] Among the respondents is Jeffrey Stout, who over the last decade has provided an extensive response to MacIntyre that addresses the situation I have been describing in literary criticism. In two review essays ("Virtue among the Ruins: An Essay on MacIntyre" and "Homeward Bound: MacIntyre on Liberal Society and the History of Ethics") and in several chapters of *Ethics after Babel: The Languages of Morals and Their Discontents,* Stout has agreed with much of the picture MacIntyre has drawn of

3. MacIntyre's work has been profitably engaged by a number of people: William Frankena in "MacIntyre and Modern Morality"; Franklin Gamwell in "Traditions of Moral Reasoning"; Stephen Holmes in "The Polis State"; J. B. Schneewind in "Virtue, Narrative, and Community: MacIntyre and Morality" and "Moral Crisis and the History of Ethics"; John D. Barbour in "The Virtues in a Pluralistic Context"; Amitai Etzioni in "Toward an I and We Paradigm"; Thomas Nagel in "Agreeing in Principle"; Richard John Neuhaus in "Traditions of Inquiry"; and Martha Nussbaum in "Recoiling from Reason."

the untidiness of current moral reasoning, but he has resisted the thesis MacIntyre has attached to that description. Stout and others have claimed that moral pluralism is the best that can be accomplished in the modern world, and that an attempt to impose one system of moral reflection — such as MacIntyre's Aristotelian and teleological one, which he advocates in *After Virtue* — is both impracticable and undesirable.

In response to such critiques, MacIntyre has revised or further articulated his proposed remedy in *Whose Justice? Which Rationality?* In this book MacIntyre has modified his thesis, arguing that productive and coherent moral critique can take place only from within a specific and fully articulated moral tradition, that his particular moral tradition has proven itself to be especially responsive and resilient, and that the great challenge of modern ethics is the problem of translating and understanding alternative languages of morality successfully. In response, Stout has praised MacIntyre as the kind of critic whose "mistaken arguments often instruct, . . . [whose] caricatures often advance the debate":

> He has performed a valuable service to his culture precisely by being the sort of person his current theory of rationality frowns on.
>   What kind is that? It is the kind who, from time to time, finds it necessary to abandon a morality so well integrated that it suffocates thought, who has the courage to take a stand for which there is not yet a convenient label or an easily defined lineage, and who has the practical wisdom to fashion a critical language for himself out of materials borrowed from many sources. All this can be done without engaging in the liberal project, aspiring to be a citizen of nowhere or ceasing to be one of us. ("Homeward Bound" 232)

This characterization of MacIntyre fits in well with Stout's earlier accounts of *bricoleurs* and *bricolage* in *Ethics after Babel* (74-78). Borrowing the terms from Claude Lévi-Strauss and Jacques Derrida, Stout adapts them in order to create an appropriate image for doing ethics in a pluralistic context. For Stout, the image of a *bricoleur* is "an apt symbol of every moralist's need to engage in selective retrieval and eclectic reconfiguration of traditional linguistic elements in hope of solving problems at hand" (293). Moral *bricolage,* in turn, is "the process in which one begins with bits and pieces of received linguistic material, arranges some of them into a structured whole, leaves others to the side, and ends up with a moral language one proposes to use" (294). In his adaptation and application of this image, Stout also uses the linguistic concepts of pidgin and creole to describe moral languages that begin as the product of the *bricoleur*'s work but eventually become fully developed moral languages (80-81, 294). We are all *bricoleurs,* says Stout, "insofar as we are capable of creative thought at all" (74); further, "all great works of creative ethical thought . . . involve moral *bricolage*" (75). In these terms, MacIntyre is a *bricoleur* to the extent that he has pieced together a moral language more nearly adequate to the challenges of the present age.

For Stout, the multiplicity of moral languages does indeed present a challenge for thinking about ethics, but each moral language has its place "in the pluralistic scheme of practices and institutions. Each serves goods of specific sorts":

> Practices like medical care and baseball are animated by talk of particular virtues and vices, of role-specific duties and the rights that correspond to them, of standards of excellence, and of goods or ends to be pursued in common. . . . The language of abomination finds use wherever distinctions between "us" and "them" or between masculine and feminine roles remain sharp and acquire a certain kind of social significance. The religious languages of morals, which used to be presupposed by everyone participating in the practice and institutions of politics, now play a more limited role there, and the religious practices in which they remain central, including theological inquiry, have moved to the margins of public life. The language of human rights, respect for persons, and justice as fairness gains a foothold in those institutions — most notably the governmental

bureaucracies, the public education system, and the secular forums of political debate — where participants cannot presuppose agreement on religious issues or full theories of the good yet still need some way to make reasoned appeals to each other. The language of cost-benefit analysis rules principally in the marketplace but in other spheres as well, wherever a course of action requires calculation and comparison of external goods and evils. (285)

In a passage such as this Stout intends to demonstrate that the contemporary profusion of moral languages appears to be more confusing than it really is, since each moral language addresses its own particular set of social practices and institutions. Where MacIntyre sees chaos (a "melange of ill-assorted fragments"), Stout sees a working arrangement of dialects and languages, each performing its own task more or less adequately.

Stout's United Nations image of complementary and harmoniously interacting language groups does not fully answer MacIntyre's complaint about Babel. Most moral problems — including such matters as medical ethics and nuclear deterrence, for example — spill over too many language borders to be addressed satisfactorily by one moral language, and part of MacIntyre's complaint then retains its cogency.

It is not necessary to resolve the dispute between MacIntyre and Stout in order to see that this dispute is crucial for any full consideration of the state of moral criticism today. The fact that there are many languages of morality, for instance, has some bearing on the confusion and disagreement I have noted. Moreover, Stout's categories of the various languages of morality can be assigned, provisionally, to some of the critics I have mentioned. Josephine Donovan's preferred kind of feminist criticism, for example, seems to depend largely on the language of "human rights, respect for persons, and justice as fairness." Wayne Booth and James Boyd White, in their use of the metaphor of books as potential friends who shape their readers, rely on the language of "particular virtues and vices, of role-specific duties and the rights that correspond to them." Russell

Kirk and John Gardner, however, employ a combination of the "language of abomination" and "the religious languages of morals" in their criticism.

Each kind of moral criticism, then, has the specific advantages — and limitations — of the particular language of morality employed for the job. It may be that further refinements of Stout's introductory description of these languages would make it somewhat easier to determine the contexts within which certain languages of morality are best suited to accomplish specific tasks.

Understanding Moral Criticism Today

Although I have been focusing on the disagreements and confusions that mark the contemporary discussion of moral criticism, it is also important to note the areas of agreement or consensus that exist. Moral criticism is the name given to a large number of critical practices which have this in common: the activity of a person who is especially interested in the moral implications of works of literature. This formulation, because it does not specify a particular kind of moral criticism as primary or normative, allows for the many varieties of moral criticism as they are actually practiced. Many moral critics are primarily interested in the effects of literature on individual readers; others focus on political implications; still others concentrate on the beliefs and intentions of the author. Some moral critics are committed to the explicit enforcement of their moral standards, while others are more or less open to the variety of moral insights that literature provides. Some critics employ the moral language of the virtues, others the moral language of rights. Some use the metaphor of literature as a potential friend; others use it as a poison or an enemy. But all such criticism is described as the activity of a person who directs his or her critical attention to the moral implications of literature.

I have chosen to frame this basic definition in terms of the "critical activity of a person" because moral criticism as it is practiced today is not a critical orientation built upon a large and coherent set of critical principles. Although Booth's constructive effort in this area is a step in the right direction, there is not yet a comprehensive theory of moral criticism. A fully developed theory may eventually appear, but moral criticism seems to be a critical approach mainly evident in its practice. This is not to say that various moral critics do not reflect on their practice, or that intelligent observers and theorists cannot discover or devise systematic approaches to moral criticism as it is practiced. But generally such reflection is local or particular, noting the strategies and practices of a moral critic, not of moral criticism in general.

In addition to being practical criticism, moral criticism is often a very personal criticism as well, in that it is frequently the expression of the full range of a person's commitments and beliefs. Lionel Trilling noted "the necessity of bearing personal testimony" as a critic and a teacher, quoting Matthew Arnold to the effect that criticism "must be apt to study and praise elements that for fulness of spiritual perfection are wanted" (9, 28). Stephen Tanner's question about Lionel Trilling — "Where did this mind come from and how did it create itself?" (*Lionel Trilling* 8) — may not be exactly the right question to ask about a moral critic. Moral criticism is the product not of the mind alone but of a "whole" person whose history and hopes have some bearing on the criticism.

Because moral criticism is personal, it is also typically a changing and developing criticism. As the context changes or as the critic's assumptions and beliefs change, the criticism also changes. Further, because moral criticism is personal, no two critics hold or use or "apply" their ideas, commitments, and beliefs in exactly the same way.

The fact that moral criticism comes to expression in so many forms makes it easy to forget that these forms have certain things in common. But most moral critics seem to agree on at least two basic assumptions. They agree, first, that works of literature may have moral content, and second, that literature thus has, at least potentially, implications for the moral life of readers. These paired assumptions, explicit in Plato's banishing of the poets from an ideal republic, are expressed by many writers, classic and contemporary, conservative and liberal, religious and secular, from Sidney to Shelley, Wordsworth to Eliot, Tolstoy to Orwell, and Booth to Gardner.

The formulations of these assumptions vary greatly, of course. Some writers focus on the author of a literary work. George Orwell has stated that "every artist is a propagandist in the sense that he is trying, directly or indirectly, to impose a vision of life that seems to him desirable" (41); T. S. Eliot has said that "the author of a work of imagination is trying to affect us wholly, as human beings, whether he knows it or not" (348). Others emphasize the lessons taught by literature. Monroe Beardsley has argued that one of the "fairly central and lasting values" of literature is its capacity to "broaden and refine our ability to understand one another" (28). Other critics exhibit these assumptions in their comments on the effects literature has on readers. Wayne Booth expresses impatience with "all the weird assertions that 'poetry says nothing' and 'makes nothing happen'"; he cites anecdotal evidence that literature changes lives. Even though such evidence may be "inherently untrustworthy," says Booth, the volume of this kind of testimony "surely cr[ies] out for critical reflection, no matter how difficult that may be" (*The Company We Keep* 278-80). John Dewey, in trying to explain "*how* poetry is a criticism of life," says,

> [It is done] not directly, but by disclosure, through imaginative vision addressed to imaginative experience (not to set judgment) of possibilities that contrast with actual conditions. A sense of possibilities that are unrealized and that might be realized are[,] when they are put in contrast with actual conditions, the most penetrating "criticism" of the latter that can be made. It is by a sense of possibilities opening before us that we become aware of constrictions that hem us in and of burdens that oppress. (346)

Basil Willey focuses on the ethical dimension of criticism:

In so far as literary study offers a training in critical evaluation, it leads straight to the question of "value." We think we understand, better than our predecessors of thirty-five years ago, how far and in what subtle ways literary criticism involves ethical assumptions; but if we admit that literary judgments are often disguised (or undisguised) ethical judgments, or that they presuppose such judgments, then we ought to be enquiring into the nature and history of moral ideas. (11)

Still others concentrate on the transactions involved in the activity of reading; Susan Suleiman examines "the kind of assent required from the reader" of fiction:

[The assent asked for] has been not only formal, but also, to varying degrees, social, political, ethical, philosophical — to use a catch-all term, ideological. Since the novel has traditionally dealt with the actions or the state of being of a set of lifelike characters, an integral part of the reader's response to novels has been an emotional reaction based on the explicit or implied judgments of the text regarding these characters or their actions. (163)

The many ways that these basic assumptions come to expression in the work of various critics point to a related fact about moral criticism: potential collaborators in the enterprise of understanding moral criticism are far afield and widely scattered. Wayne Booth's *The Company We Keep*, for instance, ranges from literary theory and ethics to philosophy and psychology in order to marshal an argument for the importance of ethical criticism. Contributions from many fields of study will continue to be important in this work. As we have seen in the example of MacIntyre and Stout, students of moral criticism can benefit from philosophical discussions about the languages of morality. Reflection on ethics can contribute to the related discussion of the nature and variety of moral criticism.

But it should also be clear that this larger "discussion" is anything but a coordinated project. The study of moral criticism is moving, piecemeal, in many directions. Reader-response criticism, for example, may yield further insights into the im-

portance and function of beliefs and assumptions for individuals
and for interpretive communities. Work in the psychology of
reading and the sociology of knowledge may provide a better
framework for understanding how readers respond to the literature they read. The old "literature and belief" discussion, so
lively and productive in the 1950s, has been brought into the
foreground again, notably in the analysis of the problem of a
reader's "ideological dissent" from the beliefs or values promoted in a work of literature (Suleiman 164). From the point
of view of cultural anthropology, Clifford Geertz has written
helpfully on the extent to which it is possible for people to
understand one another across the barriers of time and culture.
And biographical studies continue to contribute information
about the beliefs and intentions of authors, providing material
at least potentially relevant to the work of some moral critics.

Contributions in these and other areas will almost certainly enrich the continuing discussion of moral criticism. But
there is an element that is not emphasized as fully as it should
be in this discussion. A great deal of attention is being given
to the author and to the reader, to reading, ideology, and the
languages of morality; not as much attention is being given to
that particular reader who is the moral critic, and to the fact
that the moral critic is a person whose moral vision changes or
develops. Moral criticism is not only a particular kind of criticism or a theory or a set of assumptions and practices. It may
be all of these, but it is also the activity of a particular person
whose commitments and intentions will change and develop,
which will in turn impinge upon his or her work of criticism.

What is not always clear in contemporary discussions of
moral criticism is that such criticism is, in practice, a developing
and dynamic activity. Greater awareness of this fact may help
to keep some of the complaints about moral criticism in perspective. C. S. Lewis's warning about a too simple moral criticism is still current in its explanation of why moral criticism is
feared or suspected. Speaking of what he called the "Vigilant
school of critics," he noted,

You must therefore accept their (implied) conception of the good life if you are to accept their criticism. That is, you can admire them as critics only if you revere them as sages. And before we revere them as sages we should need to see their whole system of values set out, not as an instrument of criticism but standing on its own feet and offering its credentials — commending itself to the proper judges, to moralists, moral theologians, psychologists, sociologists or philosophers. For we must not run round in a circle, accepting them as sages because they are good critics and believing them good critics because they are sages. (127)

Lewis's warning need not be a condemnation of moral criticism. In fact, his warning is useful because it points to the need for readers to sharpen their ability to understand the kind of morality promoted by moral critics and used as a basis for criticism. In the same passage, Lewis conceded that "all criticism, no doubt, is influenced by the critic's views on matters other than literature" (126). Readers of criticism should ask what those views are and how they affect the criticism. It is necessary, in other words, to know more about the languages of morality used by literary critics in general. But, to paraphrase Trilling, it is also necessary to ask what a particular critical approach wants, what it wants to have happen. Further study of the "views" and commitments of critics can do a good deal to lessen suspicion and skepticism of the sort exemplified by Lewis.

Moral critics come in many varieties. Not all of them present themselves as sages. In fact, Jeffrey Stout's description of the modern moralist as a *bricoleur* seems to be more accurate. A moral critic is likely to engage in the task of "selective retrieval and eclectic reconfiguration" (*Ethics after Babel* 293) and "fashion a critical language for himself out of materials borrowed from many sources" ("Homeward Bound" 232).

Moreover, moral critics do not necessarily perform their critical work in a formulaic way, with mechanical regularity and predictability. The example of Babbitt notwithstanding, moral critics typically develop and change, not only in their critical and literary sensibilities but also in their commitments, both literary and non-literary.

PROSPECTS FOR MORAL CRITICISM

It is perhaps fortunate to take on this work in a critical climate that once again recognizes what a secular critic argued so forcefully more than twenty-five years ago: the nature of the relationship between a reader and a text allows for and may even demand something more than a strictly aesthetic response or evaluation. Passages from two essays by Lionel Trilling make this case surprisingly well, even in our situation today. In "The Two Environments," an essay he wrote in 1965, Trilling made this assessment of the achievement of the New Criticism:

> One of the commonplaces of the history of modern literature is the brilliant energy of our criticism. Yet if we judge that matter closely, after we have given criticism the praise that is surely its due, we must go on to say that its achievement has been, after all, of an elementary sort. It has taught us how to read certain books; it has not taught us how to engage them. Modern literature (it need scarcely be said again) is directed toward moral and spiritual renovation; its subject is damnation and salvation. It is a literature of doctrine which, although often concealed, is very aggressive. The occasions are few when criticism has met this doctrine on its own fierce terms. Of modern criticism it can be said that it has instructed us in an intelligent passivity before the beneficent aggression of literature. Attributing to literature virtually angelic powers, it has passed the word to the readers of literature that the one thing you do not do when you meet an angel is wrestle with him. (230-31)

In a slightly different context ("On the Teaching of Modern Literature"), Trilling addressed the same issue as it relates to the literature classroom. Faced with the prospect of teaching a new course in modern literature, Trilling said that he deliberately took evasive action:

Very likely it was with the thought of saving myself from the necessity of speaking personally and my students from having to betray the full harsh meaning of a great literature that I first taught my course in as *literary* a way as possible. A couple of decades ago the discovery was made that a literary work is a structure of words: this doesn't seem a surprising thing to have learned except for its polemical tendency, which is to urge us to minimize the amount of attention we give to the poet's social and personal will, to what he wants to happen outside the poem as a result of the poem; it urges us to fix our minds on what is going on inside the poem. For me this polemical tendency has been of the greatest usefulness, for it has corrected my inclination to pay attention chiefly to what the poet *wants*. For two or three years I directed my efforts toward dealing with the matter of the course chiefly as structures of words, in a formal way, with due attention paid to the literal difficulty which marked so many of the works. But it went against the grain. It went against my personal grain. It went against the grain of the classroom situation, for formal analysis is best carried on by question-and-answer, which needs small groups, and the registration for the course in modern literature in any college is sure to be large. And it went against the grain of the authors themselves — structures of words they may indeed have created, but these structures were not pyramids or triumphal arches, they were manifestly contrived to be not static and commemorative but mobile and aggressive, and one does not describe a quinquereme or a howitzer or a tank without estimating how much *damage* it can do.

Eventually I had to decide that there was only one way to give the course, which was to give it without strategies and without conscious caution. . . . So I resolved to give the course with no considerations in mind except my own interests. And since my own interests lead me to see literary situations as cultural situations, and cultural situations as great elaborate fights about moral issues, and moral issues as having something to do with gratuitously chosen images of personal being, and images of personal being as having something to do with literary style, I felt free to begin with what for me was a first concern, the animus of the author, the objects of his will, the things he wants or wants to have happen. (12-13)

What Trilling was describing in these essays is what many critics today assert to be obvious facts: first, that one of the ordinary consequences of the interaction of reader and text is a response to the moral concerns and imperatives which arise in the process of that interaction; and second, that it is one of the legitimate functions of criticism to consider and assess such responses. In the sixties, Trilling's reminder was for some a dramatic statement. For us today, this insistence upon the naturalness of such responses to literature may, in its turn, seem not to be "a surprising thing to have learned except for its polemical tendency." But it is not likely to be a polemical statement unless moral critics begin to claim that moral concerns are the most important or the only proper focus for the critical enterprise.

The proper question today is not whether moral criticism is allowable, but whether it can be practiced productively. For Christian critics, teachers, and readers this is a key question. How should we respond to the many and various moral criticisms we see flourishing around us? What sort of claim does each moral critic have on our attention, on our conscience? How do we negotiate the competing but overlapping tasks of reading, teaching, and writing responsibly, with so many morally charged voices urging us to consider the claims of feminism, of American Indian literature, of black literature, of Third World literature, of new religions and old heresies, of the liberation from religions? Some responses are predictable and common — confusion, or bafflement, or anger, or despair, or exhaustion, or cynicism, or promiscuous enthusiasms, or retreat into familiar practices and allegiances. Some Christian critics respond very defensively to the claim that — as whites, as Anglo-Saxons, as males, as Christians, as North Americans, as members of the middle classes, as members of an older generation, as professors — they come to the task of criticism morally compromised, if not morally crippled. At least some of the evangelical dislike of contemporary theory and criticism is "the rage of Caliban seeing his own face in a glass."

Sometimes it is possible to sense, in the background, the hope or wish that these various kinds of criticism be finished, made final, absolute. I think that frustration with the untidiness of contemporary criticism leads some critics to wish for one dominant moral criticism to appear, one with a voice so commanding that all other voices will be drowned out, so that at last we shall be released from the demand to be in the right relationship to the competing criticisms that harass us.

A second set of challenges is also apparent. How should Christian critics behave as moral critics, and how do they behave as such? What use can we make of the special insights available from Scripture, from theology, from the Christian tradition? What moral judgments of literature are Christian critics most competent to make? How likely is it that Christian moral critics will be useful moral critics?

The community of Christian scholars has not yet been able to provide anything like completely satisfying answers to this range of questions. T. S. Eliot, C. S. Lewis, Vincent Buckley, Amos Wilder, Stanley Romaine Hopper, Nathan Scott, Giles Gunn, Sally McFague TeSelle, Flannery O'Connor, Leland Ryken — these and many others have worked at providing answers to one part or another of this set of questions. Christian critics will do well to continue reading such writers and to carry the conversation onward. Basic work is needed in such areas of this subject as the nature of literature, the nature of texts, reading and readers, and the interaction of the world of the text, the world of the reader, and the world of teaching and writing about literature. In the rest of this essay, I hope to contribute to this conversation by describing and assessing certain kinds of moral criticism I think are being practiced today at Christian colleges, in and out of the classroom. Mine will be, admittedly, a partial perspective, one person's glimpse of the present moment, but it may be useful nonetheless, even if I manage to get only some of the account straight.

MORAL CRITICISM AND THE
CHRISTIAN TEACHER

Christian critics and teachers regularly cite two passages from "Religion and Literature" by T. S. Eliot, two passages that have set the tone and the agenda for much of the moral criticism practiced in Christian colleges. The passage quoted most often is this one:

> Literary criticism should be completed by criticism from a definite ethical and theological standpoint. . . . The "greatness" of literature cannot be determined solely by literary standards; though we must remember that whether it is literature or not can be determined only by literary standards. (343)

The second passage is this:

> And if we, as readers, keep our religious and moral convictions in one compartment, and take our reading merely for entertainment, or on a higher plane, for aesthetic pleasure, I would point out that the author, whatever his conscious intentions in writing, in practice recognizes no such distinctions. The author of a work of imagination is trying to affect us wholly, as human beings, whether he knows it or not; and we are affected by it, as human beings, whether we intend to be or not. (348)

These statements by Eliot are cited so regularly, and most often with such obvious approval, that I have for a long time suspected that Christian critics have assented to Eliot's description and recommendations too readily, refusing to subject them to the scrutiny that Eliot himself was willing to give them (see his preface to the 1950 edition of *Selected Essays*). I do not mean to focus on the problem of Eliot's formulation of the solution — namely, his separation and sequencing of strictly literary judgments and moral or theological judgments; others have examined that problem elsewhere. Nor do I wish to say that Eliot is wrong in saying that literature affects us "wholly, as human beings"; indeed, there seems to be greater and greater agreement on that general issue. What I do want to suggest is that Eliot's statements can easily be misappropriated by Christian critics and misused as a rationale for glib moralizing, for superficial judgments of the moral or theological rightness or wrongness of literary works. Eliot himself only rarely lapsed into this kind of uncharitable moralizing, and it is strange to see his essay adduced as a license for a Daniel come to judgment, an opportunity for literary prejudice to be added to moral triumphalism.

I think that we take Eliot's essay in a fully serious way if we go on to ask of moral criticism the question we should by now have learned to ask of every kind of criticism. If Eliot, Trilling, and others have taught us not to assume that literature is innocent of intentions, we should also have learned to doubt that criticism is similarly innocent. It is often, if not always, appropriate to ask what a critical approach wants, what it wants to have happen, what it is for and what it is against. It may be that a particular form of criticism is a simple or complex quest for a better reading of a text; it may be a form of celebration; but it may also be an act of will, a more or less systematic attempt to manipulate, direct, or control the text or the reader. Like literature, criticism affects us wholly, as human beings, and it can determine the way we approach or perceive or appropriate literature. It is because criticism can conceal signs of its ideological and methodological imperialism that it is necessary to insist on certain questions. How extensive is its explanatory power? If a critical method explains too much or too little, that is a fact about a method which we should be aware of. How adequate is it as a means of assessing the huge variety of genres and traditions that we refer to as literature? If it can account for only certain kinds of literature, only certain periods, only certain elements, then an awareness of its limits is as necessary as an awareness of what it can explain.

For most literature teachers in Christian colleges, moral criticism exists alongside many other interests and concerns.

We want students to learn something about national literatures, about genres, about literary themes and traditions, about critical approaches to literature, about themselves. And through all this learning we want them to become better and better readers, responsible and informed readers, capable not only of understanding a great variety of literary texts but also of responding to them in useful, interesting, adequate ways. What concern we may have for the moral implications of literature arises out of our awareness of the complex interaction of text, reader, and context. The college classroom demonstrates a special version of this interaction, because there the professor is often in a position to answer students' questions about a work's value or values, in a position to shape students' responses to literature. Admittedly, some part of moral criticism as it comes to expression in the classroom is submerged, silent, evident primarily in what we choose *not* to teach, based on our assessment of the abilities of the students, the purposes of the course, and our own peculiar limitations. What W. H. Auden said about writers in *The Dyer's Hand* may also have some relevance for literature professors: "All one can say is that a writer who, like all men, has his personal weaknesses and limitations, should be aware of them, and try his best to keep them out of his work" (19).

Beyond this silent or submerged moral criticism is the more visible manifestation evident when we apply moral standards directly to the literature we have decided to teach. Included here are responses to the familiar challenges posed by the subject matter of a work of literature, its characters, situations, actions, language, and attitudes or worldview, and the authorial attitude toward any or all of these elements. For some of us, it is at this level that moral criticism has its clearest task — to address the offenses of immorality, obscenity, profanity, and vulgarity, particularly if these offenses go unpunished or unrebuked in the work of literature itself. But to the extent that this sort of criticism focuses upon the indictment of surface offenses, this is surely not a complete or satisfactory job for a moral critic, especially for a Christian moral critic, who should be very aware of the possibility that literature often provides lessons that we need to learn, that it may pass judgments which are binding upon us. To paraphrase Auden, really good books read us: our lives and interests are read and judged by really good books. The action of judgment moves in both directions. For this reason, Christian professors must also be fully capable of engaging literature in the ways I mentioned earlier. They must be alert to — and respectful of — the moral sensibility that informs a work or body of work, and they must acknowledge the value of judging the adequacy of conventional ways of responding to moral concerns by allowing the work itself to judge fully and deeply.

Christian critics also bring moral concerns into play through the way they teach their courses. Lecture and discussion classes, as well as the seminar and independent study, allow moral considerations to come to the foreground. Teachers supply students with syllabi, study guides, and supplements, require short and long writing assignments, use essay questions on examinations, and direct the critical energies of their students in many other ways as well. Even if they don't consciously intend to do so, professors provide their students with regular, if unsystematic, lessons in criticism. Teachers need not devote lectures or assigned readings to the issues of morality and literature, since the persistent concerns and questions recurring throughout a course of study suggest an orientation to this subject even if professors do not explicitly announce it.

In my description, moral criticism in the Christian college classroom may look meager and/or untidy. I'm certain that it often is. Moral criticism may simply be added to the professor's many other critical concerns. Many of us habitually "cover" genre, the author, the cultural and historical context, the structure of the work itself, and the themes or ideas of the work; and finally, as a kind of afterthought, or as a duty, we make a moral assessment of the work. It should be clear that this is not adequate, neither for the work nor for the classroom nor for the larger task at hand. Moral criticism should be part of a unified and coherent response to a literary work, not one of many piecemeal and disconnected judgments.

But another reason for the meagerness and untidiness of much moral criticism is the difficulty of doing this task well at all, especially in the classroom. It is the nature of much of the literature we teach to be troubling or tendentious or even potentially offensive to someone's sensibilities. The "gather ye rosebuds" tradition of love songs and seduction lyrics generally; bawdry in Chaucer, Shakespeare, and Cummings; misanthropy and disgust with the human form in Swift; Eliot's misogyny and Pound's fascism and anti-Semitism; Flannery O'Connor's reliance upon violence and the grotesque; Auden's homosexuality — such a list is merely an indication of the kinds of challenges literature presents to teachers who consciously engage the moral dimensions of the literary experience. Such challenges can be too great, causing some teachers to abandon the task entirely, and others to become sidetracked by the moral questions, devoting all their energies to the endless problem of separating virtue from vice.

It is not necessary to yield to either extreme. This essay is not the proper place to engage the larger questions of the role of the study of literature in the Christian college curriculum, or of how to adjudicate the claims of Christ and the claims of the culture we live in, but it is surely in the context of answers to these larger questions that we can begin to see where and why and how moral criticism has a role to play in the Christian college and in the Christian life generally. My shorthand answer to such questions would involve assumptions such as the following: Christians take literary study seriously because literature can be such a powerful force in the world; because literature can promote intellectual, spiritual, and emotional growth; because we are called to be responsible stewards of all God's gifts, including the gifts of genius and craftsmanship; and because we were made in such a way as to be able to respond to the arts (and to many other things) with pleasure and joy. Christians committed to addressing and understanding the world they live in do not have the luxury of ignoring its cultural achievements and manifestations; they do not have the luxury of assuming that the arts have no claim on them; they do not have the luxury of remaining disengaged from the culture they are called to know and confront. Christians are called to make appropriate use of their various gifts, skills, resources, and knowledge. Such appropriate use will be motivated in part by obedience or response to a call to duty; it will also be motivated by gratitude for the enormous gift the arts constitute; and it will be motivated by joy, by the legitimate pleasure that the arts can promote and provide.

Within such a context, the Christian college teacher need not find the task of moral criticism to be overwhelming. That is, he or she should not teach literature as if it were a body of heretical or wicked works which need to be discredited. Nor should literature be received uncritically, as if it were simply gift or grace. Literature and the institutions for producing, receiving, and judging it are complex human and cultural activities, and as such require of the Christian an informed, thoughtful, and obedient response.

For the purposes of this essay, I am not very interested in any particular set of the various beliefs or assumptions that constitute the moral standards employed by moral critics. This area surely deserves study and exposition, but even a brief description and assessment of these beliefs would require the extensive treatment that only a separate study could provide. Even Christians, who share beliefs, hold them in different ways and assign them varying degrees of importance. Furthermore, the success of moral criticism depends not only on *what* moral standards are employed but also on *how* they are held, how they are used, and how useful they are for criticism — and this is true for each particular circumstance. For these reasons, I will conclude this essay with a brief assessment of the possibilities of moral criticism by describing its features, positive and negative, by describing what moral criticism might look like in practice. I will focus on moral criticism in the Christian college classroom, but I think that what I describe will have general relevance as well.

What should moral criticism look like if it is to be truly worthwhile for us, for literary studies, and for our students? Positively, it should have at least some of the following features.

First, it should exhibit some of what Matthew Arnold recommended as critical virtues: flexibility, modulation, patience, readiness to praise strengths and gifts wherever they appear. That is, moral criticism should be capable of taking into consideration the particular moment or cultural context addressed by a particular work of art. It is not sufficient merely to judge the morality of a work of art by the standards of a present problem, of a current issue. Furthermore, moral criticism should be capable of noting what potential benefits a work might offer our cultural situation. Moral criticism should be capable of seeing a work within large contexts, so that its place within a developing tradition of exploration or argument, its place within the development of an author's total body of work, would make a difference in the kind of judgment made.

Second, moral criticism should be aware of and receptive to the possibility of improvements or reformations of the moral standards we bring to the task of criticism. Moral critics should be capable of increasing or deepening their knowledge of what morality requires. Christian moral critics should know more fully what the life of Christian discipleship requires. Moral critics should also be aware of their tunnel vision, of their blind spots. And moral critics should be willing to be judged by the literature they read.

There are many ironies involved in this dimension of moral criticism. Some moral critics, for instance, are easily offended by the sexual content of literature, ready to judge such literature as defective and harmful, but the same critics can be only marginally aware of less visible forms of exploitation and degradation — of women, for example, because of the anti-feminist bias of a work, an author, or a tradition. Such moral critics can have very little awareness of the damage done to the exploited in the process, and can be very reluctant to face or acknowledge their own sexism, racism, or ethnocentrism. There is also the potential irony of the moral or theological critic keenly alert for blasphemy or heresy in literature but willing to view third-rate "Christian" literature, hymns, and essays as acceptable. And there is the odd irony of Christian critics who know, intellectually and doctrinally, that ours is a corrupt and corrupting culture, but who don't like literature to take a prophetic stance against our materialism, our higher consumerism, our debased taste, our vulgarity. In all such instances, a truly legitimate moral criticism would serve to close the gap between belief and practice, between intention and accomplishment.

Third, moral criticism should model for students both the necessity and the difficulty of answering basic questions about moral criticism itself: What sort of claim does moral criticism have? What authority has it claimed or earned? What does it want me to be, or do, or assume, or assent to, or value? To be fully useful, moral criticism must be reflective, capable of posing and addressing these fundamental questions about the role of moral criticism within the larger community of criticism and within the community of readers.

But not even an introductory description of moral criticism would be complete without a list of questions and concerns about how moral criticism can go wrong. Four concerns especially come to mind, concerns that I will formulate as questions for the practicing moral critic.

First, does my criticism do justice to the work under consideration? Does my critical work exhibit integrity and intelligence? Do I yield to the temptation to schematize, or stereotype, or generalize, or exaggerate? Am I guilty of acts of literary terrorism, or of settling scores?

Second, am I doing this work in a way that will allow my students or readers to develop morally, and to develop as moral critics themselves? Do I teach them to avoid moral triumphalism, an affliction that is not a real improvement on the moral olympianism they mean to oppose? Do I teach them to love literature and to demand qualities appropriate to it, and not to arm themselves for literary search-and-destroy missions? Has my criticism helped my students or readers to see that choosing to make moral judgments does not solve the problems of the moral life, but rather tends to deepen or complicate these problems? Do I acknowledge that neither moral criticism nor moral literature can guarantee the effects I desire? Do I demonstrate in my work that we cannot depend on people to respond to literature and criticism in the ways we would like them to respond?

Third, is my practice of moral criticism likely to produce an environment in which the literature I want to have will be able to thrive? Is the literature I seem to be demanding really the literature I want? Is my criticism likely to produce or encourage writers within the Christian community? For some, Plato figures as the original moral critic; because literature has the power to deny or undermine right thought, he found it necessary to banish poets from his ideal republic. Citing an "ancient quarrel between philosophy and poetry," Plato wanted to ban all poetry but "hymns to the gods and praises of famous men" in his perfect realm. "We shall be right in refusing to admit [the poet] into a well-ordered State," he commented, "because he awakens and nourishes and strengthens the feelings and impairs the reason." If we were to follow Plato's lead, we would be fostering a literary culture similar to that of the Houyhnhnms in Part IV of *Gulliver's Travels:* these superbly rational and moral horses have followed reason and right thinking to such an extent that even their language is affected — they have almost no vocabulary for evil. And their literature contains "either some exalted notions of friendship and benevolence, or the praises of those who were victors in races and other bodily exercises." While this is not exactly an idiot literature, it is far from what we really want.

Fourth, does this kind of criticism acknowledge that a moral assessment of a work may not always be an appropriate or even a desirable response to it? Critical and methodological imperialism is a temptation for moral critics, just as it is for almost any school of criticism. Moral critics must be especially alert for signs of critical agnosia in their work, the loss of ability to perceive with their other critical senses. Strikingly apposite here is Charles Lamb's complaint about theatre-goers' myopic preoccupation with "the moral point" of the "drama of common life" so popular in England, a complaint he made in "On the Artificial Comedy of the Last Century":

> We are spectators to a plot or intrigue (not reducible in life to the point of strict morality), and take it all for truth. We substitute a real for a dramatic person, and judge him accordingly. We try him in our courts, from which there is no appeal to the *dramatis personae*, his peers. We have been spoiled with — not sentimental comedy — but a tyrant far more pernicious to our pleasures which has succeeded to it, the exclusive and all-devouring drama of common life; where the moral point is everything. . . .
>
> We carry our fireside concerns to the theatre with us. We do not go thither, like our ancestors, to escape from the pressure of reality, so much as to confirm our experience of it; to make assurance double, and take a bond of fate. We must live our toilsome lives twice over, as it was the mournful privilege of Ulysses to descend twice to the shades. All that neutral ground of character, which stood between vice and virtue; or which in fact was indifferent to neither, where neither properly was called in question; that happy breathing-place from the burthen of perpetual moral questioning — the sanctuary and quiet Alsatia of hunted casuistry — is broken up and disfranchised, as injurious to the interests of society. The privileges of the place are taken away by law. We dare not dally with images, or names, of wrongs. We bark like foolish dogs at shadows. We dread infection from the scenic representation of disorder, and fear a painted pustule. In our anxiety that our morality should not take cold, we wrap it up in a great blanket surtout of precaution against the breeze and sunshine. (549-50)

Lamb's argument against the inappropriate use of moral criticism is a helpful reminder of the fact that we are not merely moral beings. Sometimes it is legitimate, even necessary, to remind ourselves of the value of sheer play, or joy, or peace, or freedom. And sometimes art can provide that sense of play, or peace, or freedom. It may be, as Lionel Trilling once claimed, that playing at the escape from the moral life may itself have moral consequences. But it is certainly true that an insistent moralism will sooner or later simply miss the point of many literary works. Lamb could say that he was "glad for a season to take an airing beyond the diocese of the strict conscience — not to live always in the precincts of the law-courts" (550), and moral critics today would be well advised to practice their trade carefully, not mistaking every literary work as an opportunity for the exercise of a heavy-handed moral judgment.

It is possible that a more nearly relaxed will would allow us to perceive the true nature of a particular work, and that under the right conditions we could make our peace with literature, perhaps even experience it as joy. We must consider that possibility. We should think of treating literature with that kind of respect as constituting a virtual moral obligation.

WORKS CITED

Abrams, M. H. "Behaviorism and Deconstruction: A Comment on Morse Peckham's 'The Infinitude of Pluralism.'" *Critical Inquiry* 4.1 (1987): 181-93.

————. "The Deconstructive Angel." *Critical Inquiry* 3.3 (1977): 425-38.

————. "From Addison to Kant: Modern Aesthetics and the Exemplary Art." In *Studies in Eighteenth-Century British Art and Aesthetics*, ed. Ralph Cohen, 16-48. Berkeley: University of California Press, 1985.

————. *A Glossary of Literary Terms.* 5th ed. New York: Holt, Rinehart & Winston, 1988.

————. "How to Do Things with Texts." *Partisan Review* 46.4 (1979): 566-88.

————. "Kant and the Theology of Art." *Notre Dame English Journal* 13.3 (1981): 75-106.

————. "A Note on Wittgenstein and Literary Criticism." *ELH* 41.4 (1974): 541-54.

————. "What's the Use of Theorizing About the Arts?" In *In Search of Literary Theory*, ed. Morton W. Bloomfield, 3-54. Ithaca and London: Cornell University Press, 1972.

Auden, W. H. *The Dyer's Hand*. New York: Random House, 1962.

Babbitt, Irving. *Irving Babbitt: Representative Writings*. Ed. George A. Panichas. Lincoln: University of Nebraska Press, 1981.

Barbour, John D. "The Virtues in a Pluralistic Context." *Journal of Religion* 63.2 (1983): 175-82.

Beardsley, Monroe C. "The Humanities and Human Understanding." In *The Humanities and the Understanding of Reality*, ed. Thomas B. Stroup, 1-31. Lexington: University of Kentucky Press, 1966.

Bloom, Alexander. *Prodigal Sons: The New York Intellectuals and Their World*. New York: Oxford University Press, 1986.

Booth, Wayne. *The Company We Keep: An Ethics of Fiction*. Berkeley: University of California Press, 1988.

————. "Criticulture: Or, Why We Need at Least Three Criticisms at the Present Time." In *What Is Criticism?* ed. Paul Hernadi, 162-76. Bloomington: Indiana University Press, 1981.

————. "Why Ethical Criticism Fell on Hard Times." *Ethics* 98 (1988): 278-93.

Bové, Paul. *Intellectuals in Power: A Genealogy of Critical Humanism*. New York: Columbia University Press, 1986.

Burke, Edmund. *Reflections on the Revolution in France*. Ed. William B. Todd. New York: Holt, Rinehart & Winston, 1959.

Clausen, Christopher. *The Moral Imagination: Essays on Literature and Ethics*. Iowa City: University of Iowa Press, 1986.

Culler, Jonathan. "Comparative Literature and the Pieties." *Profession* 86 (1986): 30-32.

————. "A Critic against the Christians." *TLS*, 23 Nov. 1984, pp. 1327-28.

Dewey, John. *Art as Experience*. 1934; rpt. New York: Capricorn Books, 1958.

Donoghue, Denis. "In Their Masters' Steps." *TLS*, 16 Dec. 1988, pp. 1399-1400.

Donovan, Josephine. "Beyond the Net: Feminist Criticism as a Moral Criticism." *Denver Quarterly* 17.4 (1983): 40-57.

Eagleton, Terry. *The Function of Criticism*. Thetford, Norwalk, England: Thetford Press, 1984.

Eliot, T. S. "Religion and Literature." In *Selected Essays*, rev. ed., 343-54. New York: Harcourt Brace Jovanovich, 1964.

Etzioni, Amitai. "Toward an I and We Paradigm." *Contemporary Sociology* 18.2 (1989): 171-76.

Frankena, William K. *Ethics*. Englewood Cliffs, N.J.: Prentice-Hall, 1963.

————. "MacIntyre and Modern Morality." *Ethics* 93 (1983): 579-87.

Frye, Northrop, Sheridan Baker, and George Perkins. *The Harper Handbook to Literature*. New York: Harper & Row, 1985.

Gamwell, Franklin. "Traditions of Moral Reasoning." *Christian Century*, 12 Oct. 1988, pp. 901-2.

Gardner, John. *On Moral Fiction*. New York: Basic Books, 1978.

Geertz, Clifford. "Found in Translation: On the Social History of the Moral Imagination." *Georgia Review* 31.4 (1977): 788-810.

Graff, Gerald. *Literature against Itself*. Chicago: University of Chicago Press, 1979.

————. *Poetic Statement and Critical Dogma*. Chicago: University of Chicago Press, 1970.

Gunn, Giles. *The Culture of Criticism and the Criticism of Culture*. New York: Oxford University Press, 1987.

Himmelfarb, Gertrude. *Marriage and Morals among the Victorians*. New York: Alfred A. Knopf, 1986.

Holman, C. Hugh, and William Harmon. *A Handbook to Literature*. 5th ed. New York: Macmillan, 1986.

Holmes, Stephen. "The Polis State." *New Republic*, 6 June 1988, pp. 32-39.

Jameson, Fredric. *The Political Unconscious: Narrative as a Socially Symbolic Act*. Ithaca: Cornell University Press, 1981.

Kirk, Russell. *Enemies of the Permanent Things*. La Salle, Ill.: Sherwood Sugden & Co., 1969.

Krieger, Murray. "In the Wake of Morality: The Thematic Underside of Recent Theory." *New Literary History* 15.1 (1983): 119-36.

Lamb, Charles. "On the Artificial Comedy of the Last Century." In *The Portable Charles Lamb*, ed. John Mason Brown, 549-58. New York: Penguin Books, 1980.

Lewis, C. S. *An Experiment in Criticism*. Cambridge: Cambridge University Press, 1961.

Lovibond, Sabina. *Realism and Imagination in Ethics.* Minneapolis: University of Minnesota Press, 1983.

MacIntyre, Alasdair. *After Virtue: A Study in Moral Theory.* 2nd ed. Notre Dame: University of Notre Dame Press, 1984.

———. *Whose Justice? Which Rationality?* Notre Dame: University of Notre Dame Press, 1988.

Merod, Jim. *The Political Responsibility of the Critic.* Ithaca: Cornell University Press, 1987.

Nagel, Thomas. "Agreeing in Principle." *TLS,* 8 July 1988, pp. 747-48.

Neuhaus, Richard John. "Traditions of Inquiry." *Commentary,* June 1988, pp. 64-68.

Nussbaum, Martha. "Recoiling from Reason." *New York Review of Books,* 7 Dec. 1989, pp. 36-41.

Orwell, George. *My Country Right or Left — 1940–1943.* Vol. 2 of *The Collected Essays, Journalism and Letters of George Orwell.* Ed. Sonia Orwell and Ian Angus. New York: Harcourt, Brace & World, 1968.

Princeton Encyclopedia of Poetry and Poetics. Ed. Alex Preminger. Enlarged ed. Princeton: Princeton University Press, 1974.

Raphael, D. D. "Can Literature Be Moral Philosophy?" *New Literary History* 15.1 (1983): 1-12.

Schneewind, J. B. "Moral Crisis and the History of Ethics." *Midwest Studies in Philosophy* 8 (1983): 525-39.

———. "Virtue, Narrative, and Community: MacIntyre and Morality." *Journal of Philosophy* 79.11 (1982): 653-63.

Siebers, Tobin. *The Ethics of Criticism.* Ithaca: Cornell University Press, 1988.

Stevens, Bonnie Klomp, and Larry L. Stewart. *A Guide to Literary Criticism and Research.* New York: Holt, Rinehart & Winston, 1987.

Stout, Jeffrey. *Ethics after Babel: The Languages of Morals and Their Discontents.* Boston: Beacon Press, 1988.

———. "Homeward Bound: MacIntyre on Liberal Society and the History of Ethics." *Journal of Religion* 69.2 (1989): 220-32.

———. "Virtue among the Ruins: An Essay on MacIntyre." *Neue Zeitschrift für Systematische Theologie und Religionsphilosophie* 26.3 (1984): 256-72.

Suleiman, Susan. "Ideological Dissent from Works of Fiction: Toward a Rhetoric of the *Roman à These.*" *Neophilologus* 60.2 (1976): 162-77.

Tanner, Stephen L. *Lionel Trilling.* Boston: Twayne Publishers, 1988.

——. *Paul Elmer More: Literary Criticism as the History of Ideas.* Provo, Utah: Brigham Young University, 1987.

Trilling, Lionel. "On the Teaching of Modern Literature." In *Beyond Culture.* New York: Viking Press, 1965.

——. "The Two Environments." In *Beyond Culture.* New York: Viking Press, 1965.

Walzer, Michael. *The Company of Critics: Social Criticism in the Twentieth Century.* New York: Basic Books, 1988.

White, James Boyd. *When Words Lose Their Meaning.* Chicago: University of Chicago Press, 1984.

Willey, Basil. *The English Moralists.* New York: W. W. Norton, 1964.

MARXIST CRITICISM

Clarence Walhout

A S A SCHOOL OF LITERARY CRITICISM, MARXISM HAS IN THE past been primarily a European development. Its influence has, of course, been felt in America, particularly in the 1930s, but this influence did not shape the major developments in American criticism. It was evident in the work of critics like Edmund Wilson, Irving Howe, and Alfred Kazin, but even for these critics Marxism was more important as a model for dealing with the social and political significance of literature than as a philosophical system. Recently, however, Marxist theory as well as criticism has gained respect worldwide and has influenced other critical movements such as poststructuralism, feminism, and New Historicism. Marxist thought, for example, provides a model of social analysis for such contemporary critics as Jerome McGann, Frank Lentricchia, and Gerald Graff. In this essay, however, we will not attempt to explore the current influence of Marxism but will examine the development of Marxist literary thought as an internally coherent tradition.

ISSUES IN MARXIST CRITICISM

Although Marxism is first of all a social theory that places a strong emphasis on economics, it has from the beginning had much to say about all aspects of human life, including art and literature. Statements about art can be found in the works of Marx and Engels and in the works of many of the early Russian followers of Marx, such as Plekhanov, Lenin, and Trotsky. The main development of Marxist literary criticism, however, was the work of university scholars and took place first in Moscow and later, after the propagandistic programs of Stalinism were enforced around 1930, in other European centers, notably Prague, Berlin, and Frankfurt. Recently its appeal is increasing in such places as the United States, England, and Australia as its ties with Russian politics are loosening and as the reputation of formalist theories of criticism continues to wane.

Marxist literary criticism is social and historical criticism rather than formalist criticism; it exists in the context of Marxist social theory and may even be thought of as an extension or a branch of social theory. In general, it builds on the assumption that literature develops out of social contexts and in some way addresses the concerns of society. The task of literary scholars is to understand just how literature is related to other kinds of social activity and how it contributes to the development of social life.

As the Marxist social ideal became the model for social development in the Soviet Union after the October revolution of 1917, literature and literary criticism came under the close scrutiny of Russian political leaders. The first major effect of this scrutiny was the growth of what came to be called social realism. This is the view that since literature mirrors and interprets social life, both literature and literary criticism should aim to improve the conditions of social life. Literature influences as well as reflects society, and therefore, like everything else, it ought to contribute to the well-being of society. It ought to help shape the ideal society as envisioned by Marxist theory. As social realism became doctrine for Stalinist thinking in the 1920s, writers and critics alike felt the pressure to work for the advancement of the Soviet state.

In its narrowest forms, this view of literature fostered propagandistic writing and led to the emigration of a number of critics who could not accept state control over art and criticism. Outside of Moscow the narrower versions of social realism did not flourish, and Marxist critics attempted to be true to Marx rather than to Stalin. These critics often refer to propagandistic and doctrinaire forms of social realism as "vulgar Marxism."

Marxist critics generally consider Georg Lukacs to be the first major spokesman for Marxist literary criticism. Much of the earlier history of Marxist criticism is summed up in Lukacs' career. He wrote his first books under the influence of Hegel, the philosopher who dominated the philosophical scene when Marx was developing his own views. Marx himself opposed Hegel but also reflected his influence. Because early followers of Marx often felt the presence of Hegel as strongly as that of Marx himself, they faced the difficulty of sorting out the implications of Marxism over against those of Hegelianism. The difference, simply put, is that Hegel viewed culture as the expression of the ideas and values that people hold, whereas Marx viewed culture as the responses of people to the material conditions of their lives. According to Hegelianism, ideas and values determine the forms of social life that people develop; according to Marxism, forms of social life determine the ideas and values that people develop. Hegel's philosophy is idealist (consciousness shapes social reality); Marx's philosophy is materialist (social reality shapes consciousness).

Lukacs' early book entitled *Theory of the Novel* (1914-15) reflects a Hegelian viewpoint in its analysis of the historical origins of the novel. In the ancient world, the Homeric epic mirrored a world that was stable and coherent because it was formed by a set of commonly held values; the epic hero was the embodiment of a social ideal. In the modern world, the epic has died because there is no social cohesiveness to sustain it. Instead, the novel arises as the expression of a new individualism. The hero of the novel is one who is in conflict with society — a victim, a maverick, a critic, an exploiter. Thus, both epic and novel are literary forms that reflect the ideas and values which a society holds, but whereas the epic reflects social unity, the novel reflects society in the throes of ideological conflict.

In Lukacs' later works, such as *The Historical Novel* (1937), the Marxist emphasis is more evident. The novel is not just the reflection of history's loss of an earlier social cohesion but is an interpretation of social values. In showing how social values are embedded in social practices, writers like Balzac reveal how literature can interpret society as well as mirror it. The best novels not only reflect the ideas that bind a society together but are also socially constructive. The novelist creates literary forms that will have an effect on social life. Lukacs' later works bear the ethical stamp that marks much Marxist criticism. They illustrate the positive, non-propagandistic qualities of social realism. For Lukacs, the best modern literature is to be found in the realistic novel, which mirrors society in order to evaluate it, to expose its weaknesses to the light of more worthy social norms.

While later Marxist critics appreciate Lukacs' work, they generally find it too heavy-handed in its moral emphasis and too insensitive to the aesthetic qualities of literature. The tension between the social and ethical emphasis of Marxism on the one hand and the increasing emphasis on artistic and aesthetic values in modern criticism on the other hand has occasioned new reflections on the role of art in society. Marxist criticism has begun to reflect an increasing preoccupation with theory in an effort to understand how Marxist practical criticism should deal with the kinds of critical assumptions being developed outside its ranks, particularly those evident in the spectacular rise of formalist criticism after World War I.

This tension can be seen in the work of Lucien Gold-

mann, a disciple of Lukacs. Goldmann attempts to understand
how it is that the literary works we consider great seem to rise
above their societies and how it is that works which mirror their
societies most realistically are often considered mediocre from
an aesthetic point of view. His answer is suggested by the term
that he used for his own theory: genetic structuralism. In great
works the author assimilates into his art cultural values that are
implicit in a society but are not always consciously recognized
by those who live in that society. This ability to reflect the
underlying values of society is what gives scope to the works of
great writers and makes them aesthetically valuable beyond
their own age. The great artist sees how various aspects of social
life are interrelated and thus stands apart from as well as within
his or her culture. Great works of art have aesthetic value
beyond their own day because they capture a vision of a society
as a whole as well as depict particular images of social life that
the artist takes directly from society. Mediocre artists render
their societies vividly but not with the interpretive vision of the
great artists. Thus, although literature has its genesis in social
life, the critic must analyze the structural and aesthetic qualities
of literature as well as its specific content in order to see how
the social value of literature extends beyond its particular place
of origin.

For other Marxists, Goldmann's effort to reconcile aesthetic theory and social theory raises as many problems as it
solves. First, it fails to solve the problem of determinism that
lurks around the model of social realism. Traditionally Marxists
conceive of society in terms of a superstructure-infrastructure
model. This model regards all of the superstructural forms of
social life — the political, legal, religious, aesthetic, ethical, and
so on — as dependent on and formed in accordance with the
infrastructure of a society, which is made up of its economic
modes of production. Fundamental to every society is the satisfaction of the basic economic needs for survival, and how a
society satisfies these material needs (its infrastructure) determines the forms that social life takes (its superstructure). The

term *genetic* in Goldmann's formula suggests a view of art that is more deterministic than later Marxists are willing to accept. They want to claim a greater degree of freedom and independence for art, to retain the materialism of Marxist philosophy without committing themselves to a simple determinism.

One way out of this dilemma is found in the work of Theodor Adorno and Herbert Marcuse. In Adorno's view, each sphere of life in the superstructure of society has its own history as well as its place in the history of society as a whole. Artists, for example, use artistic conventions that have developed historically and that do not rise directly out of the artist's own society. Although changes in these forms are influenced by the artist's circumstances and therefore by his society's infrastructure, his art cannot be explained deterministically as the direct consequence of the infrastructure. Rather, aesthetic conventions have a dialectical relationship to economic and social conventions.

Accordingly, Marxist criticism needs to understand the aesthetic conventions that form art as well as the particular social situations of the artists. Adorno, for example, whose subject is music more than literature, shows on the one hand how Schoenberg developed his modern form of serial music out of the musical traditions of the late nineteenth century and on the other hand how serial music is expressive of the social values that permeate Schoenberg's own cultural environment. This illustrates Adorno's view that art is independent with respect to its own history and dependent with respect to social history generally. It is the critic's task to interpret this dialectical relationship of various social and aesthetic influences.

Marcuse, who focuses on the social function more than on the aesthetics of art, shows that by virtue of its own traditions art can to a degree detach itself from immediate social realities and examine them critically. It does so by creating imagined and utopian societies that stand in contrast to the real society of the artist. Art, in fact, has the cultural role of creating utopian ideals that serve as negative evaluations of present society. This kind of thinking involves a radical move away from earlier forms of social realism. For Marcuse, literature is a means for social criticism rather than social propaganda. He retains the basic principles of Marxist theory but interprets them in a way that emphasizes artistic freedom rather than artistic determinism.

A second problem brought into focus by Goldmann's genetic structuralism is the old problem of Hegelian influences in Marxist thinking. Later Marxists find in Goldmann's work too great a dependence on the view that the structures of social life and the structures of art are determined by ideas and values. A number of important Marxist theorists have attempted to work out more consistently the implications of Marxist materialism. These include Louis Althusser and Pierre Macherey.

Althusser argues that the structural patterns of social life and art are not the expression of prior ideas and values but are formal principles which are implicit in the way a society carries on its social practices. They are structural patterns that can be uncovered only by analysis of a society and art; they are not pre-existent blueprints for the shaping of social life. Just as grammar does not exist before language but is implicit in actual language usage, so the structures of society and art do not precede social and artistic practices but are inherent in them. Thus, in keeping with Marxist philosophy, Althusser holds that social life and art are formed by the material conditions of life and by the infrastructural ways in which a society deals with those material conditions. The understanding of a society and its art depends on uncovering those structural paradigms that are latent in social and artistic practices. Accordingly, the literary critic sees literature as a kind of social practice that transforms in aesthetic ways the social life in which it is embedded; criticism aims to analyze the forms within which these transformations occur.

A similar line of thinking is developed by Macherey. For Macherey, the forms of art do not necessarily coincide with or exist in harmony with other social forms. Artistic structures, in fact, are typically in conflict with the dominant structures of social life; art disrupts social harmony by revealing society's incompleteness, its distance from the ideal society. Although literature cannot escape its own social contexts, it can through its fictions de-center the paradigms which exist in society — that is, writers can reveal the weaknesses of a society by their artistic struggles to express in fiction what a society does not permit in reality. The innovative and experimental nature of art means that a literary work is not the unified embodiment of social values that earlier Marxists envisioned, but a work whose "incompleteness" or forms of disunity reveal the ideological biases and limits of society.

As these brief summaries have indicated, Marxist literary criticism is a developing and dynamic movement. It takes seriously its basis in Marx's philosophy but is also vitally engaged in issues that concern contemporary literary theory and criticism generally. As previously noted, Marxist thought is influential in various kinds of postmodern criticism, including deconstructionist, feminist, and New Historicist criticism. Its long tradition of social and historical criticism offers an alternative to the various formalist models that are currently out of favor.

Much of the appeal that Marxist criticism holds even for those not committed to Marx's philosophy or political theories may be summarized by the following interrelated principles:

- an emphasis on historical criticism;
- an emphasis on the social value of criticism;
- a concern with the social function of literature;
- a view that artistic forms cannot be understood apart from the social life which is expressed through them;
- a view that artistic conventions cannot be understood apart from the history of social life which produced them;
- a view that art is to be understood as one kind of social practice;
- a view that aesthetic value is not autonomous but is intertwined with social and moral value.

MIKHAIL BAKHTIN

M. M. Bakhtin was not mentioned in the preceding historical sketch because, although he is currently perceived as one of the most important Marxist critics, he stands somewhat outside the historical mainstream. He did much of his writing in the twenties and thirties, but since he had no status in Russian universities or in Russian society, his works were not widely known and were often attributed to his friends.

His relationship to the Marxist mainstream is, in fact, rather ambivalent. On the one hand, the recent revival and popularity of his works seem a triumphant moment for Marxist criticism. On the other hand, many think his Marxism less important than the general vitality of his thought. John Frow writes, "It is an attractive path, and it will be clear from the previous chapter how strongly I have been influenced by Bakhtin (in his various voices). But although the body of his work . . . is in many ways exemplary, there are also major theoretical problems with it, and it is not clear to me that it can be unproblematically redeemed for or incorporated into Marxist theory" (97-98). Bakhtin's biographer, Michael Holquist, gives some evidence that Bakhtin retained ties with the traditions of Russian Christianity.

Bakhtin is currently riding the crest; he has been called "the greatest theoretician of literature in the twentieth century" (Todorov ix), and many non-Marxists as well as Marxists find his work profound and insightful both in theory and in practice. Since it is impossible to do justice to the scope of his thought in a few pages, I will select several ideas that seem to me to engage the Christian critic as well as the Marxist critic. Bakhtin's work reveals in many ways how the concerns of Marxist and Christian critics run in parallel courses.

Bakhtin's subject, broadly speaking, is human discourse and its deep embeddedness in the history of culture. Bakhtin argues that interdependence of discourse and social life requires that we develop a sociological poetics. He disparages formalist models of criticism that tend to divorce literature from its social moorings and its cultural complicities.

One thing that characterizes discourse is the dialectical struggle between authority and freedom. The power of authority that impinges on all of us is the power of tradition. Authoritative language — which is evident, for example, in the discourse of parents, teachers, moral leaders, religious dogmatists, political parties, and the like — establishes the order and continuity that historical experience requires. But historical experience also requires change and growth, and for this to occur, language must become "internally persuasive" and not just "authoritative." We develop as human beings when authoritative discourse yields to or joins with the power of internally persuasive discourse. Authoritative discourse, in Bakhtin's terminology, is monological; internally persuasive discourse is dialogical. In order to grow, we need to maintain a stance of openness to dialogue, for "in each of the new contexts that dialogize it, this discourse is able to reveal ever newer *ways to mean*" (*The Dialogic Imagination* 346).

The history of monological and dialogical discourses is evident not only in real life but also in literature, particularly in the history of narrative. In the history of the novel, for example, we can trace the movement from novels that speak from a single authoritative point of view (the monologic novel) to novels that speak from multiple points of view (the polyphonic novel). In this history there is a movement from authoritative viewpoints to ones in which a variety of internally persuasive voices are represented. The highest development of the polyphonic novel, in Bakhtin's view, is found in Dostoyevsky.

Placed in the context of Marxist theories of social and ideological development, these terms may seem alien — perhaps even hostile — to Christian thought. Is it not the Christian critic's obligation to judge the alluringly persuasive discourses of art in the light of the authoritative discourse of the Christian faith? Bakhtin's ideas are not, however, anti-Christian per se. Theoretically they can remind us that Christian discourse, like all discourse, is historical and contextual; the authority that Christian discourse carries must always be interpreted in the context of every new historical situation. The problem for Christian thinkers is how to understand the relationship between the authoritative word of God and the historicity of human discourses. Although Bakhtin does not focus on this theological problem, his emphasis on dialogue as the means whereby authoritative discourse can become internally persuasive discourse is a helpful model for thinking about the Christian's relationship to both Scripture and literature.

Christian literary criticism often falls into the same pitfalls that "vulgar Marxism" does — namely, that literature is simply a mirror of society or a cultural warehouse whose ideological furnishings need to be evaluated and priced. Bakhtin's view of the social history of literature, a history that is continued as long as there are readers and critics, suggests that we need to participate in the dialogue of literature and not just stand in judgment over it. Christian criticism becomes internally persuasive only if it participates dialogically in the discourse of others.

A second important idea in Bakhtin's writings is that while all literature is expressive of worldviews, these worldviews and the forms in which they are expressed cannot be understood independently from each other. Bakhtin writes, "All languages . . . are specific points of view on the world, forms for conceptualizing the world in words, specific world views, each characterized by its own objects, meanings and values. . . . This is why we constantly put forward the referential and expressive — that is, intentional — factors as the force that stratifies and differentiates the common literary language, and not the linguistic markers. . . . These external markers, linguistically observable and fixable, cannot in themselves be understood or studied without understanding the specific conceptualization they have been given by an intention" (*The Dialogic Imagination* 291-92). Although form and content can be distinguished, both are implicated in the cultural practices of historically specific societies: "For any individual consciousness living in it, language is not an abstract system of normative forms but rather a concrete heteroglot conception of the world" (293). Literature is historically situated, and its formal qualities never exist independent of ideology and are never of interest for their own sake. Aesthetic value is inseparable from social value.

This emphasis is a valuable counter to the tendency of Christian critics to regard form as "neutral" and content as the element of literature that needs to be judged by Christian norms. This tendency to separate form and content in Christian criticism comes perhaps from a desire on the part of Christians to separate the universal truths of the Christian faith from the changing forms of historical life. This desire translates into the attempt to judge form by historical standards of artistic evolution (which are neutral — that is, available to anyone) and to judge content by the non-historical standards of Christian truth. Bakhtin's view is more persuasive: all of life and art is historical, and form and content are inextricably wedded in the matrices of history.

A third idea in Bakhtin's work that is significant for Christian as well as Marxist criticism is suggested by his term *heteroglossia*. Discourse is always involved in heteroglossia, in the interplay of languages that in every society compete for attention and influence. Social voices are always in conflict and relativize one another as they become more or less persuasive to those who participate in the dialogue. According to Bakhtin, such conflict and interaction are necessary for productive changes in both society and literature: "It is necessary that heteroglossia wash over a culture's awareness of itself and its language, penetrate to its core, relativize the primary language system underlying its ideology and literature and deprive it of its naive absence of conflict" (*The Dialogic Imagination* 368).

Like Bakhtin's distinction between authoritative and internally persuasive language, these ideas may seem to be contrary to Christian thinking about truth and language, but Bakhtin's point is not that heteroglossia and dialogue destroy belief but that they sift out beliefs that lack enduring vitality. If the

Christian voice is a strong and compelling one, it has nothing to fear from participating in heteroglossia and everything to lose if it does not. When languages fail to participate in heteroglossia, Bakhtin observes, they lose touch with social realities, and "they essentially die as discourse" (*The Dialogic Imagination* 354). From the point of view of practical criticism, this is a call to read literary works not just as aesthetic objects that are expressive of static universal values but as voices in the cultural dialogue that engages all human beings. Literature is a kind of speech that comes to us from concrete historical and social circumstances and requires our dialogic response. From this point of view, the Christian critic is not the judge in a trial of literary worth but a participant in a debate over literary value.

MARXIST AND CHRISTIAN THEORY

In practical criticism, as the preceding overview makes clear, Marxists have moved from doctrinaire judgments about the ideological content of works to analyses of how literary works participate in the ongoing cultural dialogue of history. The history of Marxist literary criticism, both in theory and in practice, is instructive for Christian criticism, for both Christians and Marxists confront the task of adapting a set of beliefs and assumptions to the demands of interpretation.

That said, it is important to recognize the differences between Marxist and Christian criticism, differences that stem from the different ways in which they understand social life and the role of art in social life. These are differences in social theory and philosophy, but since social theory is so closely linked to both Marxist and Christian literary criticism, a consideration of some theoretical issues is important for the understanding of Marxist literary criticism. Indeed, most of the leading contemporary Marxist critics are social theorists as well as literary theorists.

The issues in Marxist social and literary theory are in many ways focused by the concept of ideology; this concept is the key to the understanding of social history and of literary history as a branch of social history. In the Marxist view, societies throughout history have developed economic systems of production that work to the advantage of some and to the disadvantage of others, and they have built on these systems elaborate forms of social life that serve both to carry out the economic systems and to justify those systems in the eyes of those societies. The superstructural forms of social life serve to legitimate the infrastructure on which they are based.

Since these forms of social life are not independently valuable, and since they are based on economic systems that exploit the masses of people, they may be thought of as ideological. All societies create ideologies that function as self-justifying principles for the practices of those societies. All ideologies distort the real needs of people and become agents of injustice. Ideologies are inescapable, but all must be undermined in the pursuit of justice for the whole of humanity.

Just how ideologies arise, how they function, how they can be overturned, and how extensively they reach into social life are matters of continuing debate among Marxists. The debates involve differing conceptions or definitions of ideology, for one's view of how ideology functions will depend to a large degree on how one defines ideology. It will be instructive for us to follow in broad outline the course of this debate.

One of the earliest definitions of ideology is that it is "false consciousness" — that is, a set of ideas and values which order social life in ways that do not meet the real needs of people. Certain problems with this definition soon emerged. First, it seems to imply that social practices are distinct from ideology as such, that ideology is conceptual and that social practices are brought into conformity with conceptual principles. This suggests the Hegelian view that consciousness determines reality rather than the Marxist view that reality determines consciousness. Second, this definition raises the question of how ideologies can be judged to be false — that is, it implies some standard of truth whereby consciousness can be judged to be false.

The first of these problems has led to the view now generally held by Marxists that ideology is to be defined not as consciousness but as the entire set of ideas, values, and attitudes that are implicit in social practices, or even as social practices themselves. Consciousness is not separate from social practice but is constituted by social practice. Louis Althusser goes so far as to say, "In truth, ideology has very little to do with 'consciousness'" and is better understood as "the lived relation between men and their world" (*For Marx* 233). The definition that Terry Eagleton gives in *Marxism and Literary Criticism* seems representative: "Ideology is not in the first place a set of doctrines; it signifies the way men live out their roles in class-society, the values, ideas, and images which tie them to their social function and so prevent them from a true knowledge of society as a whole" (16-17). In this definition our attention is focused on historical and social realities rather than on consciousness alone.

With this definition, however, the second problem noted becomes even more acute, for if ideology embraces all of social life as well as all of consciousness, then how can we achieve judgments about ideologies that are not themselves ideological? How can we arrive at true understanding if all of life and thought is ideological? This question lies behind the work of most of the important contemporary Marxist theorists, from Louis Althusser and Pierre Macherey to Fredric Jameson, John Frow, and Terry Eagleton.

Althusser argues that if we can achieve a valid definition of ideology per se, then we have a basis for interpreting particular ideologies as they appear in the course of history. Such a definition, he suggests, can be achieved through a structural analysis of particular ideologies. Through a comparative analysis of particular ideologies, we can derive the essential qualities or conditions for the existence of all ideologies. These conditions are illuminated most fully in Marxist social theory. The difficulty with this approach, however, as many assessments of structuralist thinking have shown, is that comparative analysis of particular societies is itself a kind of interpretation which occurs within a given society. Even structural definitions of ideology are based on interpretations from within ideology. Definitions depend on interpretation and cannot achieve status as the necessary ground for interpretation.

Pierre Macherey approaches the issue by suggesting that literature distinguishes itself from ideology by standing in opposition to it. Although as a social production it cannot rise above ideology, it can create imaginative images that point to differences between itself and the ideological forms of social life. It cannot speak in the name of some non-ideological truth, but it can create a form of "incompleteness which enables us to identify the active presence of a conflict at its borders" (155). Literature creates a gap — an "otherness," a "silence," an "absence" — between itself and ideology. Thus, literature reveals the limits of the ideology that produces it. While this view suggests a theory about how literature serves to expose the limits of ideology, it does not offer a criterion for defining ideology or for judging the truth of the critiques of ideologies found in literary works.

A rigorous attempt to deal with these questions can be found in *The Political Unconscious* by Fredric Jameson. Jameson agrees with Macherey that analysis of how literary works function as social critique is important, but he also stresses that the evaluation of such critiques requires that we reach beyond the ideology of the society which produces those literary works. He agrees with Althusser that structural analysis is important for our understanding of ideology, but he also argues that in order to overcome the circularity of the structuralist model, we need to take the bigger step of developing a philosophy of history, for only if we have an understanding of history can we interpret the social functions of ideology and literature as they develop and change in the course of history. In Jameson's view, history sets the boundaries or limits of experience and understanding; we cannot escape history. Accordingly, all theories arise out of or within history and must take a theory of history as the starting point for thought.

For Jameson, Marxism represents the best theory because it is the only one that has consistently based its thinking on the material conditions which history imposes on social life. We can understand the nature of ideologies by analyzing the historical conditions that are evident in the rise and evolution of ideologies. And thus we can understand literature — which is the expression of ideology in particular historical circumstances — in the light of the Marxist theory of historical development. Marxism is ultimately a theory of history that illuminates both social theory and literary theory.

However, a theory of history from within history confronts the same problem of circularity that is confronted by a theory of ideology from within ideology. Because of this circularity, every theory of history falls short of offering absolute rational proof. Jameson recognizes that no such proof is available, but he argues that by broadening the hermeneutical circle to its ultimate limit — namely, history — we can gain a broader perspective and see the necessity of taking a Marxist view.

A somewhat different conclusion is reached by John Frow in his *Marxism and Literary History*. Accepting the postmodernist conclusion that theorizing necessarily entails circular reasoning, Frow attempts to rethink Marxism in the light of that conclusion. He writes, "Anyone now working with and committed to Marxist theory will have to use concepts which are insecure, tentative, exploratory; will have to recognize the need to draw upon bodies of thought elaborated outside Marxism, and often this will demand an arduous process of reworking alien categories; will have to be deeply suspicious of some of the central categories of Marxism itself" (5).

Frow adopts the postmodernist view that understanding always takes place in language and that understanding is therefore contained within and by discourse. We cannot step outside discourse to find some absolute basis for judgment and truth; analysis of society, of literature, of history, of ideology requires analysis of the kinds and domains of discourse we use to think about such things. Such analysis, in Frow's view, reveals that we use discourse to impose control over our world and hence to exercise power over it. The study of social discourse is the study of the uses of power; ideology is the discourse of power. Frow acknowledges that his concept of power, like Jameson's concept of history, may be vulnerable because it fails "to account for its own conditions of possibility" (51), but he argues nevertheless that by focusing on the discourse of power, we can avoid traditional Marxist assumptions about the universality of reason, and we can accept the paradox that the best critique of ideology arises out of that discourse which has the most explanatory power (51). Marxism, Frow argues, needs to face the challenge of demonstrating the explanatory power of its own discourse and to do so on the basis of observation and interpretation of social history rather than an appeal to absolute principles of reason and historical change.

Frow's acceptance of an epistemological skepticism has not been characteristic of mainline Marxism. Traditionally, Marxists have held that ideology can be contrasted to science. Science achieves knowledge of the workings of the material world, and the methods of science applied to society can achieve social knowledge. Marxists have traditionally thought of Marxism as a science of social life or a science of history. It may be, therefore, that Frow has stepped over the line which has traditionally set the limits for Marxist theory. But his skepticism is increasingly felt among Marxist theorists and is central to contemporary Marxist debate.

This debate helps to focus the difference between Marxist and Christian thinking. Christianity has long held the view, contrary to traditional Marxism, that understanding finds its basis in belief. The contemporary questioning of the foundations of rational thought, while remaining a critical problem for Marxism, lends indirect and unintentional support to traditional Christian conceptions of the nature of knowledge, formulated, for example, in Augustine's dictum *credo ut intelligam*. A Christian view of the limits of rational thought and the ways in which beliefs function in understanding can be found in Nicholas Wolterstorff's *Reason within the Bounds of Religion*.

The role that belief plays in rational discourse enables us to pitch the dialogue between Marxism and Christianity at the level of their respective assumptions and primary beliefs. There are many areas of common concern to be found among Marxists and Christians, but there are fundamental differences as well at the level of their foundational beliefs about the nature and meaning of history and social life. The conflict between Marxism and Christianity is a conflict between two belief systems. Although they share many common concerns in the practice of literary criticism, specific literary judgments will diverge according to the differences in the basic beliefs that govern their practices.

These differences, which follow from Christian theism and Marxist atheism, can be briefly suggested by an examination of the term *material* as it is used by Marxists. Marxism's claim to be a materialist philosophy does not imply a denial of all spiritual reality or spiritual value; it implies only that there is no spiritual reality or manifestation of spirit independent of the concrete realities that shape our lives. *Material* is not synonymous with *natural;* it means, rather, that all human existence is historical and that we cannot escape from or reach beyond history. All existence is *material* in the sense that everything, including art and philosophy and religion, exists as part of or is contained within the processes of history. The contrast to *materialism* is *idealism*. Marxism opposes all idealist philosophies which hold that understanding and value are dependent upon an ideal reality which exists outside and beyond the limits of history.

Because of its profound belief in the reality of God, Christianity holds a non-materialist philosophy and in that regard is an opponent of Marxism. Nevertheless, there is value in reflecting on the significance of the term *material* for Christian think-ing. In a Christian view, too, everything that is human is his-torical. Not only are human beings held within the limits of history; they are intended to be historical. For the Christian as well as for the Marxist, there is no human activity that escapes the constraints of the material historical world. In the biblical view, human beings are neither divine nor spiritual beings; they are creatures made for and placed within the material limits of historical existence.

Therefore, the basic difference between Christianity and Marxism is not suggested by the opposition "spiritual/material." Rather, it is suggested by differing conceptions of the sources, motives, and goals of our material-spiritual experiences in his-tory. Christianity holds that human beings belong to a created order which is sustained by and always stands in relation to the Creator God, whose existence is metaphysically autonomous. Therefore, all understanding and value are to be defined in terms of the relationship of human beings to the divine Creator as he is revealed in the Christian scriptures.

In contrast, Marxism holds that our historical identity as human beings is formed entirely by and within the material (i.e., historical) order of existence. Spiritual values arise as human beings exercise their powers of consciousness in a con-tinuing struggle to master the forces of the material world. Spiritual life is defined not in relation to a transcendent God but in relation to the conditions of the concrete material world. These conditions are thought to be at the primary level economic or economic/political; that is, social organization for the purpose of survival and mastery is regarded as the most basic of human activities.

The implications for literary criticism are immense even though they can be only hinted at here. Marxist critics will examine the history of literature to understand how writers have responded to the social and economic conditions of cultural life. Christian critics will examine the history of literature to understand how writers have responded both to the social conditions of life and to the reality of a divine being who transcends the material world. These concerns will be further shaped by more specific implications of Marxist and Christian teachings. A Marxist will develop his or her interpretation using such characteristic concepts as infrastructure/superstructure, dialectical oppositions, class struggle, and revolution. The Christian will develop his or her interpretation using such characteristic concepts as biblical revelation, the cultural mandate, the Incarnation, sin, and redemption. While both Marxists and Christians recognize the importance of social and historical forces in literary works, they will interpret these forces in different ways. The task of Christian literary scholars is to elaborate both theoretically and practically how a biblical perspective on these differences illuminates an understanding of literature, history, and culture.

WORKS CITED AND CONSULTED

(Titles with an asterisk are recommended as introductions.)

Althusser, Louis. *For Marx*. London: Allen Lane, 1969.

————. *Lenin and Philosophy*. New York: Monthly Review Press, 1971.

*Arvon, Henri. *Marxist Esthetics*. Ithaca: Cornell University Press, 1973.

Bakhtin, M. M. *The Dialogic Imagination: Four Essays*. Ed. Michael Holquist. Austin: University of Texas Press, 1981.

————. *Marxism and the Philosophy of Language*. Cambridge: Harvard University Press, 1986.

Benjamin, Walter. *Illuminations*. New York: Schocken Books, 1969.

*Bennett, Tony. *Formalism and Marxism*. New York: Methuen, 1979.

*Eagleton, Terry. *Marxism and Literary Criticism*. Berkeley: University of California Press, 1976.

Frow, John. *Marxism and Literary History*. Cambridge: Harvard University Press, 1986.

Jameson, Fredric. *Marxism and Form*. Princeton: Princeton University Press, 1971.

————. *The Political Unconscious*. Ithaca: Cornell University Press, 1981.

Lukacs, Georg. *Realism in Our Time*. New York: Harper & Row, 1964.

McGann, Jerome J. *The Romantic Ideology*. Chicago: University of Chicago Press, 1983.

Macherey, Pierre. *A Theory of Literary Production*. London: Routledge & Kegan Paul, 1978.

Todorov, Tzvetan. *Mikhail Bakhtin: The Dialogic Principle*. Trans. Wlad Godzich. Minneapolis: University of Minnesota Press, 1984.

Williams, Raymond. *Marxism and Literature*. Oxford: Oxford University Press, 1977.

PSYCHOLOGICAL CRITICISM: FROM THE IMAGINATION TO FREUD AND BEYOND

Alan Jacobs

INTRODUCTION

O F ALL THE APPROACHES TO LITERATURE NOW CLAMORING for our attention, psychological criticism is perhaps the most difficult to define and to isolate, for it speaks with many voices. The patterns of thought and language fostered by modern psychology are pervasive in our intellectual culture, so that one cannot pursue any literary issue very far before concepts or terms of psychology begin to enter into the discussion. We may attribute this state of affairs chiefly to the influence of Sigmund Freud, whose ideas — however discredited by more recent developments in psychology — still provide us with a kind of lingua franca for discussing the projects and peculiarities of the human mind. Even Christians, who tend to fear Freud (along with Marx and Nietzsche) as a "master of suspicion" (to use Paul Ricoeur's phrase), make frequent use of Freudian ideas — the unconscious, repression, defense mechanisms, and so on — and have eagerly embraced the therapeutic culture whose roots are in Freud.

Literary scholars have had no more success in ridding themselves of the Freudian apparatus than anyone else, even if it persists in transmuted forms in their thought and work. The archetypal criticism that Professor Ryken discusses elsewhere in this volume derives from Jung's theories of how the unconscious works, but Jung's idea of the unconscious in turn derives from Freud. And such indebtedness is not confined to explicitly psychological forms of criticism. Where, for instance, would Marxist theorists be without Freud? For they use his theories of internal struggle to explain how we bourgeois readers suppress our class allegiances and thereby enable ourselves to pretend that *our* canons, *our* ways of reading, *our* interpretations possess a "natural" or inherent authority. Likewise, feminist critics appropriate Freudian analytical techniques to unmask sexual bias in writing, reading, and theorizing; and deconstructors often use Freudian terms to explain how we deny the inevitability of the interpretive abyss.

Given an influence so pervasive, this essay must confine itself to those theories and practices which announce their primary allegiance to be with psychology or psychoanalysis. Among these, the majority will be Freudian, not only because of the evident power of Freud's conceptual structures, but because Freud, more than any scientist of the mind, was profoundly interested in the psychology of artistic creation. As Frederick Crews has said, "Psychoanalysis is the only psychology to have seriously altered our way of reading literature. . . . To dwell at length on the possible literary implications of [other approaches] would be to say more than the psychologists themselves have been able to say" (*Out of My System* 4).

Nevertheless, let us be historically aware: there was intelligent — even brilliant — psychological criticism before Freud; he did not produce his ideas about art and literature in a vacuum, nor were they altogether without precedent. We must investigate the origin of some of his ideas in Romantic aesthetics, placing particular emphasis on the concept of the imagination (which has, of course, exerted considerable influence among Christian literary critics). In fact, we will discover that the concept of the imagination is as central to psychological criticism as Freudian thinking, and that the two have significant points of contact. A broad historical overview, then, from Coleridge to the present day, will constitute the greater part of this essay, and will set the stage for reflections upon possible Christian responses to the history thus described.

One further note on method is needed. The varieties of psychological criticism have focused attention not only on authors and readers but also on characters and speakers within the literary text. In fact, the psychological analysis of character probably constitutes the quantitatively predominant form of psychological criticism. Nevertheless, it will suffer an almost complete neglect in this essay, a state of affairs that requires some explanation. The chief reason for this neglect is that character analysis has fallen into serious disfavor in this age of theory. As Meredith Anne Skura writes in *The Literary Use of the Psychoanalytical Process,* "Though it had seemed only natural to Freud to treat characters like people, the New Critics were beginning to distrust all character analysis even while he was writing; it was not long before almost all critical realism gave way to a general belief that characters, whose traits were determined not by analyzable 'personalities' but by the requirements of the text, were only parts of a design" (29). There are, then, two closely linked components to this fall from grace: first, the formalist emphasis on the *textuality* of literature that began only with the New Criticism and that finds its culmination (it would appear) in deconstruction; and second, an increasing suspicion of the *mimetic* possibilities of literature, of its ability genuinely to represent "real life."[1] Character analysis is by no means dead, but its currently dubious status necessitates its neglect in an essay as pressed for space as this one.

---

1. This skepticism about the representational potential of literature has been far greater among literary critics than psychologists. For instance, Harvard University's Robert Coles — best known for his *Children of Crisis* series — habitually uses novels and short stories as texts in his psychology classes because of his belief in their power to illuminate psychological realities otherwise rarely revealed.

BEFORE FREUD: COLERIDGE AND THE IMAGINATION

Let us begin our history with a heuristic fib: psychological criticism begins with Samuel Taylor Coleridge.

The inaccuracy of this statement is obvious: the discussions of poetic inspiration in several of Plato's dialogues (especially the *Ion*) surely constitute a kind of author psychology, while Aristotle's descriptions of audience responses to tragedy equally surely mark the beginnings of a psychology of reception. But Plato's views are hardly congenial to the modern mind, and Aristotle's comments, aside from being confined to a single dramatic genre, are too sketchy to be widely useful. Only with the development of a genuine modern psychology — that is, one congruent with post-Renaissance and post-Reformation notions of selfhood and personal identity — by John Locke and his heirs did genuine psychological criticism become possible. And indeed, the eighteenth century would produce a number of thorough accounts of poetic (and, more broadly, aesthetic) creation, culminating in Alexander Gerard's *Essay on Genius* (1774), which, according to M. H. Abrams, "remained for a century the most comprehensive and detailed study devoted specifically to the psychology of the inventive process" (157).

Why, then, do I insist on my allegedly heuristic lie? Because Coleridge's work exemplifies a new trend, a new element in the equation: an organicist theory of poetic imagination. The key words here are *organicist* and *imagination* — they mark the divergence of Romantic thought from previous treatments of the subject.

Earlier notions of poetic invention had been based on Locke's concept of the "association of ideas": the task of the poet is to combine in novel ways the ideas already present in his mind. Furthermore, in the aftermath of the Newtonian achievements in physical mechanics, both celestial and terrestrial, the process of mental combination was increasingly understood in mechanistic terms. The most important faculty

a poet can possess, in this pre-Romantic view, is *judgment* —
the ability to decide what combinations of ideas are the most
pleasurable and instructive. Thus there is in this view no such
thing as poetic *creation;* the poet works with that which is
presented to his senses.

Coleridge produced his famous distinction between (the
associative) *fancy* and (the autonomously powerful) *imagination*
in order to refute, or rather to transcend, the Lockean approach.
Needless to say, the process by which the imagination works is
inexplicable in the mechanistic terms favored by eighteenth-
century thinkers; thus Coleridge — most clearly in Goethe's
debt here — replaces those terms with a vocabulary derived
from the growth and development of living things, especially
plants. Like plants, the products of the imagination grow and
develop according to their own inner impulses and directives;
the directions they take are, in the best sense of the term,
"natural." They give the appearance of disorder only to the mind
unduly constricted by self-imposed rules, the mind that understands and accepts only the pedestrian combinations of fancy.

The influence of this fundamental distinction persists to
this day. Since Coleridge, has there been any intellectually rep-
utable attempt to explain the process of poetic invention? Even
John Livingston Lowes, whose famous study entitled *The Road
to Xanadu* sought to discover the sources of virtually every name,
object, and image in Coleridge's own "Kubla Khan" and "The
Rime of the Ancient Mariner," could not explain by what
alchemy the poet turned his leaden sources into poetic gold.
Perhaps Lowes did not *want* to explain it. It would appear that
Coleridge had made the imagination into a Holy of Holies
which none dare investigate. And the religious metaphor is not
flippant, for there is an important sense in which Coleridge's
imagination performs a number of functions formerly reserved
for God himself: from now on, we will hear nothing of the old
poetic *inspiration* in the sense that Plato and, later, the Christian
poets up to Milton's time spoke of it — that is, a divine source
breathing power into the poet. After Coleridge, if the term

inspiration is used, it refers not to some external source of poetic authority but to the energy inherent in the poet's own mind. One may, like Shelley, ascribe this energy to the "spirit of the age," but it remains utterly immanent, having no definable existence outside the person.[2]

Coleridge's theory of the imagination is perhaps the most powerful myth of poetic freedom ever devised, for it defines the imagination as immune to any outside force. This theory simultaneously justifies the two prevalent Romantic conceptions of the poet: on the one hand, the all-powerful visionary, "the unacknowledged legislator of the world"; and on the other hand, the asocial mystic withdrawn in self-contemplation, the pure aesthete more common in later Romantic thinking. Neither figure is susceptible to the tensions and depredations of history, and thus is free to work out interior fate (and, in the first model, the fate of the world) with, if need be, fear and trembling, but in any event alone. Thus, for many years after Coleridge the psychology of literary creation was reduced to a series of meditations on the sheer mystery of poetic invention.

2. One of the best accounts of the shift from inspiration to imagination is provided by Owen Barfield in "The Psychology of Inspiration and Imagination," Chapter 3 of *Speaker's Meaning*. Barfield rightly demonstrates that the shift is more complex than the constraints of space have allowed me to suggest: "Perhaps all our endeavors to say something fruitful about imagination can best be seen as a struggle to reject the old concept of inspiration — and yet somehow retain it — to reject the old superindividual psychology and at the same time to develop an individual psychology which is viable for the phenomenon of art" (79-80).

The most thorough historical overview of the subject is Thomas McFarland's *Originality and Imagination*, and in his preface McFarland makes it clear that the Romantics, especially Coleridge, developed their whole concept of the imagination as a substitute for what they considered — or implicitly understood — to be a bankrupt concept of the human soul. "Indeed, as 'soul' became weaker, they [i.e., 'originality' and 'imagination'] became stronger" (xi). This linkage provides another insight into the relations between inspiration and imagination.

FREUD

When Freud, a century after Coleridge, turned his attention to the problem of poetic creation, little had changed. The poet-as-aesthete had completely superseded the poet-as-legislator, but that change was probably a foregone conclusion after the failures of the French Revolution; Wordsworth's *Prelude* (even in its 1805 version) traced just such a progression. In any event, Coleridge's conception of poetic imagination by now was a given, and few theories had arisen to challenge the Romantic poet's self-definition.

Freud threatened to alter that situation. His recognition that all human behavior is motivated, that we never do anything for no particular reason, led him to ask diligently why the poet writes. And perhaps, if one could discover that, one might also discover *how* the poet's imagination produces its effects. This is the burden of his most significant essay on poetic creation, "The Relation of the Poet to Day-Dreaming."

The essay begins with an introductory treatment of the linkage between children's play and adult daydreaming; Freud only gradually works himself around to the subject of poetry. When he does, he prefaces his remarks by insisting on an apparently familiar distinction: "we must distinguish between poets who, like the bygone creators of epics and tragedies, take over their material ready-made, and those who seem to create their material spontaneously" (50). This sounds very much like Coleridge's pairing of fancy and imagination — but with some important differences.

Of the poets in the first category, Freud says that their "material is derived from the racial treasure-house of myths, legends, and fairy-tales. . . . [I]t seems extremely probable that myths, for example, are distorted vestiges of the wish-phantasies of whole nations — the age-long dreams of young humanity" (53). (Clearly, this is a version of Coleridge's fancy, but the associative processes are now complicated by the workings of the unconscious.) Most of Freud's literary essays are devoted to such stories, folktales, and folktale motifs in literature, but he seems to find the authors of such works less interesting than the prototypical Romantic poets who seem to create, like God, ex nihilo — just as Coleridge found the products of fancy less remarkable than those of imagination.[3] Perhaps the analyst faces more of a challenge in confronting the inner struggles of specially gifted individuals than in confronting those common to the whole human race.

In the essay at hand, there is no doubt that it is the "imaginative" poet (in Coleridge's sense) that Freud is interested in, and the beginning of the essay promises a critical examination of the poet's claims to imaginative creativity. Freud's very language — "those who *seem* to create their material spontaneously" (my italics) — reveals his intention to turn a suspicious eye on the poet: Might the process be less spontaneous, and hence more amenable to critical and scientific analysis, than it would at first appear? Might the magic mountain of the imagination be scalable, despite the warnings of poets perched at the top?

The conclusions Freud reaches are by now familiar: the writer, especially the writer of fiction, projects his own conflicts into story, objectifies them by casting them into character and event. If we but look beneath the surface of the literary artwork, we find "His Majesty the Ego, the hero of all day-dreams and all novels" (51). Further, Freud suggests an explanatory scheme for the poetic impulse, a scheme that he expects research eventually to bear out: "Some actual experience which made a strong impression on the writer had stirred up a memory of an earlier experience, generally belonging to childhood, which then arouses a wish that finds a fulfillment in the work in question, and in which elements of the recent event and the old memory should be discernible" (52).

---

3. Coleridge sometimes denied any hierarchy involving fancy and imagination, claiming that the two are simply different. But he was far from consistent on this point, and in practice he elevated the imagination far above fancy. See McFarland, *Originality and Imagination* 148-50.

Now, this is virtually as far as Freud goes in "The Relation of the Poet to Day-Dreaming." The essay is a brief one, and he does not claim its conclusions to be firm: of the little formula I just quoted, he says, "I myself expect that in reality it will prove itself to be too schematic, but that possibly it may contain a first means of approach to the true state of affairs" (52). Yet, despite Freud's obvious caution, this is an essay which his literary and critical followers have taken very seriously, and not without reason. It has had two powerful implications that we must look at.

The first implication arises from Freud's linking of the artist with the daydreamer or fantasist, a linkage based on the substantial research, about which Freud is confident, that he had done on daydreaming. But where did he get this information about daydreaming? After all, "the adult . . . is ashamed of his day-dreams and conceals them from other people; he cherishes them as his most intimate possessions and as a rule would rather confess all his misdeeds than tell his day-dreams" (46). It turns out that there is one class of people upon whom "a stern goddess — Necessity — has laid the task of giving an account of what they suffer and what they enjoy. These people are the neurotics; among other things they have to confess their phantasies to the physician to whom they go in the hope of recovering through mental treatment" (47). The relation between the poet and the daydreamer, then, is more precisely the relation between the poet and the neurotic; in fact, we might even say that these are normally the only groups of people to whose fantasies we have access.

Some may argue — after all, this is what Freud implies — that the comparison is forced upon Freud by our unwillingness to reveal our daydreams. But one might also wonder if both the poet and the neurotic may be seen as persons whose fantasy lives are out of control and force themselves to outward expression. "If phantasies become over-luxuriant and over-powerful, the necessary conditions of an outbreak of neurosis or psychosis are constituted; phantasies are also the first preliminary stage in the mind of the symptoms of illness of which our patients complain" (49). Might not such over-luxuriance also result in an "outbreak" of poetry? Freud does not directly make this link himself, but he leaves it there to be made; and in the coming Age of Anxiety, the period when a sense of the existential absurd marked the man of true awareness, the unification of art and neurosis was perhaps inevitable.

Thus many poets and critics accepted with grim satisfaction this link between the poet and the neurotic. But others rejected it, most notably Lionel Trilling, who rightly understood that in making such an implication Freud was not applauding the poet but rather condemning him. Freud, Trilling explains in a 1941 essay called "Freud and Literature," saw the poet as a creator of illusions, illusions that might gratify him and his readers — and that were not dangerous so long as they did not pretend to be anything *more* than illusions — but that nonetheless were not to be praised. "For Freud there are two ways of dealing with external reality. One is practical, effective, positive; this is the way of the conscious self . . . and it is the right way. The antithetical way may be called . . . the 'fictional' way. Instead of doing something about, or to, external reality, the individual who uses this way does something to, or about, his affective states" (41).[4] Finally, Trilling argues, there is no way to get around one of Freud's most fundamental distinctions:

4. Compare this with a distinction made later by Frank Kermode: "We have to distinguish between myths and fictions. Fictions can degenerate into myths whenever they are not consciously held to be fictive. In this sense anti-Semitism is a degenerate fiction, a myth; and Lear is a fiction. Myth operates within the diagrams of ritual, which presupposes total and adequate explanations of things as they are and were; it is a sequence of radically unchangeable gestures. Fictions are for finding things out, and they change as the needs of sense-making change. Myths are the agents of stability, fictions the agents of change. Myths call for absolute, fictions for conditional change" (*The Sense of an Ending* 39). As Frank Lentricchia has pointed out, this is not only an attack on religion but also and more pointedly an attack on Northrop Frye's critical system and an attempt to replace it with a system based on the philosophical poetry of Wallace Stevens (32).

For Freud there exist "the polar extremes of reality and illusion. Reality is an honorific word and it means what is *there;* illusion is a pejorative word and it means a response to what is *not there*" (41). The poet is inevitably on the side of illusion.

The second implication of Freud's seminal essay returns us to the question that we thought Freud might be able to answer: How does the imagination work? If Freud's direct statements in the essay at least sketch a theory of *why* the poet writes, does he tell us *how* the poet, or the poetic imagination, manages to produce poetry? Freud phrases the problem in an interesting way. He knows, from his experience as an analyst, that when people reveal their fantasies to us, "they repel us, or at least leave us cold" ("The Relation of the Poet to Day-Dreaming" 53). How, then, does the poet in revealing his fantasies make them pleasurable to us? Freud provides two partial answers. First, the writer "softens the egotistical character of the day-dream by changes and disguises"; in other words, he projects those fantasies into characters and events that do not have an obvious link to him. Second, "he bribes us by the offer of a purely formal, that is, aesthetic, pleasure in the presentation of his phantasies" (54).

Some readers may protest that Freud hasn't really answered the question he promised to answer: we still do not know how the writer makes these projections pleasurable (for they are not pleasurable simply because they can't be linked to their author), or how aesthetic form is created or received. Indeed, Freud admits just this point: "How the writer does this is his inmost secret" (54), he says, obviously implying that it is a secret even to the writer himself. Elsewhere, he makes it clear that psychoanalysis "can do nothing towards elucidating the nature of the artistic gift, nor can it explain the means by which the artist works" (quoted by Crews, *Out of My System* 10). May one say, then, that for all his suspicion Freud has not managed to destroy or discredit the Romantic view of poetic imagination? Is not the poet's "How" still a mystery inaccessible to rational analysis?

We must answer "Yes." But while poetic invention remains inexplicable, Freud has nonetheless given a mortal wound to the imagination, for he has denied it its cherished autonomy. The whole purpose of Coleridge's conceptual innovation was to protect the poetic mind from external attack, from history and event. But Freud attacks the imagination at the one place it cannot defend: within the mind itself. The imagination does not act with autonomy, but rather is motivated — as all human behavior is motivated — by the need to resolve internal tension and conflict. One must say, then, that Freud ultimately denies the distinction between fancy and imagination: all mental activity is derivative and dependent, though some of it may *seem* autonomous and spontaneous. Even the greatest poet works with building blocks given to him by experience and temperament; there is no imaginative *creation* in the strict sense. We might even say that Freud returns to pre-Romantic days: he forces those of us who would discuss poetic invention to shift our attention back to the questions of *judgment* that dominated eighteenth-century thinking. For if those building blocks are already there, then the poet's task is to decide how to combine them.

The difference between Freud's view and the pre-Romantic view is that for Freud judgment is determined not by a single and whole "self" but by internal *conflict* between id, ego, and superego, each hoping to wrench the decision-making authority away from the others. Thus the question of judgment becomes much richer and more complex than it had been — and as a consequence more amenable to critical analysis.

If Freud himself had not found the key to unlock the mysteries of the imagination, his psychoanalytic method promised that that key could not remain forever hidden. For there was little that Freud did not promise: psychoanalysis was for him the one absolutely certain, all-powerful hermeneutic. There was no feature of human behavior that could, in the end, remain inaccessible to it.

Freud's implicit dethronement of the imagination

spawned a whole race of critics eager to discuss the multiple motivations determining any literary text. He provided a vocabulary that, at least in the view of some, does justice to the richness and complexity we find in literature itself. This was Trilling's claim, despite his reservations: "The Freudian psychology is the only systematic account of the human mind which, in point of subtlety and complexity, of interest and tragic power, deserves to stand beside the chaotic mass of psychological insights which literature has accumulated through the centuries" ("Freud and Literature" 32). But it would appear that the price to be paid for this system was the loss of the Romantic privileging of the imagination — and perhaps of the imagination itself. For it is clear that Freud, despite his admiration for the poets, considered the secrecy shrouding their work to have but a short time remaining to it before it yielded to psychoanalysis.

As Frederick Crews writes, "If, as an heir of the Romantic movement, Freud sometimes credited art with a visionary truth, as a bourgeois, a scientist, and a utilitarian he suspected it of unreality and evasion" (*Out of My System* 6). Ultimately, his investigations into the motives of literary production and, by extension, the motives of literary reception — indeed, of all human behavior — fostered a spirit of criticism and analytical rigor that dominates current thinking about literature. Freud's suspicious attitude toward artistic production gives critics a kind of rhetorical — dare we say psychological? — leverage over authors that they have been understandably unwilling to relinquish.

FREUD'S INHERITORS: HOLLAND, LACAN, BLOOM

If Freud's writings on literature focused on the psychology of the author, the rest of his writings have encouraged a reader-centered criticism, and our major critical inheritance from him comes in this sphere. Without going too deeply into a subject that, as I have said, is covered elsewhere in this volume, I would like to sketch three of the many reasons for this influence.

The first involves Ernest Jones, Freud's American disciple, who made a foray into literary criticism with an essay on *Hamlet* entitled "The Death of Hamlet's Father" (published in various versions between 1910 and 1949). In speaking of Shakespeare's alleged Oedipus complex and its alleged expression in the character of Hamlet, Jones commits a pair of errors that often threaten those who would study the psychology of invention: he assumes that it is possible to psychoanalyze the dead, and he assumes that the Romantic notion of poetry as the spontaneous overflow of powerful emotion is universally applicable. Once the New Critics began to disabuse us of the latter notion by suggesting that there can be poetry which is not pre-eminently self-expressive, the former assumption became much less tenable. (It had always been problematic to a degree — Freud himself disavowed it, arguing that psychoanalysis without the application of the technique of free association is impossible.)

A second reason for the neglect of author psychology may also be traced to the New Critics — more precisely to their attacks on the recoverability of authorial intention and on the usefulness of that intention, even if recoverable, as a guide to interpretation. Since their critique of intentionalism was widely accepted and remains widely accepted even now that New Criticism has fallen from favor, the critic investigating authorial psychology always must deal with significant resistance to his method.

Third, we should consider a dominant feature of Freud's anthropology: his emphasis on our hermeneutical imperative. Freud's whole theory of internal struggle and development may fruitfully be understood in hermeneutical terms, for that theory conceives of each individual as continually striving to interpret his or her experience in a way that will resolve conflicts. Mental health results from a coherent and orderly *reading* of experience — the kind of reading provided, say many analysts, only by a thorough and successful psychoanalysis. Therefore, it might be expected that we bring to the reading of books the same needs and many of the same hermeneutical techniques.

This third insight is the foundation of the criticism of Norman Holland, perhaps the best-known American practitioner of orthodox psychoanalytical criticism. Holland does not neglect the psychology of the author altogether, but it plays a minimal role in his work, and he is careful to avoid the obvious pitfalls. In his *Poems in Persons: An Introduction to the Psychoanalysis of Literature* (1973), he devotes his chapter on the author, "A Maker's Mind," to a thorough reading of the American modernist poet "H. D." (Hilda Doolittle). Why? Because H. D. underwent analysis with Freud himself and left a record of her experience. Asks Holland, "How can we know a poet's or novelist's mind except tautologically — by the very poems and fantasies whose creation we want to explain? We can't — with one unique exception: H. D." (6).

This "unique exception" aside, Holland turns his attention to a study of the reading process, as is indicated by the titles of his most significant books: *The Dynamics of Literary Response* (1968) and *Five Readers Reading* (1975). The former text is his chief contribution to criticism, for it is there that he presents his complete model of how we respond to literature, and why we respond as we do. "A literary text has implicit in it two dimensions," he says: "one reaches 'up,' toward the world of social, intellectual, moral, and religious concerns; the other reaches 'down,' to the dark, chthonic, primitive, bodily part of our mental life." But, having made this statement, Holland immediately corrects it, for it implies an objectivity of description of which we will be suspicious if we are alert to motives: "The text itself is only a series of words — it is we who stretch it in these two directions. Unconsciously or half-consciously, we introject it, taking it into us as, at the most primitive level of our being, we long to incorporate any source of gratification" (*The Dynamics of Literary Response* 310). Literary response for Holland, then, is determined by what Freud called the pleasure principle: "Literature transforms our primitive wishes and fears into significance, and this transformation gives us pleasure" (30). Our reading of literature is conditioned by our need to defend ourselves against pain — Holland understands literary genres as different types of defense mechanisms — and our desire to achieve pleasure and gratification. Literature is particularly valuable to us in this regard because while we "introject" it we also may control it, keep it at a certain distance. "The pleasure we experience is the feeling of having a fantasy of our own and our own associations to it managed and controlled but at the same time allowed a limited expression and gratification" (311-12).

When Holland says that literature consists merely of words on a page, words that readers invest with meaning and significance, he is doing little more than justifying his own interest in literary response. But most of the major moves in recent criticism, especially structuralism and deconstruction, take that notion much more seriously than Holland does. For the deconstructors in particular, texts do not consist even of words: they are instead comprised of a series of black marks on white paper. Words are *mental* constructs, agreed-upon interpretations of those marks that lack intrinsic meaning. If psychological criticism was to survive in the contemporary theoretical climate, it had to find some way of reconciling itself with what has been called the "linguistic turn" in literary study. Many critics feel that one figure successfully brings together psychoanalysis and the new radical linguistics: Jacques Lacan, the inscrutable Frenchman.

To explain Lacan's theories is a task beyond my powers, for he is indeed a paragon of opacity. Compared with Lacan, Jacques Derrida writes with the lucidity of a latter-day Dr. Johnson. This much is clear: the purpose of much of Lacan's writings is to outline a semiotic theory of the self — that is, a psychoanalysis based upon our acquisition and use of language and upon the nature of language itself. (I say "the nature of language itself" because, in Lacan's view, existence precedes essence and language precedes existence. Our language is here before we are and thus shapes — or rather dictates — the resources of our minds.) In this theory, Lacan combines Freud's mechanisms of desire and pain, loss and compensation, with Derrida's understanding of the linguistic sign as a token of absence. For Lacan, the very existence of language indicates loss or absence, for we need speak only of that which we do not have. In Terry Eagleton's words, "Our language 'stands in' for objects: all language is in a way 'metaphorical,' in that it substitutes itself for some direct, wordless possession of the object itself" (166). Eagleton continues, "[For Lacan] all desire springs from a lack, which it strives continually to fill. Human language works by such lack. . . . To enter language, then, is to become a prey to desire" (167). Whereas Holland — and Freud too — thought that the reading of literature could provide genuine satisfaction, Lacan considers that impossible, or possible only as an illusion, which he, like Freud, rejects. Because literature is built of language, it signifies nothing but its inability to signify: it is a perpetual testimony to perpetual emptiness. "Imagination" is merely a word, a tool for self-deception. And how could it be otherwise, when the very self that imagines is linguistically inaccessible? The word "I" is just as empty as any other — no more empty than any other, it is true, but since it is this word to which we give the greatest responsibility, the responsibility of indicating who we are, its emptiness is the hardest to take. "I think, therefore I am," said Descartes; Lacan replies, "I think where I am not, therefore I am where I do not think" (166). To think is to enter the field of signification, signification that never comes to rest in meaning. And there is no refuge from this play of signifiers even in non-linguistic action, for all action, all objects, are recognized by the mind only as signifiers: Lacan replaces Freud's interest in "phallic symbols" with the assertion that the phallus itself is a symbol, "the signifier of desire" (288). Freud once said that sometimes a cigar is just a cigar, but for Lacan a cigar is *never* a cigar: it is a signifier, in fact a signifier of a signifier, and so on ad infinitum.

These are melancholy conclusions, to be sure, but they are increasingly common as deconstruction becomes just another part of our intellectual landscape. Lionel Trilling had tried to rescue literature from Freud's linkage of the writer and the neurotic by arguing that there is a key difference between the two: the author controls his fantasy, while the neurotic is *controlled by* his fantasy. (See "Art and Neurosis," *The Liberal Imagination* 155-75.) But in the aftermath of Heidegger and Derrida and Lacan, all of whom insist that language, which precedes us, determines not only what we say but who we are, who can still believe that the poet is in control of anything? Surprisingly, there is at least one critic who believes that the greatest insights of Freudian psychoanalysis may be used — in defiance of Lacan and Derrida and, indeed, of much of Freud's own work — to reclaim the poet's power of self-determination, perhaps to reclaim the imagination itself. That critic is Harold Bloom.

The keynote of Bloom's criticism is struck in the first sentence of *The Visionary Company* (1961), his famous historical and critical survey of the poetry of the major English Romantics: "Blake died in the evening of Sunday, August 12, 1827, and the firm belief in the autonomy of a poet's imagination died with him." The funereal tone of the declaration indicates the mournful regret with which Bloom reports this fact. And in surveying contemporary criticism — some years later in his career, in 1975, after Theory had announced itself as a possible escape from any critical impasse — Bloom clearly sees a widespread lack of respect for the imagination's long-cold corpse. Particularly in deconstruction Bloom finds an emphasis on language that excludes the human mind altogether from the study of poetry, and this is a movement that he protests with some heat. We suffer a profound "humanistic loss," he argues, if we give in "to those like Derrida and Foucault who imply

. . . that language by itself writes the poems and thinks. The human writes, the human thinks" (*A Map of Misreading* 60).

Bloom's statement clearly marks his refusal to accept any contention that the source of poetry lies anywhere outside the poet. But whether that refusal implies genuine imaginative autonomy is another matter. For the very sentence I just quoted has a different feel when quoted in full: "The human writes, the human thinks, and always following after and defending against another human, however fantasized that human becomes in the strong imaginings of those who arrive later upon the scene" (60).

In that sentence we find the full complexity of Bloom's account of how poems come to be written. Bloom begins with what he calls a "dyad," the paired figures of precursor and ephebe (or acolyte — "ephebe" is from Wallace Stevens). The young poet whose embryonic career seems thwarted by the influential presence of a mighty precursor who will not die hardly seems to exemplify imaginative autonomy. "A poet," Bloom argues, "is not so much a man speaking to men as a man rebelling against being spoken to by a dead man (the precursor) outrageously more alive than himself" (19). But the "rebelling" is significant, and betokens a shift in the balance of power: the ephebe begins to transmute and transform his precursor by means of "strong imaginings," deliberate misreadings or (to use Bloom's term) "misprisions" which the ephebe uses to gain leverage over that mighty poetic spirit. In his first book on this subject, *The Anxiety of Influence* (1973), Bloom enumerates and defines the methods which, he argues, the ephebe uses to misread and revise his precursor. (These six "revisionary ratios" are extremely technical — in fact, they have become bywords of critical obfuscation; we need not explore them here.)

For our purposes, the key point in all this involves Bloom's revision of the Freudian picture of how the person encounters and deals with the world. As we have seen, Freud defines mental health as the ability to accept and orient oneself to reality; mental illness is the succumbing to illusion. Bloom, however, dispenses with the whole conceptual structure of health and illness. For him, the issue is simply survival: will the poet (as a poet) eat or be eaten by his precursor? Most poets, Bloom implies, are swallowed by their precursors, defeated by their "belatedness"; they don't even put up a fight. (Bloom cites T. S. Eliot as a poet whose various influences take complete possession of him, leaving him utterly without strength.) Others fight with their precursors only to lose. But the strong poet survives by accommodating reality to his imagination, misreading and revising the father-poet who would threaten his imaginative autonomy. If this is an illusion — and Bloom accepts deconstruction just enough to question the existence of an interpretive standard according to which we might distinguish reality from illusion — then it is an illusion to be welcomed, for it enables the poet to avoid Romanticism's greatest horror: a self not only defined by something external to it but *aware* of that definition.

In this light, Bloom's purpose is clear: to admit the power of and use the insights of Freudian analysis for the purposes of literary criticism, but at the same time to argue that there is a place where the imagination can take refuge from Freudian criticism. Most poets — indeed, almost all poets, says Bloom — are explicable in terms of Freudian conflict. Even the strong poet in his immature "ephebe" phase is explicable in those terms. But eventually that strong poet wins out — he defeats the precursor, thus resolving all conflict and winning through to a place beyond the reach of analysis. There he is not explicable in any terms other than the ones he sets for himself, for if he can defeat the precursor, he can defeat any of us. He forces us to succumb to the power of his imagination; he becomes "the unacknowledged legislator of the world." (Let us remember that Bloom's favorite poet is Shelley.)

Bloom's theory is actually a bizarre extension of Freud's implied relation between art and neurosis. By using the methods of neurosis — the mental reconstruction of the world and its inhabitants, willful misreadings and misinterpretations, and so on — the strong poet preserves his poetic faculty inviolate. Thus, in the most prominent recent exemplar of psychological criticism, Freud's vision of the self in inevitable conflict with the world merges, however oddly, with the Romantic "belief in the autonomy of the poet's imagination."

PSYCHOLOGICAL CRITICISM AND THE CHRISTIAN SCHOLAR

From this historical survey, it should be clear that two necessities rule the Christian scholar who would become involved with psychological criticism: first, the theories of Freud must be confronted and mastered; and second, the usefulness and power of the concept of the imagination must undergo profound reconsideration and revaluation.

To the first point. In many ways, the Freudian hermeneutic of selfhood is not so different from that of Christianity. If Freud is a master of suspicion, it is also true that Christians knew, long before Freud, to be suspicious of announced motives and self-justifications. We have always recognized that our souls have many disguises and concealments, that the ways of our hearts are crooked. The wise Christian is, like the Freudian psychoanalyst, an archaeologist of the self, a seeker after the vital but deeply hidden truths about ourselves. But are the "truths" sought for the same in each case?

Paul Ricoeur, in his magisterial *Freud and Philosophy*, points out that Freud explicitly disavowed a teleology — a conviction of the right and proper goals of personhood — to accompany his archaeology: psycho*analysis* is not to be followed by psycho*synthesis*, the taking apart not to be completed by a putting back together (460).[5] But the Christian scholar who

5. Ricoeur is here referring to Freud's essay entitled "Lines of Advance in Psychoanalytic Therapy" (1918), found in *The Standard Edition of the Complete Psychological Works of Sigmund Freud* 17:160.

uses a version of psychoanalytical method to study the activities of reading and writing is not allowed the luxury of forgetting the *telos* of the individual, his purpose and destiny. Reinhold Niebuhr rightly linked "the nature and destiny of man" in his study of that title; it is not permissible to study the one without dealing with the other.

In fact, according to Ricoeur, it is not *possible* to do so: "In order to have an *archē* a subject must have a *telos*" (459). Therefore, according to Ricoeur, psychoanalysis does indeed have a teleology; it is just hidden, implicit, undeveloped. And what does this teleology consist of? Ricoeur implies that it may be summed up in a single phrase of Freud's: "Woll Es war, soll Ich werden" ("Where id was, there ego shall be").[6] In other words, Freud sees the individual as (at least ideally) driving toward the right and proper control of the ego over the unbridled id.

But in what sense may we say that such control is "right" and "proper"? On what grounds does Freud, the (self-described) empirical scientist, intrude an "ought" into the discussion? In order to justify this teleology, Freud finds himself forced to go beyond his early work, to go (as the title of a later book has it) "beyond the pleasure principle." The replacement for the pleasure principle, or rather its superior, becomes the *reality* principle. Ego ought to control id because this facilitates a coming to terms with reality, with the way the world is. Thus, for Freud it becomes the patient's *responsibility* to come to terms with reality; mental illness (and Freud could be just as cold-blooded about this as it appears) is simply an abdication of that responsibility.

This demand upon the patient is what Philip Rieff calls Freud's "ethic of honesty," and he bases upon it his staggering claim that Freud is the greatest moralist of this century. But it

6. This is taken from the *New Introductory Lectures on Psychoanalysis* (*The Standard Edition of the Complete Psychological Works of Sigmund Freud* 22:80).

should be clear that there are two things wrong with this "ethic." First of all, honest interpretation can be no more than a preparation (though a necessary preparation) for ethical action. Oddly enough, Rieff recognizes this: "Freud's is a penultimate ethic tooled to the criticism of ultimates. It regards the disposition of human potentiality as a matter beyond prescription" (*Freud* 354). But is not such prescription necessary if ethics — and hence a psychoanalysis keyed to the reality principle — is to be more than a matter of arbitrary personal choice? Which leads us to the second problem: Freud conceives of ethics in purely individualistic terms. There is no hint of the person's responsibility to anyone or anything other than his or her own self-understanding. If Rieff is correct in his interpretation of Freud, Freud's willingness to stop his ethical imperatives at this point derives from a confidence in the goodness of human nature that is especially staggering coming from such a "master of suspicion": "Psychoanalysis shares the paths of truthfulness common to rationalist doctrines. People ought to be forthright. If they express their true natures, goodness will take care of itself" (354). A method that offers so sanguine a view of human nature is a shallow archaeology indeed.

This survey should suggest that the radical disjunction between the Freudian and the Christian archaeologies is in fact determined by an equally radical disjunction between teleologies. If the Freudian teleology may be summed up in the sentence "Where id was, there shall ego be," the Christian teleology may be equally tersely expressed in the answer to the first question of the Westminster Catechism: the chief end of man is "to glorify God and enjoy Him forever." The difference between these statements necessitates a difference in analytical practice, and — to return to the real subject of this essay — a difference in the practice of psychological criticism. The Freudian approach leads us to believe that the profound ambivalence Nathaniel Hawthorne exhibits toward his Puritan forebears is a result of conflict between the id's desire to be free from moral strictures and the superego's unbridled authoritarianism; but will the Christian critic agree? Similarly, will the Christian, aware that the Church is the Bride of Christ, understand the sexual language of John Donne's "Batter My Heart, Three-Personed God" in the same way the Freudian does? The profound disagreement between these two views of the origin and end of the person militates against agreement. Christian psychological criticism must take a different road from Freudian criticism at precisely the point where their views of the "nature and destiny of man" diverge, and it must not look back.

I hesitate to begin discussing my second subject, for I know that the imagination is a treasured concept for many Christian scholars of literature. There are many reasons for this attachment — it is worth reflecting on the many hidden relations between evangelical Christianity and Romantic aesthetics — but the most important, in my opinion, is the enormous influence of Dorothy Sayers' book entitled *The Mind of the Maker*. This book emphasizes the similarities between poetic invention and divine creation in order to suggest that through the contemplation of the poetic imagination we may come to a closer understanding of God's mind, since God has made our minds in the image of his own. Such understanding is indeed a noble goal, but the analogy between poetic and divine creation may not be close enough to justify its use as a fundamental explanatory tool.

In my view, W. H. Auden is perhaps the only Christian critic of repute to have recognized both the uses and the limitations of this analogy. In a famous aphorism he says, "Every beautiful poem presents an analogy to the forgiveness of sins." But what is usually ignored in approving citations of that phrase is the remainder of the sentence in which it occurs: " . . . an analogy, not an imitation, because it is not evil intentions which are repented of and pardoned but contradictory feelings which the poet surrenders to the poem in which they are reconciled" (71). This distinction between the imitative and the analogous is crucial, as Auden explains:

> The poet's activity in creating a poem is analogous to God's
> activity in creating man after his own image. It is not an imi-
> tation, for were it so, the poet would be able to create like God
> *ex nihilo;* instead, he requires pre-existing occasions of feeling
> and a pre-existing language out of which to create. It is
> analogous in that the poet creates not necessarily according to
> a law of nature but voluntarily according to provocation. (70)

In making this distinction, Auden is rightly dissociating himself, as a Christian, from the dominant Romantic tradition, best
exemplified in English by Coleridge. M. H. Abrams has forcefully demonstrated that Goethe and August Schlegel, among
others, were instrumental in promulgating the view that poetry
can constitute "a second creation, . . . not a replica nor even a
reasonable facsimile of this world, but its own world, *sui generis,*
subject only to its own laws" (278). Coleridge is clearly following them when he states, in the *Biographia Literaria,* that "the
primary IMAGINATION [is] a repetition in the finite mind
of the eternal act of creation in the infinite I AM" (I:304).

The sources of this idea are difficult to trace; Abrams
locates them in the great humanists of the Italian Renaissance,
though he notes that the concept was far less important for
them (and for their English heirs, such as Philip Sidney) than
it would become for the Romantics (272ff.). However, Dorothy
Sayers claims — without providing evidence — that the idea is
not only essential to aesthetic theory but also distinctively
Christian: "This idea of Art as *creation* is, I believe, the one
important contribution that Christianity has made to aesthetics" ("Towards a Christian Aesthetic" 13).

But Auden's distinction suggests to the contrary that the
concept may at some point come into direct conflict with Christianity, chiefly through its neglect of the inherent constraints
and conditions of human work. In this vein, Nicholas Wolterstorff argues that "divine creation, rather than being an illuminating model for what goes on in artistic creation, in fact
seriously distorts it." It does so by saying nothing "about the
social realities of art — nor indeed, about its cultural and ma-

terial realities" (465). One might add that it also trivializes and oversimplifies psychological realities: for all their profound flaws, the models of internal tension and conflict favored by Freud and his followers at least help to correct Sayers' and the Romantics' uncritical celebration of artistic production. (It is worth noting that Coleridge himself, according to his daughter Sara, struck out the comparison between God's creation and the poet's in one of his annotated copies of the *Biographia* [I:304n.].)

The alliance between Christianity and Romanticism on this point is easy enough to explain. As we saw earlier, Coleridge and his German predecessors argued for the autonomy of the imagination and the creative power of the artist in order to protect the poetic mind against the threat of Enlightenment rationalism: if poetic activity consists only in the combination and presentation of feelings, ideas, and words that the poet has inherited, then surely it is vulnerable to rational analysis. Is it any surprise, then, that Christian scholars of literature would readily accept the same notion, since they feel threatened by precisely the same enemy? And is it not clear that a merely analogous relationship between creation and poetic invention would do them no good, since it is only through maintaining the freedom of the imagination from earthly, historical contamination that the rationalistic Beast may be kept at bay?

The linking of imaginative and divine creation provides the foundation for all the key features of the doctrine of the imagination: that it generates its own distinctive kind of truth (unchallengeable by other kinds of truth, especially the scientific and the theologically dogmatic); that it proceeds from a faculty of mind clearly distinguishable from the faculties that produce rational thought and moral judgment; that it brings order out of the chaos of experience. But each of these positions is, from the Christian perspective, dubious.

If the poet's act of creation is like that of God, then it begins with chaos, a world void and without form. This is indeed the Romantic view: thus the first chapter of John Livingston Lowes' *Road to Xanadu* is called "Chaos," the last "Imagination Creatrix." But is this view consonant with the Christian doctrine of the sovereignty of God? Is it not more accurate to say that experience, however chaotic it may appear, always possesses an order waiting to be revealed through the knowledge of God — or at the very least to be accepted through faith in his purposes? Even so, the Christian acceptance of the order-out-of-chaos doctrine is easily explicable in the terms we have set forth: for if the poetic mind but recognizes an order that is already there, its truly creative function is lost, and it is thrown back on perception and judgment, both of which might be empirically examined.

The other two points are closely related, since the distinction between rational and imaginative truth is often justified by an appeal to "faculty" psychology. Unfortunately, this belief in faculties — separate compartments of mental action, as it were — derives directly from the philosophy of Kant and his successors, who had a great influence on the development of psychology in the nineteenth century (an influence that extended to Freud). Obviously, given dramatic advances not only in psychology but also and more importantly in neurophysiological research, this is no longer a justifiable basis for a theory of the mind. However, there are recent developments in the study of the brain that may revive a kind of faculty psychology. The much-discussed discoveries about the different roles of the left and right sides of the brain are as yet too vague and general to help students of poetic psychology, especially since the evidence of these discoveries is ambiguous: the right side of the brain is associated with artistic ability and visual imaging, but the left side is responsible for the use of language; and the division of faculties is in no sense absolute. Nevertheless, were literary scholars to devote attention to such research, it would mark a welcome change from their normally anti-empirical habits of mind.

In fact, what Freudian psychoanalysis and the Romantic doctrine of imagination share is precisely this disregard for, or lack of interest in, empirical standards of support and evidence in psychological investigations. In the former case, the disregard is covert — psychoanalysis has always unjustifiably claimed a scientific foundation, as Sir Karl Popper famously demonstrated three decades ago (a critique recently taken up and developed by Frederick Crews) — while in the latter it is overt. Furthermore, the former is a hermeneutics of pure suspicion, while the latter is a hermeneutics of pure faith (faith in the powers of intuition over against reason). But the similarities are nonetheless significant. The proponent of each viewpoint wishes to make compelling assertions about how the poetic mind works — and sometimes about how the reader's mind works — without having to be burdened with providing support for those assertions. In the current intellectual climate, Freudians making such demands on the faith of their readers get little respect; what, then, may Christians hope for? And are Christian scholars of literature willing to continue along the path that, since the Enlightenment, has proved so dangerous for Christians in every discipline: the gradual abandonment of more and more methods and areas of cultural investigation to our opponents? Dietrich Bonhoeffer rightly condemned this procedure by showing that it confines God to the "gaps" in our knowledge, gaps which are getting smaller in size and fewer in number. The gradual confinement of literature to a place on the periphery of culture may be far less important, but it is no more welcome; and too-frequent recourse to an anti-empirical "imagination" brings just such confinement.

Psychological criticism has a great deal to offer the Christian scholar, but only, I think, if he or she abandons the fear of empirical investigation that has for too long haunted our thinking about poetic invention. We must not, like the Freudians, claim explanatory powers that we cannot substantiate; on the other hand, we must not be too quick to resort to anti-explanatory invocations of the "mystery of poetic creation." Right now, it seems to me, psychological criticism from a Christian perspective is virtually non-existent. If it is to come to life, that life must come from a vivid awareness of current debates about creativity, the workings of the mind, and the nature of the brain. The chief difficulty for the scholar of literature who wishes to achieve such awareness is that these disciplines are currently riven by factious disputes: the recently published *Oxford Companion to the Mind* (1988) almost failed even to appear in print, so violent were the disagreements between its editors about, for instance, whether there is such a thing as the "mind."

But there is one significant contributor to these fields who is not only a fine scientist but also an extraordinary writer and a man of extraordinary sensibility: Oliver Sacks. In books such as *The Man Who Mistook His Wife for a Hat* (especially its section on "Excesses," devoted to people who possess "an excess or superabundance of function" [87]) and *Seeing Voices: A Journey into the World of the Deaf* (which turns out to be an extended meditation on the neurological and psychological roots of language), Sacks strikes a much-needed balance between the desire to know and the willingness to confess — and confess with wonder — ignorance. He possesses what too many Christian intellectuals lack: the insight to distinguish between genuine mysteries and intellectual puzzles. Such insight will be gained only by those who will risk exploring apparent mysteries to their very hearts, knowing that a genuine mystery cannot be debunked or trivialized. Christian psychological criticism could do worse than to follow Sacks' example.

WORKS CITED

(Titles with an asterisk are recommended as introductions.)

Abrams, M. H. *The Mirror and the Lamp*. New York: Oxford University Press, 1953.
Auden, W. H. *The Dyer's Hand*. New York: Random House, 1962.

Barfield, Owen. *Speaker's Meaning*. Middletown, Conn.: Wesleyan University Press, 1967.

Bloom, Harold. *The Anxiety of Influence*. New York: Oxford University Press, 1973.

*———. *A Map of Misreading*. New York: Oxford University Press, 1975.

———. *The Visionary Company*. Rev. ed. Ithaca: Cornell University Press, 1971.

Coleridge, Samuel Taylor. *Biographia Literaria*. Ed. James Engell and W. Jackson Bate. 2 vols. Bollingen Series LXXV. Princeton: Princeton University Press, 1982.

*Crews, Frederick. *Out of My System*. New York: Oxford University Press, 1975.

———. *Skeptical Engagements*. New York: Oxford University Press, 1986.

Eagleton, Terry. *Literary Theory: An Introduction*. Minneapolis: University of Minnesota Press, 1983.

*Freud, Sigmund. "The Relation of the Poet to Day-Dreaming." In *On Creativity and the Unconscious*, 44-54. New York: Harper & Row, 1958.

———. *The Standard Edition of the Complete Psychological Works of Sigmund Freud*. Ed. and trans. James Strachey et al. 24 vols. London: Hogarth Press and the Institute of Psycho-Analysis, 1966-74.

Holland, Norman N. *The Dynamics of Literary Response*. New York: W. W. Norton, 1968.

———. *Five Readers Reading*. New York: W. W. Norton, 1975.

———. "A Maker's Mind." In *Poems in Persons: An Introduction to the Psychoanalysis of Literature*. New York: W. W. Norton, 1973.

Jones, Ernest. "The Death of Hamlet's Father." In *Literature and Psychoanalysis*, ed. Edith Kurzweil and William Phillips, 34-39. New York: Columbia University Press, 1983.

Kermode, Frank. *The Sense of an Ending*. New York: Oxford University Press, 1967.

Lacan, Jacques. *Écrits: A Selection*. Trans. Alan Sheridan. New York: W. W. Norton, 1977.

Lentricchia, Frank. *After the New Criticism*. Chicago: University of Chicago Press, 1980.

Lowes, John Livingston. *The Road to Xanadu: A Study in the Ways of the Imagination*. 1927; rpt. Boston: Houghton Mifflin, 1955.

McFarland, Thomas. *Originality and Imagination*. Baltimore: Johns Hopkins University Press, 1985.

Ricoeur, Paul. *Freud and Philosophy*. Trans. Denis Savage. New Haven: Yale University Press, 1970.

Rieff, Philip. *Freud: The Mind of the Moralist*. Garden City, N.Y.: Anchor Books, 1961.

————. *The Triumph of the Therapeutic: Uses of Faith after Freud*. New York: Harper & Row, 1966.

Sacks, Oliver. *The Man Who Mistook His Wife for a Hat*. New York: Simon & Schuster, 1985.

————. *Seeing Voices: A Journey into the World of the Deaf*. Berkeley: University of California Press, 1989.

*Sayers, Dorothy. *The Mind of the Maker*. New York: Harcourt Brace, 1941.

————. "Towards a Christian Aesthetic." In *The New Orpheus: Essays toward a Christian Poetic,* ed. Nathan Scott, 3-20. New York: Sheed & Ward, 1964.

Skura, Meredith Anne. *The Literary Use of the Psychoanalytical Process*. New Haven: Yale University Press, 1981.

*Trilling, Lionel. "Art and Neurosis." In *The Liberal Imagination: Essays on Literature and Society,* 155-75. 1950; rpt. Garden City, N.Y.: Anchor Books, 1957.

*————. "Freud and Literature." In *The Liberal Imagination: Essays on Literature and Society*. 1950; rpt. Garden City, N.Y.: Anchor Books, 1957.

Wolterstorff, Nicholas. "Evangelicalism and the Arts." *Christian Scholar's Review* 17 (June 1988): 449-73.

READER-RESPONSE THEORIES

Michael Vander Weele

Literary criticism has always involved three ines-capable elements: the author, the work, and the reader. Reader-response criticism regards the third of these elements as the most crucial for criticism, for criticism always begins in the first instance with reading. The current interest in reader-response theory derives not only from this fact, however; it also comes from contemporary skepticism about our knowledge of authors' intentions, from philosophical problems with the formalist view of the autonomy of artworks, and from the diversity of interpretations that cluster around individual works. If the meaning of a work cannot be grounded in reliable knowledge of intentions or texts, then the role of the reader becomes a more crucial issue in literary criticism. Although reader-response theories differ among themselves, they all emphasize the centrality of the reader in the literary experience.

To distinguish the concerns of reader-response theories from those of other theories of literature, Raman Selden (3) refers to the diagram of linguistic communication that Roman Jakobson developed in the late 1950s:

```
                    CONTEXT
ADDRESSER           MESSAGE          ADDRESSEE
                    CONTACT
                    CODE
```

The first four factors on this diagram will seem familiar to most readers. Jakobson described the final two this way: "A CODE [is] fully, or at least partially, common to the addresser and addressee . . . and . . . a CONTACT [is] a physical channel and psychological connection between the addresser and the addressee, enabling both of them to enter and stay in communication" (357). Although "code" usually refers to a lexical range, it could also refer to the larger requirements of genre, which are shared, at least in part, by addresser and addressee.

Selden relates the concerns of reader-response criticism to the right-hand side of the diagram (ADDRESSEE), opposite the Romantic emphasis on genius (ADDRESSER), with Marxist, formalist, and structuralist criticism located between. Although the diagram is usually read from left to right, reader-response critics argue that it must be read from right to left: the addressee hypothesizes about the addresser by interpreting the context, message, and code of the work. This heuristic scheme helps us to see the radical shift in direction of reader-response criticism. The first part of this chapter will also show its relationship to a long-standing tradition of interest in the reader as one element in the enterprise of criticism. Positioning reader-response criticism historically as well as analytically will help us evaluate its development within three main categories: psychological, social, and intersubjective theories of reader response.

A LONG HISTORY OF ATTENTION TO RESPONSE

Rhetoric, which emphasizes communication and audience, has a much longer tradition than aesthetics, which after the Romantics emphasized the work and its author. Rhetoric has always emphasized the effectiveness of speech or writing when used for specific occasions. Accordingly, it has been keenly interested in the effects of speech and writing on listeners and readers. This was especially so in the Christian tradition, for after Augustine's discussion of classical rhetoric in *On Christian Doctrine,* purpose and audience became more important than matching style to subject (Kennedy 157).

An early instance of the attention given to reader response within the Christian rhetorical tradition can be found in Book XII of Augustine's *Confessions.* Augustine states that he would rather have a reader respond to the truth the reader found in his writing than have the reader be able to duplicate his understanding of that truth. This generous view of truth developed out of a view of Scripture that allowed for multiple and historically developing meanings. Augustine describes Scripture, for example, as "a spring which is all the more copious because it flows in a confined space. . . . From the words of Moses, uttered in all brevity but destined to serve a host of preachers, there gush clear streams of truth from which each of us . . . may derive a true explanation of the creation as best he is able, some choosing one and some another interpretation" (XII.27). To the simple, Augustine adds, Scripture is like a fledgling's nest; but to others, who are like birds already reared, "the words of Scripture are no longer a nest but a leafy orchard, where they see the hidden fruit. They fly about it in joy, breaking into song as they gaze at the fruit and feed upon it" (XII.28). Scripture, in short, will speak to the various needs and capabilities of individual Christian readers.

Such a view of Scripture endured at least until the seventeenth century. One finds it enunciated, for example, in the meditations and expostulations of John Donne's *Devotions upon Emergent Occasions* (1624). In Expostulation 19 Donne writes, "Oh, what words but thine can express the inexpressible texture and composition of thy word; in which, to one man, that argument that binds his faith to believe that to be the word of

God is the reverent simplicity of the word, and to another, the majesty of the word; and in which two men, equally pious, may meet and one wonder that all should not understand it, and the other as much that any man should." The multiple capacities of Scripture were not forgotten in reading others or, as in Augustine's case, in imagining how others might read you. What was important, however, was not so much multiplicity as the direction of interpretation, not so much accuracy as the incorporation of reading into one's life.

If we turn our attention from Scripture to nonscriptural texts, our best example of the view of readers' responses comes from Dante, who was greatly influenced by Augustine and who greatly influenced Donne. The risks of reading can be seen in the *Divine Comedy*, in Paolo and Francesca's literal identification with Arthurian romance and the eternal restlessness of their roused desire (*Inferno* 5) — and, on the other hand, in Statius's misreading of the fourth eclogue of Virgil, which begins his journey to God (*Purgatory* 22). The attempt to defuse reading by separating it from the rest of life is just as filled with risk. If we don't read with our lives, we share the plight of Dante's "neutral angels" in *Inferno* 3 (Freccero 110-18) and Dante's "neutral authors" in *Purgatory* 24 (Mazzotta 207-17), a plight likely suggested to Dante by John's description in Revelation 3 of the lukewarm Laodiceans.

For Augustine and Dante, language is always linked to desire. In the *Confessions* the infant is the one who reaches out in desire of something. In that reaching out, language is born as the cry of both lack and desire. Since that desire is never satisfied within the boundaries of language and human existence, the human soul on earth is always restless. But this restlessness may have a positive function, according to Augustine, since he believes that the human soul is permeable by the language of others, whether of God or of friends. In fact, Augustine describes God both as the Word and as the end of all desire, which establishes the deep connection between language and desire. The same link between language and desire can be seen in Dante. To return to the examples of Francesca and Statius just mentioned, both the seductive reading of Arthurian romance and the efficacious reading of Virgil are described as "kindling" the reader. Reading is never neutral; the erotic (including a theological eros) and the poetic are always related in this Augustinian tradition.

The rhetorical tradition that had emphasized teaching (Bruns), both of the will and of the intellect, had placed great emphasis on the reader's response. In poetry this response focused on pleasure, the handmaiden of instruction, and on desire, which moved the will to seek understanding. However, after belief in the interrelatedness of all aspects of creation began to fade, and the new science shifted its focus from purpose to function — movements Donne struggled to understand in the early seventeenth century — the refinement of objective representation on the one hand and subjective feelings on the other hand began to replace teaching as the primary goal of interpretation.

In the eighteenth century, the shift away from rhetoric was evident in the rise of the new "science" of aesthetics. Alexander Baumgarten, who first used the term *aesthetics* for his philosophy of the fine arts, still held the spectator (or reader) as a proper focus of his study, though he was more interested in understanding the arts in relation to one another. Aesthetics quickly turned to the question of genius, however, and then to formal properties of the artwork that called for disinterested contemplation. In terms of Jakobson's diagram given at the beginning of this chapter, attention shifted from the addressee to the addresser and the work. One still finds in Kant and Schiller considerable attention paid to the partaker, as well as to the creator, of art. Schiller, for example, emphasized the way an aesthetic education prepared one for a time that needed but did not encourage change. This emphasis, however, was directed toward the sensibility more than to the social and moral education of the reader, which had been emphasized in the much longer tradition of rhetoric.

Cicero's influence on the reception of classical rhetoric in the Middle Ages and the Renaissance assured its continuance as a civic art. But by the late eighteenth and nineteenth centuries, reading was considered a private matter. The science of aesthetics respected that privacy and increasingly focused on the formal elements of the literary work, elements which, it was hoped, everyone could agree upon.

CHANGING VIEWS OF CONVENTION AND NATURE

The New Criticism of the 1940s and 1950s seemed to continue the tradition of aesthetics. Its practitioners hoped to achieve an objective criticism by separating study of the work from the intention of the addresser or the affect on the addressee (Beardsley and Wimsatt). But by the 1960s the "objective" study of the "separated" work appeared to be more an exclusionary act of the will than the intellect's guarantor of objectivity.

Today's reader-response criticism, more a movement than a school, follows a heightened awareness of the separation between custom and nature, between social conventions and a natural order of reality. In *Convention: 1500–1750,* Lawrence Manley has detailed the history of Western views of convention. According to Manley, the roots of a separation between custom and nature go back at least to the late Renaissance recognition of difficulties in adapting "the supposedly natural norms of classical technique to the special rhetorical demands of the European setting" (12) and to the late seventeenth-century insistence on the relativity of non-scientific knowledge (13). These developments began to divide cultural values and poetic precedent on the one hand from nature on the other. Convention lost any sense of bipolar tension between the objective and the social. It came to be "contrasted as a social phenomenon to what is more objectively either universal or unique." Thus neoclassical authors could challenge convention because it was not universal, while Romantics could argue against convention because it was not unique. In either case, convention came to be seen as a social construction whose development was more arbitrary than natural. As a result of the widening split between the objective and the social, we see "a disintegration of the essentially harmonious relationships among readers, nature, and precedents" (2-3).

Using the terms of Manley's summary, we can describe the New Criticism as an attempt to rule out both the conventional and the idiosyncratic, the historical and the personal, in literary criticism. Reader-response theories rule both back into the interpretive process, but no longer with confidence in their "essentially harmonious relationships." While the New Critics wished to transcend conventions (viewed only as social phenomena), reader-response critics wish to expose conventions, especially those conventions that had seemed as natural as "the organic unity of the poem." The New Critics had used this (unrecognized) convention to oppose other conventions that seemed more dangerous to them. The rallying cry that had seemed natural and objective to the New Critics came to be seen as a harmful convention by many critics writing after 1959.

Contemporary criticism thrives on the suspicion that conventional readings are not natural readings and, indeed, that readings which pretend to be natural or objective must be denaturalized through psychological or sociopolitical analysis. Even before the work of modern semiotics, Freud, Nietzsche, and Marx had raised questions about the existence of *natural* laws or *natural* understanding in the human sciences. Today semiotics shares the same goal: to expose the process whereby cultural codes arrogate to themselves the status of the natural.

In late structuralist theory, the suspicion of "natural" or "objective" readings was accompanied by an emphasis on the links between one work of literature and all other written works. In this view, the meaning of a particular text could not be governed by that text alone, for the meaning of one work would depend upon the reader's associations with other literary and non-literary texts. The content of these associations was unpredictable. Intertextual meaning depended upon the *reader's* re-combining activity as much as it depended upon the *writer's* combining activity. That re-combining activity is viewed in different ways by different reader-response critics. Some of those ways emphasize the reader's subjectivity; others emphasize anonymous social forces that impinge upon and partly determine the reader.

THE SPECTRUM OF READER-RESPONSE THEORIES

Although reader-response theories have no single philosophical starting point, they can be grouped into three categories: psychological, social, and intersubjective. These quite diverse approaches all commonly resist the clear separation of reader and text. They would all challenge, for example, the opening paragraph of Beardsley and Wimsatt's classical essay on "The Affective Fallacy":

> We believe ourselves to be exploring two roads [i.e., the intentional fallacy and the affective fallacy] which have seemed to offer convenient detours around the acknowledged and usually feared obstacles to objective criticism. . . . The Affective Fallacy is a confusion between the poem and its *results* (what it *is* and what it *does*), a special case of epistemological skepticism, though usually advanced as if it had far stronger claims than the overall forms of skepticism. It begins by trying to derive the standard of criticism from the psychological effects of the poem and ends in impressionism and relativism. The outcome . . . is that the poem itself, as an object of specifically critical judgment, tends to disappear. (my italics)

More than any other essay, this one focused the debate between reader-response critics and the New Critics, the defenders of objectivity.

The terms of debate that Beardsley and Wimsatt set up in this introduction include "objective criticism," "relativism," "psychological" effects (which we might also call "subjectivism"), and a strong division between existence and action ("is" and "does," "poem" and "results"). These terms would be challenged by all three kinds of reader-response criticism.

Norman Holland and David Bleich, for example, who have developed psychological models of understanding, question whether there is a difference between the poem and its results. They call into question the independence of the poem and argue that the reader creates the poem in the process of interpreting it. Unlike the New Criticism, which is interested in the ideal reader, Holland and Bleich are interested in actual readers with differing backgrounds that make for different readings. As for the possibility of an objective criticism, Holland and Bleich would respond that there is no objective text, no origin of voice independent of the reader for the reader to listen to. Instead, all reading and all criticism are subjective. To suppose otherwise is to accommodate the rhetoric of literary criticism to a scientific ideology. Holland and Bleich would also discredit the work of an "objective criticism" that did not give the same careful attention which they give to actual readers and their reading processes. In their view, the text is a set of conventions that has no meaning apart from the unique individual reading it. Meaning is tied not to these conventions but to the identity of the individual. Nature rests in the unique individual; the text by itself is lifeless convention. Any literary approach that desires to be at all objective would have to study the construction of meaning by individual readers.

Finally, Holland and Bleich might well admit that criticism is relative and impressionistic, insofar as readers always begin with motivations. In Holland's terms, those motivations consist of defenses, expectations, fantasies, and transformations: "One can think of these four separate principles as emphases on one aspect or another of a single transaction: shaping an experience to fit one's identity and in doing so, . . . avoiding anxiety, . . . gratifying unconscious wishes, . . . absorbing the event as part of a sequence of events, and . . . shaping it with that sequence into a meaningful totality" (342).

Relativism and impressionism can also be related to the nature of the reading process as analyzed by Bleich. He emphasizes three key elements in this process: perception, affect, and association. As a professor, Bleich assigns and collects "response statements" from students who answer these three questions after reading a poem or a story: (1) What do you make of this? (perception); (2) What did you feel when reading it? (affect); and (3) What personal associations did you make while reading it? (association). (The three questions correspond to Beardsley and Wimsatt's charges of relativism, impressionism, and the confusion of the poem with its results.) Bleich uses the response statements in later discussion as the "motivational substrate" of the subsequent interpretive judgment, a judgment whose connection to personal response and motivation remains explicit. Thus both Holland and Bleich believe that the individuality of the reader directs the reading process. Accordingly, they argue, teachers and critics ought to give more attention to that individuality.

We should ask at least three questions about the psychological approach to criticism — questions about the relationship of literature to desire, to society, and to the classroom.

First, we have seen the close link between desire and language/reading in Dante and Augustine. But what happens to this relationship if, as Erich Auerbach claimed in his study of *Madame Bovary* (488-92), desire in the modern world is freefloating, not linked to specific objects and events, nor defined politically, historically, or religiously? Might our readings become more indistinct — that is, merely personal — even as their differences multiply? This seems to be true of Raymond Carver's characters in *What We Talk About When We Talk About Love* (1981) when they try to interpret their own and others' speech. Carver suggests even in his title that his characters' speech is our own, but then he positions his readers so that they are dissatisfied with this inadequate language of desire. But whereas Carver's fiction, especially his later fiction, confronts its readers with questions of judgment and value, psychological criticism has neither measure nor place for correctives. Further, one can ask whether the reader's self-knowledge is the goal of literary study, as the psychological approach to reader-response criticism assumes, or whether the psychological approach short-circuits some other kinds of knowledge we think important to literary study. For a Christian these might include the relation of literature to community and the influence of religious practices, both liturgical and social, on literature.

Second, are literary works isolated or social? If they are social, then does the socialization of the reader occur during the reading experience or after it? Similarly, if the individual is primary and consensus follows individual perception, how can we account for agreement between individuals? These questions would not have occurred to most authors and readers outside of the Western tradition or prior to the last two hundred years, as a quick consideration of Cicero and Augustine, Chaucer and the Gawain poet, and Dryden and Pope would make clear. To them, separating perception and socialization would not have been imaginable. Nor, perhaps, should it be for us.

Third, how does the instructor conduct his or her class after the response statements to a literary work are shared? One might talk about the class discussion itself and the dynamics behind it, but this seems to move too quickly to a metacritical activity. Or one might emphasize the self-knowledge gained in exchange with other students, but this seems an inadequate goal for literary study. Neither strategy resolves the difficulty of moving from individual to communal response — or at least of accounting for that movement according to the psychological model of reading.

The social model of reader-response criticism, in contrast to the psychological model, emphasizes reading conventions that the reader participates in and can exert control over once they are brought to consciousness. Both Jonathan Culler and Stanley Fish emphasize literary competence rather than individualized reading, competence that comes from participation in and understanding of a cultural tradition of reading. Faced with Beardsley and Wimsatt's "Affective Fallacy," they too would deny a split between the poem and its effects and would, like Holland and Bleich, emphasize the poem as experience. Unlike Holland and Bleich, however, Culler and Fish would study the systems that govern the production of textual meaning. Within such systems the individual reader and the constraining text lose their independent status.

Culler and Fish would give up the claim of "objective criticism" less easily than those following a psychological approach would. They emphasize historically qualified but shared reading conventions that enable one to gain competence as a reader. This establishes a field of scientific inquiry for literary study; however, that inquiry is limited to relational structures rather than content. One can infer from Culler's *Structuralist Poetics* (174) that description of relational structures may be historically objective, and that description of the most basic models for relational structures may even be universally objective, but that interpretations of the content of individual poems are not objective but relative to the structural conventions of one's society. Accordingly, interpretations are not the proper subject matter for criticism. Culler would oppose blanket charges of relativism and impressionism and would search for the common interpretive strategies or conventions that underlie a multiplicity of meanings.

We should ask at least two questions about the social model of reader-response theory sketched here. First, does it adequately deal with the importance of specific interpretations of literature? How would the teacher, for example, direct class discussion after shared reading conventions had been isolated and identified? Raman Selden states that there is "something narrow about a theory which treats interpretative moves as substantial and the content of the moves as immaterial" (121). This is especially true for those literary works like *The Divine Comedy* which make strong claims for their didactic value. Furthermore, are not shifts in reading strategies at least in part explained by the interpretations readers make of the content of literary works? The second major question to ask is this: Even if self-knowledge is not the only or even the primary goal of reading literature, should it not be at least part of that enterprise? And does that not require a way to talk about personal judgments, however socially informed?

The social and the psychological models provide two poles for reader-response theories. The intersubjective model — associated with European phenomenologists like Wolfgang Iser and Hans Robert Jauss but also with the American critic Louise Marie Rosenblatt — emphasizes neither the unique individual nor shared conventions but the negotiation between the two.

Iser emphasizes the temporal process of reading whereby we constantly adjust our expectations and fill in gaps in the text. These interpretive adjustments are more important to reading (and to teaching) than is a fixed meaning that can be read back into the text at every point. For Iser, a novel such as *Tom Jones* represents not objects whose prior reality is faithfully represented in the text but elements that are partly determined by the text and partly left to the reader's construction. The interplay of what is determined and what is constructed puts into play the norms, value systems, or worldviews of the author (who creates the work in a particular historical and cultural context) and of the reader (who reads in a different context). For Iser, therefore, the reading process involves the interaction of text, social reality, and reader. The contest between the viewpoints of the extra-literary world can be played out only through the reader's experience of the text: "The reader's existing consciousness will have to make certain internal adjustments in order to receive and process the alien viewpoints which the text presents as reading takes place. This situation produces the possibility that the reader's own 'worldview' may be modified as a result of internalising, negotiating and realising the partially indeterminate elements of the text" (Selden 114). The reader tries to resolve the tensions between various viewpoints by combining those viewpoints into "a consistent gestalt." Moving through the reading process, the reader is guided by the text but is also constantly interpreting and constructing the meaning of the text. Thus the text has no objective reality apart from the reading of it. Iser writes that "the perspective [the reader] assumes at any one moment becomes the 'theme' that is read against the 'horizon' of the previous perspectives in which he [or she] had been situated" (97).

Steven Mailloux, a former student of Stanley Fish, praises Iser's interest in "the anthropological side of literary criticism," but he doubts that Iser moves us far enough away from American text-centered criticism: "The emphasis on textual constraints and the prestructuring of effect, combined with the lack of examples of differing interpretations and significant changes in readers, will make it quite easy for Iser's theory to be grafted onto the American critical tradition without really affecting the text-centered, often a-rhetorical criticism and theory that tradition fosters" (*Interpretive Conventions* 56). This assessment notwithstanding, Iser's theory does call attention to socio-historical realities that situate the text and the reader, and it does give as much attention to the world as to the view implied in "worldview."

Hans Robert Jauss extends the influence of reader-response theories from literary criticism to literary history. In his "reception aesthetics," Jauss argues that both intrinsic and extrinsic approaches to literary history — approaches that treat literature as art or literature as a reflection of history — are built on a production model of literature that emphasizes various influences on the construction of a text but ignores the various influences on literary reception. Both approaches to the history of literary productions occlude the influences that help books gain a reading. Jauss urges his readers to supplement or displace literary history based on a production model with literary history based on a reception model.

In the past literary critics have searched for influences on reception that would account for shifts in the popularity of such poets as Donne, Herbert, Blake, Smart, and Browning, or for developments such as the rise of the novel. Like Iser, Jauss makes use of the phenomenological notion of a "horizon of expectations" and looks at both intra-literary and extra-literary expectations. Study of intra-literary expectations could include the development of a literary genre at any historical moment — of tragedy, for example, at the time of *Death of a Salesman*. It could also include expectations established by other works of the author or by other contemporary authors. But one could study not only the horizon of literary expectations but also the extra-literary horizon of social and political experience. For *Death of a Salesman* these might include post–World War II views of business, of women, and of American ideals such as progress and individualism that were sometimes in conflict with each other.

Jauss's call for attention to the history of reception is a worthwhile challenge to Christian students of literature. It might mean, for example, comparative study of extra-literary practices and the reception of a literary text — something J. A. Burrow undertakes when he relates the experience of *Sir Gawain and the Green Knight* to late medieval practices of penance. Such an approach mediates the relationship of literature to doctrine by giving attention to specific religious *practices*, both those familiar to the author's contemporary readers and those familiar to the author's subsequent readers.

The history of reception might require looking behind intertextual influences to the social practices that support them. One might ask why *Pilgrim's Progress*, Part I (the narrative of the solitary Christian), became a powerful influence on the novel, while Part II (the narrative of Christiana, who gathers to herself a community of children and fellow pilgrims) has much less force in both confessional and secular literature. Why was the reception of these two works such that the first remains a strong influence on the novel even into the nineteenth century (*Jane Eyre* is one example), while the second, more Chaucerian narrative has never attained the status of a model for later fiction? Such questions cannot be addressed if literary influence is isolated from social practice. If one adopts Jauss's view, the historical emphasis of the teacher of literature points toward a better understanding of the present. Teacher and class have to allow the literary work to call into question the present horizon of expectations as formed by literary and extra-literary practices.

Jauss, even more than Iser, is able to show the cooperation of text, reader, and the particular historical situation in which they meet. He spends less time than other reader-response theorists speculating about the relationship of text to reader. Instead, he describes that relationship at a particular time and how it changes over time, making the issue not an epistemological one but a social and historical problem.

Louise Marie Rosenblatt's work similarly broadens the context of communication in literature. Her early work, *Literature as Exploration*, was published in 1938, at about the same time as the early work of the New Critics. In it, she argued that a literary work is best understood as an event or transaction between the reader and the text. Both the reader and the text have social pasts (and social futures) that organize the transaction between them, which we call a literary work. While *Literature as Exploration* had some influence in the schools, the New Critics won the approval of those doing English studies at colleges and universities, who gave Rosenblatt little attention until after the New Criticism seemed in the 1960s to have run its course. Since that time three editions of her seminal work have been published under the sponsorship of the Modern Language Association. Although the new reader-response criticism of the 1960s and 1970s was in general associated with the work of Rosenblatt, in *The Reader, the Text, the Poem: The Transactional Theory of the Literary Work* (1978) she distances herself from the psychological model of reader-response criticism. She also opposes structuralist and deconstructionist theories of reading. Her work derives from William James, who influenced Edmund Husserl and, through Husserl's student Roman Ingarden, the work of both Iser and Jauss.

In "The Literary Transaction," Rosenblatt argues against deconstructionists, who, because they are "unable to believe in an absolute unmediated reality . . . see an extreme relativism as the only alternative" (70). To counter deconstruction, she points to

John Dewey's effort to "counteract the dualism that spoke, for example, of an 'interaction' with the environment, implying separate, self-contained entities acting on one another" (70). Dewey introduced the term "transaction" to designate a reciprocal relationship between humans and nature as aspects of a total situation (71), a view reinforced, according to Rosenblatt, by modern ecology and philosophy of science as well as by her own efforts to describe the transaction between reader and text as more than "separate, self-contained entities acting on one another."

Rosenblatt also opposes the view, stemming from Ferdinand de Saussure, that language is a self-regulating system of signifiers and signifieds detached from any notion of reference, since such a view encourages one to think of language "simply as an ungrounded code, an abstract, arbitrary system" (71). Again she returns to the American tradition of pragmatism, this time to the work of Charles Sanders Peirce, in order to provide a "triadic formulation" of language: sign, object, and interpretant. "A sign," Peirce wrote, "is in a conjoint relation to the thing denoted and to the mind. . . . The sign is related to its object only in consequence of a mental association, and depends upon a habit" (3:360; cited by Rosenblatt in "The Literary Transaction" 71). According to Rosenblatt, this triadic model, with its emphasis on human habit, re-opens the study of interpretation to personal responses and social forces. It helps us describe literature as communication, not as an isolated aesthetic product. Rosenblatt argues that a transactional theory emphasizes neither autonomous text nor unbounded subjectivism: "[It] saves us, on the one hand, from the deconstructionist's focus on the text as an autonomous semiotic entity of unbounded potentialities and, on the other hand, from the subjectivism that concentrates on the reader's response [alone]" (79). Rosenblatt believes that habit, shaped by personal and social forces, holds text and reader in relationship to each other from the beginning and guarantees that they remain interdependent.

THE USES OF READER-RESPONSE THEORIES

The practical implications of reader-response theories are diverse and sometimes contradictory. While the New Critics championed modernist and seventeenth-century poetry, and the American deconstructionists return again and again to re-readings of the Romantics, the work of reader-response theorists does not cluster around a particular set of texts. Hans Robert Jauss is a German medievalist. Wolfgang Iser studies the eighteenth-century British novel. Stanley Fish claims seventeenth-century poetry as his special province. Jonathan Culler is a leading interpreter of Flaubert, though he has moved away from individual interpretations. Even a development such as "spectator aesthetics" in Shakespearean criticism is related to reader-response criticism. This is one sign of the strength of recent emphases on readers' responses. Another is attention to reader response in fields such as American studies and women's studies, where such attention has often joined forces with feminist criticism or the New Historicism.

The great strength of the psychological model for reader-response theories is pedagogical — its involvement of individual readers. "Response statements" such as those used by David Bleich can help students clarify their responses to a novel or poem. Response statements can enrich and deepen the reading experience, especially if they interrupt that experience rather than follow it. Examining such statements allows the teacher to emphasize the process of reading, just as we have learned to emphasize the process of writing. What is dangerous about a psychological model is its suggestion that literary communication is a private matter. Such an approach typically emphasizes the autonomous freedom of the student but then has to take a laissez-faire approach to social, political, and religious issues.

The social model of reader response emphasizes power more than autonomy. According to this view, strong social forces surround us, shape us, and are inseparable from us — whether we know it or not. We gain some measure of control over these forces when we become conscious of them. So, too, we gain some measure of control over our own reading and writing when we become aware of how shared strategies are used for better or for worse. Such knowledge helps us see how the world of public discourse works and might help us find a place in that world. This attention to social convention is at least as important as attention to the individual process of reading. However, it too easily slights attention to content and to personal response.

The reader-response movement has also expanded our sense of literary history, not only by emphasizing particular readers at particular times and places but also by attending to both literary and extra-literary expectations. Two images are especially helpful. The first is that of the "horizon." It suggests the dual significance of past and present contexts for reading as well as the testing that goes on within the reading experience (Jauss's sense that historical emphasis helps us judge present expectations). The other image sometimes associated with the historical and social side of the reader-response movement is that of a "cultural conversation." This term is an adaptation of Kenneth Burke's description in *The Philosophy of Literary Form* of the "unending conversation" that we are born into:

> Where does the drama get its materials? From the "unending conversation" that is going on at the point in history when we are born. Imagine that you enter a parlor. You come late. When you arrive, others have long preceded you, and they are engaged in a heated discussion, a discussion too heated for them to pause and tell you exactly what it is about. In fact, the discussion had already begun long before any of them got there, so that no one present is qualified to retrace for you all the steps that had gone before. You listen for a while, until you decide that you have caught the tenor of the argument; then you put in your oar. Someone answers; you answer him; another comes to your defense; another aligns himself against you, to either the embarrassment or gratification of your opponent, depending upon the quality of your ally's assistance. However, the discussion is inter-

minable. The hour grows late, you must depart. And you do depart, with the discussion still vigorously in progress. (110-11)

Steven Mailloux ("Rhetorical Hermeneutics" 637) changes Burke's "unending conversation" to "cultural conversation" to emphasize the social character of our effort to understand the situation that we were born into and that we try to shape. Teaching literature and composition should mean, in the first instance, helping our students find a voice within the conversation that surrounds them.

EVALUATION AND NEW DIRECTIONS

The description of the rhetorical tradition — particularly the Christian rhetorical tradition — at the beginning of this chapter and the later description of the spectrum of reader-response theories should make it evident that attention to reader response can be personal or social, constructive or skeptical, ahistorical or historical. To end this chapter, I will try to project where the reader-response movement is going and what Christians can learn from it, offering these judgments in hopes of furthering discussion rather than concluding it.

The energy of the reader-response movement today lies in efforts to make it more socially and historically responsible and less of an epistemological puzzle. As reader-response criticism becomes more interested in social and historical questions, its concerns are being assimilated by a wide range of critics — so much so that the reader-response movement is losing its identity. This is a sign not of its weakness but of its strength. Its concerns are affirmed, for example, in the work of the cultural anthropologist Clifford Geertz, who argues convincingly that the ability to view a Quattrocento painting or to hear a contemporary Moroccan poem is as much a cultural artifact as the elements that go into the composition of such works. In addition, critics are increasingly dissatisfied with the dyadic model of linguistics (the model limited to signs and signifieds) that Ferdinand de Saussure proposed and that structuralism and deconstruction adopted. Feminists and Marxists and minority critics who cannot give up the question of reference are more likely to give Louise Marie Rosenblatt a sympathetic hearing. Contemporary fiction (e.g., that of Italo Calvino, John Barth, John Fowles) and contemporary poetry (e.g., that of Adrienne Rich, John Ashbery, Norman Dubie) have also taken a more rhetorical turn that brings to the fore the act of enunciation and the audience's role in that act. This, too, gives credence to the reader-response argument that reader and text cannot be viewed as separate entities interacting with each other but are entities already in relation to each other through a larger, historical and linguistic environment.

The question that reader-response theorists face today is whether they adequately consider the act of enunciation. Can they, for instance, comment adequately on the concrete social situation of the act of enunciation (cf. M. M. Bakhtin)? And what can they say about the status or nature of the enunciator, the producer of literary language as a social product (cf. Michel Foucault)? Linda Hutcheon described the challenge to reader-response theory this way: "When the locus of meaning shifts from Romantic author to formalist text to the reader and, at last, to the whole act of enunciation and its 'situating' in discursive practice, then we have finally moved beyond formalism and even beyond reader-response theory per se" (42).

Christians can accept this challenge. Too often a formalist paradigm of literature, modified by historical and theological concerns, has seemed our only hedge against subjectivism. But desire and interest cannot be screened out of the act of reading, as the early Christian tradition understood very well. A more pressing matter might be the nature of desire today. Today, when desire has fewer constraints, it is also less daring and less definite. The relationship of individual desire to politics and history — a relationship Dante thought clear enough — has become unclear. One can no longer assume an overarching relation between nature, society, author, reader, and precedent. That relationship has become a theoretical and, even more, a practical matter, a task for Christians to undertake.

This task requires our effort, imagination, and faith. Help can come from several sources — two of which I will mention here. First, the rich tradition of Christian thought can help us, though it must be appropriated critically, with questions of sign theory, intentionality, the relationship of literature to society, and other central issues of literary debate. The notion of "horizon" may serve as a reminder of our relation to that tradition. A horizon distinguishes without separating. It always suggests a dual function, so that a questioning of a text or tradition is also a questioning of our own understanding. The image of a "cultural conversation" is a second source of help. It reminds us that textual meaning is always interpreted and has significance in a particular cultural situation, the cultural situation that we were placed in to understand and to shape. It emphasizes sympathetic listening and participation rather than detachment and isolation. Christians need both to listen to others and to make their voice heard by others — not any voice that can get a hearing, not a private voice, and certainly not a pre-established voice, but one whose speech attends to God and to the communities he has placed us within.

Reader-response theory does not aim for uniformity of interpretation, nor does it assume that uniformity is possible; it does, however, help to account for the diversity of interpretations and to encourage participation in a community of interpreters. Such a goal is a worthy one for Christians, who wish to stand both within their own traditions and within culture at large.

WORKS CITED

Auerbach, Erich. *Mimesis: The Representation of Reality in Western Literature.* Trans. Willard Trask. Chapel Hill: University of North Carolina Press, 1980.

Augustine. *Confessions.* Trans. R. S. Pine-Coffin. London: Penguin, 1961.

———. *On Christian Doctrine.* Trans. D. W. Robertson. Indianapolis: Bobbs-Merrill, 1958.

Beardsley, Monroe C., and W. K. Wimsatt, Jr. "The Affective Fallacy." *Sewanee Review* 57 (1949): 31-55.

Bruns, Gerald L. "The Problem of Figuration in Antiquity." In *Hermeneutics: Questions and Prospects*, ed. Gary Shapiro and Alan Sica. Amherst: University of Massachusetts Press, 1984.

Burke, Kenneth. *The Philosophy of Literary Form: Studies in Symbolic Action.* Baton Rouge: LSU Press, 1941.

Burrow, J. A. *A Reading of Sir Gawain and the Green Knight.* New York: Barnes & Noble, 1966.

Culler, Jonathan. *Structuralist Poetics: Structuralism, Linguistics, and the Study of Literature.* Ithaca: Cornell University Press, 1975.

Donne, John. *Devotions upon Emergent Occasions.* Ed. Anthony Raspa. New York: Oxford University Press, 1987.

Freccero, John. *Dante: The Poetics of Conversion.* Ed. Rachel Jacoff. Cambridge: Harvard University Press, 1986.

Geertz, Clifford. "Art as a Cultural System." *MLN* 91 (1976): 1473-99.

Holland, Norman. "Transactive Criticism: Re-Creation through Identity." *Criticism* 18 (1976).

Hutcheon, Linda. "A Poetics of Postmodernism?" *Diacritics* 13 (Winter 1983): 33-42.

Iser, Wolfgang. *The Act of Reading: A Theory of Aesthetic Response.* Baltimore: Johns Hopkins University Press, 1978.

Jakobson, Roman. "Closing Statement: Linguistics and Poetics." In *Style in Language*, ed. Thomas A. Sebeok. Cambridge: MIT Press, 1960.

Kennedy, George. *Classical Rhetoric and Its Christian and Secular Tradition from Ancient to Modern Times.* Chapel Hill: University of North Carolina Press, 1980.

Mailloux, Steven. *Interpretive Conventions: The Reader in the Study of American Fiction.* Ithaca: Cornell University Press, 1982.

————. "Rhetorical Hermeneutics." *Critical Inquiry* 11 (June 1985): 620-41.

Manley, Lawrence. *Convention: 1500-1740.* Cambridge: Harvard University Press, 1980.

Mazzotta, Giuseppe. *Dante, Poet of the Desert: History and Allegory in the Divine Comedy.* Princeton: Princeton University Press, 1979.

Peirce, Charles Sanders. *Collected Papers.* Vols. 3-4. Ed. Charles Hartshorne and Paul Weiss. Cambridge: Harvard University Press, 1933.

Rosenblatt, Louise M. "The Literary Transaction." In *The Creating Word*, ed. Patricia Demers. Lincoln: University of Nebraska Press, 1986.

————. *Literature as Exploration.* 4th ed. New York: MLA, 1983.

————. *The Reader, the Text, the Poem: The Transactional Theory of the Literary Work.* Carbondale: Southern Illinois University Press, 1978.

Selden, Raman. *A Readers' Guide to Contemporary Literary Theory.* Lexington: University Press of Kentucky, 1985.

Suggested Reading

In addition to the works listed in Works Cited, the following books would be helpful for further study of reader-response theories:

Freund, Elizabeth. *The Return of the Reader: Reader-Response Criticism.* New York: Methuen, 1987.

Holub, Robert C. *Reception Theory: A Critical Introduction.* New York: Methuen, 1984.

Jauss, Hans Robert. *Toward an Aesthetic of Reception.* Trans. Timothy Bahti. Minneapolis: University of Minnesota Press, 1982.

Suleiman, Susan, and Inge Crosman, eds. *The Reader in the Text: Essays on Audience and Interpretation.* Princeton: Princeton University Press, 1980.

Tompkins, Jane, ed. *Reader-Response Criticism: From Formalism to Post-Structuralism.* Baltimore: Johns Hopkins University Press, 1980.

HERMENEUTICS

Roger Lundin

S EVERAL THINGS MAY COME TO MIND WHEN THE CHRISTIAN critic hears the word *hermeneutics*. First, he or she is likely to recognize the term because of its long association with the interpretation of the scriptures within the Christian tradition. Indeed, even those with little theological training realize the importance that hermeneutics has for the understanding of the scriptural text. This is especially true for evangelical Protestants, who are people of the Book and are likely to recognize the importance of interpretive principles for the understanding of God's truth.

The word *truth* calls to mind another common assumption about the word *hermeneutics*. It is that the person who studies hermeneutics does so for the purpose of discovering the way to the right interpretation. New Criticism, archetypal criticism, feminist criticism, and Marxist criticism — all discussed in separate chapters in this book — often advocate special ways of reading works of literature, and many who practice these techniques offer interpretive keys with which to unlock the mysteries of texts. Set alongside these schools of criticism, "hermeneutics" may appear to be one more school of criticism claiming to have discovered the right way to read.

But to see hermeneutics in this way — as a critical school

prescribing the means of right interpretation — is to miscon-
strue the work done in hermeneutical theory in recent decades.
As carried out by Martin Heidegger, Paul Ricoeur, Hans-Georg
Gadamer, and others, that work has sought to be descriptive
rather than prescriptive. Its goal has been not to develop a
specific interpretive scheme but rather to understand what we
do when we interpret a book or a human action. To be sure,
this work has implications for the study of literature as well as
for theology and social practice, and I will refer to some of these
implications later in this essay. For now, I will claim that hermeneutical thinking in our century has been primarily concerned with understanding the nature of interpretation rather
than with devising a method to be employed in the quest for
the right reading of a text.

Similarly, I hope to explain how contemporary hermeneutical thinking has moved well beyond a discussion of the
scriptures in its attempts to describe human understanding. The
major practitioners just mentioned — Heidegger, Ricoeur, and
Gadamer — all came to their thinking about hermeneutics out
of specific confessional Christian traditions. Each, however,
moved beyond the insights of his tradition to make more
general statements about the practice of interpretation. The fact
that each seemed to move "beyond belief" may give us pause
as we consider the implications of hermeneutical thinking for
evangelical Christians.

In this essay, my goal is to sketch several of the main
definitions of the hermeneutical enterprise. Then, after examining some of the origins of hermeneutical thinking, I will take
a look at crucial figures and issues of our century. Finally, having
attempted to delineate some of the implications of this thinking
for Christian reflection upon literature, I will conclude by assessing the potential, both positive and negative, of contemporary hermeneutical theory.

THE SCOPE OF HERMENEUTICS

In an excellent book on the subject entitled *Hermeneutics,* Richard Palmer outlines "six modern definitions" of the word *hermeneutics* (33-45). His divisions reveal interesting things. They show that hermeneutical theory is grounded in the history of efforts by the Christian church to understand and apply the message of the Bible. More specifically, Palmer's categories reveal the fact that self-conscious reflection upon the nature of interpretation is largely the product of the early modern era and the culture of Protestantism. Both hermeneutics as biblical exegesis and hermeneutics as philological method date back to the seventeenth and eighteenth centuries.

Although questions of exegesis and interpretation are as old as the history of doctrines of revelation, only in the seventeenth century did hermeneutics arise as a specific concern in itself. At that time, we in the West began to separate exegesis clearly from hermeneutics; the former was actual commentary, while the latter was the study of the rules, methods, or theories governing that study. Under the influence of rationalism in the eighteenth century, hermeneutics became the study of the linguistic and historical tools needed for the discovery of those timeless scriptural truths that were consistent with the rational values of the era.

Two of Palmer's definitions of hermeneutics deal with major issues of the nineteenth century. In this period, hermeneutical efforts were directed toward making the interpretation of human actions as systematic as the study of the natural world had become in the physical sciences. "Hermeneutics as the science of linguistic understanding" grew out of the monumental work of the German theologian Friedrich Schleiermacher, whose goal was to outline a science of all human understanding. Schleiermacher sought to uncover the rules governing all attempts to interpret texts, and in his theory, hermeneutics was finally cut off from its explicit scriptural roots. No longer the limited study of biblical interpretation, it sought

to become a project of universal significance. One individual
strongly influenced by Schleiermacher, Wilhelm Dilthey, attempted to establish a universal science of the study of human
art, action, and writing.

The final two categories listed by Palmer are of twentieth-
century origin, and they are both reactions against the rational
and empirical definitions given to hermeneutics in the previous
two centuries. Palmer describes these modern views as "hermeneutics as . . . existential understanding" and "hermeneutics
as a system of interpretation." The influence of Martin Heidegger is inestimable in this period. Because he was convinced of
the impoverished consequences of rationalism and empiricism,
Heidegger set himself nothing less than the goal of rethinking
the hermeneutical enterprise in its entirety. His radical reassessment would in turn prove to be of great importance to Hans-
Georg Gadamer and Paul Ricoeur.

In a survey of the landscape of the past three centuries of
hermeneutical reflection, two things stand out. First, modern
hermeneutics — and, indeed, most contemporary textual study
— is deeply rooted in the events of the Renaissance and the
Reformation. Out of Protestantism grew the concern to delineate
clear rules of interpretation and to develop an exact science of
human understanding. By taking the question of interpretation
out of the framework of ecclesiastical authority and locating it in
the transaction of the reader and the text, Protestantism increased
the need for principles to guide interpretation. In the absence of
institutional authority, there arose a clear need for rules.

The second thing we see is that the story of modern
hermeneutical thinking has been one of relentless emancipation
and expansion. Especially since Schleiermacher, hermeneutics
has been cut loose from its theological moorings, and this has
led hermeneutical reflection to explore many hitherto uncharted
waters. Once hermeneutics had become the universal science
of understanding, it was no longer explicitly tied to problems
of Christian revelation and interpretation. Some contemporary
hermeneutical thinkers, particularly Ricoeur and Gadamer,

have tried to return the question of the sacred to our thinking about interpretation, but they have done so against great odds. For three centuries, intellectual life in the West has moved in the direction of human autonomy. To renew a sense of the sacred within a secular society is a most difficult matter.

ROMANTICISM AND HERMENEUTICS

Anxiety over hermeneutical questions increases dramatically when accepted principles of interpretation have lost their hold on the readers of texts, thus making the meaning of revered works appear to have become opaque. When the meaning of authoritative works seems obvious, few will speculate about the nature of understanding; when classic texts seem to have lost their connection to present life, however, hermeneutical anxiety grows. One such period of anxiety came in the final decades of the eighteenth century, at the end of the Enlightenment and the beginning of the Romantic age. Powerful political and intellectual forces conspired to widen the gap between modern interpreters and the authoritative texts of antiquity. How was someone who was trained in Newtonian science, committed to philosophical rationalism, and enthralled by the radical possibilities unleashed in the French Revolution going to understand classics that spoke of fate and radical human evil, that were filled with demons and angels and other fantastic creatures?

In the face of such difficulties, Friedrich Schleiermacher sought to reformulate in a dramatic way the hermeneutical problem. For Schleiermacher, misunderstanding was not an isolated phenomenon but a universal fact of the reading process.[1] He held that we are forced to interpret because of our

1. For my reading of Schleiermacher and his influence, I am particularly indebted to Gadamer's *Truth and Method* (184-97), Ricoeur's "Task of Hermeneutics," and Weinsheimer's *Gadamer's Hermeneutics* (136-43). According

natural inclination to misunderstand that which has been said
to us in speech or writing. And since misunderstanding is the
norm and not the exception, Schleiermacher argued, what we
need is a set of rules to govern all interpretation of texts. We
need methods to correct our practice.

Schleiermacher further argued that the goal of interpretation is not to arrive at a sound judgment about the claims to
truth made in the statements or writings of another individual.
Instead, because he considered art, philosophy, and theology to
be primarily the creative expressions of human individuality,
Schleiermacher conceived of interpretation as the attempt to
get inside the mind of the author of the work we are reading,
viewing, or hearing. For Schleiermacher, interpretation became
an act of psychological divination. "It is ultimately a divinatory
process, a placing of oneself within the whole framework of the
author, an apprehension of the 'inner origin' of the composition
of a work, a re-creation of the creative act" (Gadamer 187).

Schleiermacher formulated his hermeneutical perspective
at the same time that the Romantic movement was establishing
itself in English literature, and the parallels between the German theologian and the English poets are striking. Like
Schleiermacher, the Romantics focused upon the question of
individual genius. They recast the definition of truth, seeing it
not as something discovered through rational reflection or given
in special revelation, but rather as the creative projection of
highly imaginative individuals. John Keats stated this
eloquently in a well-known letter to a friend:

> I am certain of nothing but of the holiness of the Heart's
> affections and the truth of Imagination — What the Imagination

to Weinsheimer, "For Schleiermacher the possibility of misunderstanding is
universal. The distance and alienation that prevent immediate understanding
and foster misunderstanding are not confined to written texts composed in
the distant past; they obtain in conversation as well. The alienation of historical distance in Schleiermacher's view is merely a special instance of the
more general, indeed universal, alienation of I and Thou" (137).

seizes as Beauty must be truth — whether it existed before or not — for I have the same idea of all our Passions as of Love they are all, in their sublime, creative of essential Beauty. . . . The Imagination may be compared to Adam's dream [*Paradise Lost*, VII:452-90] — he awoke and found it truth. . . . (Bate 237-38)

Under the significant influence of German Romantic idealism and English Romantic poetry, the nineteenth century undertook a dramatic revision of the question of interpretation. When we read a book, it was now claimed, we are not encountering a word of truth that comes to us from without. Instead, we are facing a creative projection of truth that has arisen from within another human being. In understanding that creation, we cannot rely upon our membership in a community or tradition to mediate its unique truth for us. Precisely because it is the projection of individual genius, that truth can be understood only through our sympathetic identification with the one who has created it. To comprehend what that person has said, we must try to see the world through his or her eyes.

This model of the interpretive process has dominated hermeneutical thinking for almost two centuries, whether in the Victorian humanism of Matthew Arnold, in the high modernism of the early decades of this century, or in the various critical schools spawned by the academic study of literature in the past fifty years. Texts are expressions of deep human feeling, the product of individual or collective genius and need. To understand them, we need to set aside our prejudices and enter as fully as possible into their worlds. This involves establishing some form of communion with the authorial mind behind the work or somehow moving into the alien world of the work of literature.

The important thing is that we do this without depending upon our traditions or assumptions to serve as guides. Since the whole point is to understand the unique expression that another person has created, what purpose could our own beliefs serve in the process? Instead of prejudices, we need techniques to help us learn how to avoid inevitable misunderstanding as we move into the alien world of another individual's under-standing. Literary study is "a type of schooling," writes Gerald Bruns in a recent unpublished essay:

> Its theme is the mastery of a canon of texts, and there is a long-standing consensus as to what this mastery looks like. One masters a text by situating it in a context and then discovering the connections between the two: text and context. . . . And by doing these things we comply with the basic rule of Romantic Hermeneutics, which is, as Schleiermacher says, 'To understand the text at first as well as and then even better than its author.' . . . We learn to ask of the text how it is made, how it works, how its elements combine or fly apart, or how the internal disposition of its parts compares with other texts taken in this same analytical spirit. . . . The text, like mind or culture, is rule-governed.

After Schleiermacher and the Romantics, then, the goal of reading increasingly became an objective yet sympathetic analysis of the text, and the goal of this analysis was to make it possible for the interpreter to engage in self-dispossession. We read to leave our selves behind. And to see how pervasive this conception has become and how it has influenced even those who would otherwise deplore many aspects of Romanticism, we might briefly consider the case of C. S. Lewis. Near the end of his life, Lewis wrote a curious book on literary theory, *An Experiment in Criticism*. In its final pages, Lewis explains why we ought to read fictional stories even though they might arouse in us harmful vicarious feelings. "The nearest I have yet got to an answer is that we seek an enlargement of our being," he claims. "We want to see with other eyes, to imagine with other imaginations, to feel with other hearts, as well as with our own" (137). And what is the source of this desire? Nothing less than our wish to break free of the prisons of our own isolating consciousnesses:

> We are not content to be Leibnitzian monads. We demand windows. Literature as Logos is a series of windows, even of doors. One of the things we feel after reading a great work is

'I have got out.' Or from another point of view, 'I have got in';
pierced the shell of some other monad and discovered what it
is like inside. . . .

The man who is contented to be only himself, and therefore
less a self, is in prison. My own eyes are not enough for me, I
will see through those of others. . . .

In reading great literature I become a thousand men and yet
remain myself. Like the night sky in the Greek poem, I see
with a myriad eyes, but it is still I who see. Here, as in worship,
in love, in moral action, and in knowing, I transcend myself;
and am never more myself than when I do. (138, 140-41)

This passage from Lewis demonstrates how strong is the
hold of the thinking of Schleiermacher and the Romantics, even
in the thinking of someone whose understanding was as profoundly orthodox as Lewis's was.

THE TWENTIETH-CENTURY DEBATE

The redirection of hermeneutical thinking in the modern world
was prompted in part by the failure of Romantic hermeneutics
to develop a convincing method of textual interpretation. Hermeneutics as a science of human understanding foundered upon
the rock of actual practice. In biblical criticism, the social sciences, history, and literary study, a myriad of conflicting
methods arose, each claiming authority and exclusivity. Rather
than leading to the discovery of a unified method, the quest
for a technique of certainty spawned countless competing
means of interpretation. Hermeneutical thinking since Heidegger has sought ways of moving beyond this impasse.

Before turning to several key figures in the modern debate,
however, we need to move back several centuries to consider
certain philosophical origins of contemporary hermeneutical
thought. We do so because of the dramatic influence of René
Descartes upon our modern conceptions of knowledge and

understanding. In a famous passage outlining his process of philosophical reflection, Descartes described how he sought to get at the truth of things by setting aside all of his preconceptions about God, the world, and the self. He came to the point where he doubted everything save the fact that he was doing the doubting. *Cogito, ergo sum:* upon this single certainty — that *he* existed because *he* consciously doubted — Descartes sought to ground his structure of mathematical, philosophical, and theological certainty.[2]

What has made Descartes so crucial for the history of hermeneutical thinking has been the influence of his conviction that we must undertake the quest for knowledge independent of the influence of authority and tradition. By establishing a dichotomy between knowledge and prejudgment, Descartes helped to create our modern longing for method. Method was to do the work of displaced traditions and authority. As Schleiermacher was to argue more than a century later, Descartes claimed that the human intellect needs clear-cut methods to correct its slovenly practices. Knowledge is discovered in the transactions between the *unassuming* self and everything that stands over against that self. "Descartes paves the way for making the relevance of the knowing self the center of thought," explains the German theologian Helmut Thielicke. "Henceforth every object of thought, understanding, perception, and indeed will and belief, is related to the conditions contained for these acts in the subject that executes them. . . . Man, then, always stands over against what he observes; he is always himself a theme" (34, 35). The Cartesian imperative is behind the intellectual traditions of the Enlightenment and Romanticism, which, in turn, have had vast influence upon modern theorizing.

In what may be the most important work on hermeneutics in our century, *Being and Time,* Martin Heidegger challenges the foundational assumptions of Cartesianism. As a treatment of the

---

2. For a comprehensive and balanced study of modern theories of selfhood, knowledge, and interpretation, see Taylor, *Sources of the Self.*

history of Western metaphysics, *Being and Time* raises a number of provocative questions, many of which must remain beyond the purview of this essay. Here I will concentrate upon Heidegger's claims about interpretation, which have been of great importance in contemporary hermeneutical thinking. Whether one directly opposes or endorses Heidegger's thought, it is undeniable that his reflections on hermeneutics have shaped the debate about interpretation for more than half a century.

In simplest terms, we might say that Heidegger radically questions the Cartesian and Enlightenment claims about our ability to cast aside our pre-understanding as we search for knowledge. For Heidegger, such a bracketing of our assumptions is impossible, because there is, he argues, no such thing as direct, unmediated perception. All of our judgments of things are informed by prior conceptions that we hold, even if we do not recognize that we hold them. "In interpreting," he points out, "we do not, so to speak, throw a 'signification' over some naked thing which is present-at-hand, we do not stick a value on it. . . . In every case this interpretation is grounded in *something we have in advance*" (190, 191).

This is the famous *hermeneutical circle*. The paradox is that, in a sense, one must already *understand* something before beginning to interpret it. The claim Heidegger makes is that we never come to the interpretation of any book, object, or event with a blank mind, because prejudgments inform all our mental activities. We may regret this state of affairs, Heidegger explains, "*but if we see this circle as a vicious one and look out for ways of avoiding it, even if we just 'sense' it as an inevitable imperfection, then the act of understanding has been misunderstood from the ground up. . . .* What is decisive is not to get out of the circle but to come into it in the right way" (194, 195). To Heidegger, the undeniable existence of the hermeneutical circle means that what Descartes sought to do is impossible. We cannot set aside our "fore-understanding" of reality, for if that were not in place, the world would be for us an unintelligible series of events and objects. As Alasdair MacIntyre writes in

After Virtue, "a world of textures, shapes, smells, sensations, sound and nothing more invites no questions and gives no grounds for furnishing any answers" (79-80).

The French philosopher Paul Ricoeur has made a similar point on a number of occasions, perhaps most forcefully in an early work, *The Symbolism of Evil.* In this probing study of the language of human shame and guilt, Ricoeur denies the possibility of what he calls "pure reflection." Philosophical analysis in the Cartesian tradition claims to be able to ponder the truth free of all mythical and symbolic encumbrances. But in this process, Ricoeur claims, "pure reflection" abstracts itself from life: "the reflection is pure, but it leaves everyday reality outside, insofar as man's everyday reality is 'enslavement to the passions'" (347). The Cartesian claim of a radical new beginning is belied by the fact that all of our thinking is rooted in language which is saturated with the history of human shame and glory. When we pick up a word in order to use it to express our individual meaning, that word is already charged with a history of significance. When it comes to "thinking about thought," Ricoeur argues, "the illusion is not in looking for a point of departure, but in looking for it without presuppositions. There is no philosophy without presuppositions" (348).

That last sentence could well serve as a summary of the conviction guiding the work of another important hermeneutical theorist, Hans-Georg Gadamer, who in *Truth and Method* explores the implications of Heideggerian insights for the process of reading and interpreting. Gadamer offers a model that stands in sharp contrast to what I have called the Cartesian ideal of self-dispossession — that is, the claim that to understand the truth about something, we must first remove our prejudices. Behind the ideal of disinterestedness, Gadamer detects a pervasive "prejudice against prejudice" that is the "global demand of the enlightenment."

According to Gadamer, Heidegger correctly saw that rather than being an impediment to right understanding, as Cartesianism and the Enlightenment would have it, *prejudice* (as *pre*-judgment) is the only foundation upon which any appropriate understanding can build. Although the word *prejudice* now has understandably strong negative connotations, in the history of law the word has long meant something far different from "groundless assumption." As Gadamer notes, "In German legal terminology, a 'prejudice' is a provisional legal verdict before the final verdict is reached." Only through the Enlightenment critique of religion did the word come to mean "'unfounded judgment'" (270). According to Gadamer, "the fundamental presupposition of the enlightenment" is the belief that "a methodologically disciplined use of reason can safeguard us from all error. This was Descartes' idea of method" (277). By denigrating prejudice, the Enlightenment tradition established "a mutually exclusive antithesis between authority and reason." This antithesis has been a potent factor in the intellectual and political life of the West for the past several centuries.

By denying that there can be a perfectly disinterested, perfectly *rational* reading of another person, of the natural world, or of a text, Gadamer questions the very foundations of the Enlightenment tradition. He would agree with those who call for us to engage in rational reflection and the critical scrutiny of presuppositions. But he would emphasize that such activities can take place only after the crucial initial act of understanding has occurred. Long before we understand ourselves or our world through detached, critical reflection, "we understand ourselves in a self-evident way in the family, society and state in which we live. . . . That is why the prejudices of the individual, far more than his judgments, constitute the historical reality of his being" (276).

According to Gadamer, each of us belongs — through language and the patterns of behavior to which language points — to communities and extensive traditions. For Gadamer, to deny the supremacy of Cartesian reason is not to celebrate subjectivity or irrationalism. When we deny the claim of reason to have established adequate foundations for thought, we do not become solipsistic entities shut off from communion with the outer world and locked within our isolating prejudices. If we leave the world of Descartes, we need not become the "Leibnitzian monads" that C. S. Lewis feared. We are never alone in language, because all of us have received hosts of assumptions about ourselves and the nature of things. Through language, we are connected to vast communities, past and present, whether or not we are even aware of these connections.

Rather than standing as impediments to right understanding, then, "prejudices" are the basis of all understanding. The goal of all thinking — and reading — should not be to cast these assumptions aside in order to take on those belonging to another person. (Recall the argument put forth by Lewis: "The man who is contented to be only himself, and therefore less a self, is in prison. My own eyes are not enough for me, I will see through those of others.") Rather, the goal of thinking should be to test, clarify, modify, and expand our assumptions, to bring them more in line with a more comprehensive truth.

According to Gadamer, understanding is a form of dialogue in which the horizon of our prejudices is fused with that of the text we are reading or the individual with whom we are conversing, as we both attend to the object or truth in question: "The task of hermeneutics is to clarify this miracle of understanding, which is not a mysterious communion of souls, but sharing in a common meaning" (292). Accordingly, to understand another person or a book or a painting is not so much a matter of putting on another's spectacles in order to see how the object appears to "other" eyes; it is more a matter of looking with an "other" upon the object until a common understanding emerges.

To summarize: modern hermeneutical reflection calls into question the Cartesian and Enlightenment claims for the supremacy of skeptical detachment and rational reflection. On a practical level, hermeneutics has questioned whether such complete detachment is a possibility. Do we ever read with all of our assumptions held in abeyance? Do we completely set aside our beliefs when we enter the alien world of a text? To such questions, hermeneutical theory responds with a convincing "No."

On a deeper level, modern hermeneutical thinking has asked whether the Cartesian ideal is a desirable or necessary one. Does the fact that knowledge is shaped by "prejudice" mean that we are doomed to hold nothing but mere opinions? Is the influence of authority or tradition upon a belief enough to deny that belief any status as knowledge? Again, those who understand Heidegger's critique would answer such questions in the negative. When considering the implications of contemporary hermeneutical reflection, Christian thinkers should continue to remind themselves of the larger issues at stake in the struggle between hermeneutics and the dominant Cartesian tradition in the modern world.

HERMENEUTICS AND CHRISTIAN LITERARY STUDY

Although the promise and the peril of Heideggerian thinking for biblical hermeneutics have been explored thoroughly for several decades, only recently has hermeneutical theory begun to have an appreciable influence upon literary study. Furthermore, in Anglo-American literary study, Heidegger has come down to us more through the influence of Jacques Derrida than through that of either Hans-Georg Gadamer or Paul Ricoeur. Derrida, who differs from Gadamer and Ricoeur in his reading of Heidegger, is discussed in the chapter on deconstruction.

As we begin to consider the potential of hermeneutics for literary study, we would do well to remind ourselves of an important fact: hermeneutical theory does not offer another method for reading texts. This is significant, since academic literary study in our century has consisted of a procession of competing theoretical schools that have had a shared fascination with technique. From New Criticism to myth criticism, structuralism, Marxism, feminism (to a certain degree), Freudianism, and poststructuralism, literary criticism and theory have seemed preoccupied with developing systematic techniques to employ in the reading of texts.

Considering the nature of intellectual life in the university and the modern penchant for innovation at almost any cost, the rapidity with which one school of criticism has replaced another should perhaps not be surprising. One of the powers of hermeneutical theory may be its ability to help us comprehend the history of our fascination with interpretive systems. The major intellectual and social forces of the modern world — Cartesian rationalism, Baconian empiricism, Protestantism, the Enlightenment, and the Romantic movements in England and America — have been in agreement about the need to deny the claims of authority and tradition in the realm of knowledge. As we employ a radical skepticism and rely on our creative intellectual freedom, we are supposedly enabled to discover truths that are independent of our communal commitments or any authority outside the self. Hermeneutical thinking challenges these assumptions, and by forcing us to realize our vast debt to our cultural (linguistic) past, it may help us develop a more balanced approach to the passing fads of methodical literary study.

Hermeneutics may help us achieve this balance, in part, by enabling us to appreciate the legitimacy of principled pluralism in literary study. Ricoeur is particularly instructive on this point. In *Freud and Philosophy*, he argues for the hermeneutical significance of those whom he calls the great modern "masters of suspicion" — Marx, Nietzsche, and Freud:

> If we go back to the intention they had in common, we find in it the decision to look upon the whole of consciousness primarily as "false" consciousness. They thereby take up again, each in a different manner, the problem of the Cartesian doubt, to carry it to the very heart of the Cartesian stronghold. The philosopher trained in the school of Descartes knows that things are doubtful, that they are not such as they appear; but he does not doubt that consciousness is such as it appears to itself; in consciousness, meaning and consciousness of meaning coincide.

Since Marx, Nietzsche, and Freud, this too has become doubt-
ful. After the doubt about things, we have started to doubt
consciousness. (33)

After Marx, Freud, and Nietzsche, Ricoeur is arguing, we
would be most naive to believe that there was only one legitimate way to read a text.[3] Ricoeur is not arguing for the comprehensive truth of, say, a Marxist or a Freudian interpretation
of existence. In fact, as supposedly exhaustive explanations,
these two "readings" of human experience all but cancel each
other out. Instead, Ricoeur is pressing the claim that modern
interpretation must account for the fact that written texts
embody not only those conscious meanings willfully put into
them. They also give evidence of economic interest, the working
of the subconscious, and the presence of a will to power. In
"Existence and Hermeneutics," Ricoeur explains that rival hermeneutical schemes display the "dependence of the self — its
dependence on desire glimpsed in an archaeology of the subject,
its dependence on the spirit glimpsed in its teleology, its dependence on the sacred glimpsed in its eschatology" (24). There
are many stories that one can tell about a book or a human
action — about its physical and psychic origins in the subter-
ranean regions below consciousness, about its purposive moral
and aesthetic activity, and about its spiritual destiny and mystery. Many of these stories may complement one another and
thus give a fuller picture of human experience without radically
conflicting with one another.

While hermeneutical criticism may assist us by revealing
the ground for a principled interpretive pluralism, it cannot be
of much help in formulating a specifically Christian response
to literature. Although the three main figures I have discussed

---

3. The acknowledgment that multiple meanings might exist for a single
text is not, of course, an exclusive development of modern hermeneutical
thinking. For example, medieval Catholicism developed an elaborate scheme
of "fourfold interpretation." For a succinct discussion of medieval interpretive
beliefs and practices, see Ozment's *Age of Reform, 1250-1550*, 63-72.

in this chapter had extensive training in Protestant theology, none has been overtly Christian in his work. Heidegger seems clearly to have left Christian faith behind and to have replaced it with something like a linguistic mysticism, especially in his later writings. Both Ricoeur and Gadamer frequently say things that might lead one to believe them to be Christian theorists, but in each case the references to the Christian faith often seem to remain tantalizingly obscure.

To explain the relationship of the major hermeneutical theorists to Christian belief and practice, we need to consider an anomaly. In this century, all of these theorists — Heidegger, Gadamer, and Ricoeur — have asserted the failure of the Cartesian ideal of grounding knowledge independent of tradition, specifically the Christian tradition. Nevertheless, in confronting what they consider to be the epistemological poverty of twentieth-century thought, these three theorists have self-consciously worked as philosophers rather than as theologians. They have sought the starting point for reflection not within the life of the church or revelation, but rather within the resources and residue of language itself. Consequently, any Christian critic employing the insights of the hermeneutical theorists will need to engage critically their conceptions of truth and their assumptions about the meaning of religious language in the modern world. While Christians from different traditions have different emphases, all Christians concerned with orthodoxy agree that truth comes to us through Scripture and through the revelation of God in the history of his dealings with his people. But in philosophical hermeneutics, Scripture and tradition tend to be conflated and to become a *linguistic tradition* that *embodies* (instead of *pointing to*) the truth.

Helmut Thielicke discusses at length the limitations of modern hermeneutical models for the individual committed to Christian orthodoxy. "To the degree that theological interest focuses on appropriation," writes Thielicke, "faith becomes a matter of understanding" (155). In spite of its efforts to break out of the confines of Cartesianism, Thielicke claims, the

Heideggerian tradition has remained bound to the question of the human subject. For example, though Heidegger and Gadamer seek to ground the interpreting self in tradition, their break with Cartesianism consists more of an acknowledgment of the power of the collective human consciousness, subtly manifested in the history of language, than of a discovery of a revelatory truth imparted to humanity. Thielicke describes the difference between a strictly "hermeneutical" understanding of Scripture and more orthodox, confessional claims about it: "Being an active rather than an interpretive or 'apophantic' word, God's Word changes the self rather than disclosing it. Hence it does not permit of prior principles of understanding. As the existence which is being understood is given up to death, so its principles of understanding are given up to death" (156).

Gerald Bruns, one of the most perceptive contemporary interpreters of Heidegger and Gadamer, argues that the truth which is disclosed within history is confined to history and does not reach beyond it. He writes, "These versions [of the truth of anything as it is disclosed in the process of interpretation] are not representations of anything hidden behind or beneath history, or at history's end. They are just whatever makes its appearance in time, which is all, I believe, that anything ever does" (14). Such a view of truth runs counter to the Christian conception of the creative and revealing word of God, who was before all time and will be all in all at the end of the age. Truth is not simply something that *emerges from* or is *disclosed in* history; in historic Christian theology, it has always been something *revealed* to men and women *in* history by the one who claims to be the author of history.

Although it cannot supply us with a specifically Christian response to literature, hermeneutical theory can provide us with substantial support in our theoretical reflection and our practice as Christian critics. By emphasizing the situated nature of knowledge and the validity of tradition, hermeneutical theory can help Christian critics bring the discussion of literature back into history and social reality. At the same time, it can provide validation for the practices we engage in as critics who interpret from within specific theological and liturgical traditions. Although it may not specifically endorse the Christian perspectives we bring to our reading, hermeneutical theory does provide a telling justification for our bringing such perspectives to bear upon the books we read.

While the question of the relationship of hermeneutics to the Anglo-American critical tradition could be adequately treated only in an essay by itself, I can perhaps at least sketch the outlines of a "hermeneutical" response to that tradition.[4] As a number of recent studies have claimed, one way of viewing literary theory since the Romantic age is to see it as a history of formalism in various guises.[5] Whether symbolist, modernist, New Critical, or even poststructural, this "formalism" has tended to isolate and then exalt the aesthetic category; to make sharp distinctions between "poetic" discourse and all other forms of discourse, and, in recent years, to collapse all discourse into poetic discourse; to make light of literature's didactic functions and to celebrate instead its ability to give pleasure; and finally, to emphasize the self-contained, non-referential nature of either the individual work or the whole body of literature (Northrop Frye), or to speak of all of language as non-referential.

By returning literature to history and human action, hermeneutical theory helps to release literature from some of the binds into which Romantic thinking has led it. For example, by demonstrating how all human "readings" of experience, including those "readings" that constitute works of imaginative literature, are rooted in prior assumptions, hermeneutical theory calls into question the claims of disinterestedness which have governed aesthetics for two centuries. In addition, hermeneutical theory renews interest in the questions of the truth claims of a work of art, and does so after a long period in which the

4. For a fuller treatment of this subject, see my article entitled "Hermeneutics and the Romantic Tradition."

5. See Graff's *Literature against Itself,* Hartman's *Beyond Formalism,* Lentricchia's *After the New Criticism,* and McGann's *Romantic Ideology.*

formalist tradition has largely discounted such claims as tangential or irrelevant. And finally, hermeneutics has the potential to release us from a too narrow definition of the discipline of *English*. That is, by forcing us to rethink our assumptions concerning the supposedly radical distinction between scientific knowledge and aesthetic knowledge, hermeneutics may enable those of us who study literature to appreciate the rich possibilities of dialogue between our discipline and such fields as history, philosophy, theology, and the social sciences.

In many instances, the alternative to a hermeneutical understanding is sobering. In poststructuralism, for example, we discover similar insights about the historically situated nature of all human use of language. But the "moral" that many poststructuralists draw from this is quite different from that which someone like Hans-Georg Gadamer would claim. For Gadamer, the fact that writing and interpretation are grounded in tradition does not mean that they are the subjective opposite of authentic, scientific knowledge; to accept such a conclusion would be to grant primacy to the Enlightenment dichotomy between reason and authority, tradition and truth. For poststructuralists, however, to say that scientific and aesthetic knowledge are grounded in tradition is to say that they are not knowledge at all but tropes and tropes alone. And if all assertions and assumptions are tropes, and all tropes are untrue, the conclusion is obvious.

It is from an impasse such as this that the insights of the hermeneutical tradition may be able to deliver us. It commends itself to us because it offers us as Christian literary critics a coherent way of defending what we do without making us rely on untenable assumptions about language. Furthermore, hermeneutical theory provides us with one meaningful way of bringing questions of truth and moral commitment back into the center of our discussion of literature. By refusing to accept the aestheticized definition of art dominant since the Romantic age, hermeneutic reflection offers a means of conceiving of literature without either trivializing it or unduly exalting it.

We must remember, however, that hermeneutical theory cannot offer a specific method for the reading of literature. Instead, it may provide a justification for and understanding of the various uses to which we might put literary works. And we also must remain aware of our need to engage hermeneutical theory, like all theories, in a critical dialogue. There is no more reason for Christian students of literature to accept hermeneutical theory uncritically than there is for us to adopt poststructuralism, feminism, or Marxism without question, or than there was for us to embrace New Criticism and archetypal criticism with largely uncritical eagerness. If we engage theory, we must do so critically. To do less than that would be to sacrifice the distinctives of our Christian faith for a very questionable gain.

WORKS CITED

(Titles with an asterisk are recommended as introductions.)

Bate, Walter Jackson. *John Keats.* Cambridge: Harvard University Press, 1963.

Bruns, Gerald. *Inventions: Writing, Textuality, and Understanding in Literary History.* New Haven: Yale University Press, 1982.

*Gadamer, Hans-Georg. *Truth and Method.* 2nd ed. Original translation revised by Joel Weinsheimer and Donald G. Marshall. New York: Crossroad, 1989.

Graff, Gerald. *Literature against Itself: Literary Ideas in Modern Society.* Chicago: University of Chicago Press, 1979.

Hartman, Geoffrey. *Beyond Formalism: Literary Essays, 1958-1970.* New Haven: Yale University Press, 1970.

Heidegger, Martin. *Being and Time.* Trans. John Macquarrie and Edward Robinson. New York: Harper & Row, 1962.

Lentricchia, Frank. *After the New Criticism.* Chicago: University of Chicago Press, 1980.

Lewis, C. S. *An Experiment in Criticism.* Cambridge: Cambridge University Press, 1961.

Lundin, Roger. "Hermeneutics and the Romantic Tradition." *Christian Scholar's Review* 13.1 (1983): 3-18.

McGann, Jerome. *The Romantic Ideology: A Critical Investigation.* Chicago: University of Chicago Press, 1983.

*MacIntyre, Alasdair. *After Virtue: A Study in Moral Theory.* 2nd ed. Notre Dame: University of Notre Dame Press, 1984.

Ozment, Steven. *The Age of Reform, 1250-1550: An Intellectual and Religious History of Late Medieval and Reformation Europe.* New Haven: Yale University Press, 1980.

Palmer, Richard E. *Hermeneutics: Interpretation Theory in Schleiermacher, Dilthey, Heidegger, and Gadamer.* Evanston: Northwestern University Press, 1969.

*Ricoeur, Paul. "Existence and Hermeneutics." In *The Conflict of Interpretations: Essays on Hermeneutics,* trans. Kathleen McLaughlin, ed. Don Ihde, 3-24. Evanston: Northwestern University Press, 1971.

———. *Freud and Philosophy: An Essay on Interpretation.* Trans. Denis Savage. New Haven: Yale University Press, 1970.

———. *The Symbolism of Evil.* Trans. Emerson Buchanan. Boston: Beacon Press, 1967.

*———. "The Task of Hermeneutics." In *Hermeneutics and the Human Sciences,* trans. and ed. John B. Thompson, 43-62. Cambridge: Cambridge University Press, 1981.

Taylor, Charles. *Sources of the Self: The Making of the Modern Identity.* Cambridge: Harvard University Press, 1989.

Thielicke, Helmut. *The Evangelical Faith.* Vol. 1, *Prolegomena: The Relation of Theology to Modern Thought-Forms.* Trans. and ed. Geoffrey Bromiley. Grand Rapids: Eerdmans, 1974.

Weinsheimer, Joel. *Gadamer's Hermeneutics: A Reading of "Truth and Method."* New Haven: Yale University Press, 1986.

DECONSTRUCTION

Alan Jacobs

THE LEGACY OF STRUCTURALISM

JACQUES DERRIDA PRESENTED THE PAPER THAT INAUGU-
rated deconstruction — "Structure, Sign, and Play in the Discourse of the Human Sciences" — at a Johns Hopkins University Conference in 1966. But although in the next year he
published two books of seminal importance, *De la grammatologie*
and *L'Ecriture et la différence,* they did not appear in English
translation until much later: *Of Grammatology* was published in
1976, *Writing and Difference* in 1978. By this time, Derrida's
thought had developed — though perhaps not in radically new
directions — and the work he was doing then, such as *La Carte
postale* (1980), has only recently become available in English (*The
Post Card,* 1987).

The disorienting echo effect of this situation — as though
Derrida were working on Alpha Centauri and we American
scholars (those unable to read Derridean French, anyway) were
waiting at Houston's Mission Control for radio transmissions
to crawl, at a mere 186,000 miles per second, to our anxious
ears — has been mitigated somewhat by Derrida's willingness
to write numerous essays in English. But it remains the case
that his major works have been written in French and then

translated slowly and painstakingly by British and American scholars into English, with the result that Derrida's enormous American reputation rests almost exclusively upon work he did twenty years ago or more. It therefore makes sense that this essay should focus its attention on that work, even though to do so may not be altogether fair to Derrida. After all, this is an essay on deconstruction, and deconstruction as an intellectual movement in the American academy has not remained within Derrida's control or subject to his direction; moreover, what people in this academy *think* Derrida stands for has had far greater practical consequence than what he has actually written. It is a point not without ironies.

As I noted, the first salvo of deconstruction, "Structure, Sign, and Play," was fired in 1966. That fact too holds certain ironies, for the purpose of the conference at which it was presented was to introduce structuralism into American university life. The conference's organizers, Richard Macksey and Eugenio Donato, sought (pardon their syntax) "to bring into an active and not uncritical contact leading European proponents of structural studies with a wide spectrum of American scholars" (ix). Presumably they did not expect that a young (age 36) and to this point virtually unknown French philosopher would announce that structuralism had come to a dead end. But that is what Derrida did.

A bit of background is in order. Structuralism had found its origins in the work of the Swiss linguist Ferdinand de Saussure, whose key move was to insist that what linguists had called the sign — for example, the word "shoe" — needed to be divided into two parts, the *signifier* and the *signified*. The signifier is the set of sounds, or written marks, that is taken to designate an idea or concept; the signified is that idea or concept. Saussure reminded his students (he never published his work; it was compiled after his death from his students' notes) that the connection between the signifier "shoe," whether written or spoken, and the concept it represents is purely arbitrary. We could call a shoe a "plox" if we so desired, as long as we kept two things in mind: (1) there would need to be general agreement within the linguistic community that "plox" indicated this concept, and (2) the signifier "plox" must be distinguishable from all other signifiers, for the meaning of any given signifier lies *only* in its difference from others. As for the shoe itself, that object lying in the closet or encasing my foot, Saussure called it the "referent" and insisted that linguistics as such had no concern with it whatsoever. Furthermore, Saussure insisted that the job of linguistics was to study language *synchronically* — that is, to explore a system of signifiers as it exists at one given time, namely now (this in order to distinguish linguistics from philology, which studies the historical development of language, and thus considers it *diachronically*). In short, Saussure proposed to treat language as a structure, as though it were a set of physical objects arranged in space, in order that we might better understand the relations between its component parts.

Eventually, readers of Saussure came to realize that it was not just language that could be studied in this way — or rather, that almost all cultural practices could be understood as languages, possessing the equivalents of grammar and syntax in their rules of formation or organization. Thus the anthropologist Claude Lévi-Strauss proposed, in a famous essay — "The Structural Study of Myth" — to make such a study and then went on to analyze, among other things, table manners and cooking in the same way. Similarly, Vladimir Propp in 1928 suggested that all folktales could be understood as being constructed from a series of elements that he called "spheres of action" and "functions." And four decades later, A. J. Greimas would suggest that such tales could be broken down into but six fundamental structural units that he paired off and called *actants:* Subject and Object, Sender and Receiver, Helper and Opponent.

By the time of the aforementioned Johns Hopkins conference organized by Macksey and Donato, structuralism had become a dominant method in the humanities and the social sciences in France but had made little impact in the United States. Frank Lentricchia has suggested that this neglect can be explained, in the field of literary criticism at least, by the enormous influence of Northrop Frye, whose all-encompassing archetypal system bears significant resemblance to structuralism (158-59). Frye had already cornered that market, so when his authority began to wane in the early seventies, American scholars were not interested in turning to what seemed to be only a rather different version of the same old game. Although they may not have known it, they were ready for a new figure to come on stage and announce that the long reign of formalism — whether in the shape of the New Criticism, Frye's archetypal criticism, or structuralism — was over.

JACQUES DERRIDA

So what *was* Derrida's quarrel with structuralism? In "Structure, Sign, and Play," it manifests itself in a critique of Lévi-Strauss. One element of that critique will give a pretty clear sense of Derrida's modus operandi. In his early book entitled *The Elementary Structures of Kinship* (1949), Lévi-Strauss had emphasized a distinction fundamental not only to anthropology but to Western thought in general — the distinction between nature and culture. Derrida summarizes Lévi-Strauss's handling of this crucial opposition thusly: "That belongs to nature which is *universal* and spontaneous, not depending on any particular culture or on any determinate norm. That belongs to culture, on the other hand, which depends on a system of *norms* regulating society and is therefore capable of *varying* from one social structure to another" (253). This seems clear enough. But then Lévi-Strauss comes upon what he calls a "scandal": the incest taboo. It is universal and in that sense is subject to being called natural, but on the other hand it belongs to the "system of norms" which determine the functioning of particular societies and in that sense deserves to be called cultural. Lévi-Strauss's response to this paradox is to acknowledge that the incest taboo compromises the distinction between nature and culture but does not render it useless. The distinction retains an instrumental or heuristic value, even though it does not achieve the stature of absolute truth. Says Derrida, in a formulation that may be read to praise or condemn: "Levi-Strauss will always remain faithful to this double intention: to preserve as an instrument that whose truth-value he criticizes" (255).

Derrida admires Lévi-Strauss's ability to discover this paradox, but he is not comfortable with Lévi-Strauss's putative escape from it. For Derrida, the incest taboo does not merely compromise the validity of the nature/culture dichotomy; it renders it empty and void. Among the issues at stake here is that essential feature of Western thought, the law of non-contradiction: A does not equal not-A. Nature and culture are opposed to one another by their very definition; in fact, the one has meaning only by virtue of the other. (We should recall here Saussure's claim that meaning lies only in *difference*.) You cannot have nature without culture any more than you can have male without female, or a center without a margin, or an inside without an outside. In all such cases, each term of the polarity means something only in contrast to the other term; yet, Derrida argues, by that very fact each term requires the other in order to mean anything. The apparent opposition masks a profound interdependence.

Thus, when it becomes clear that there are facts or situations which cannot be made to conform to a given opposition, like the one between nature and culture, it is not simply a matter of a concept being demoted from Truth to Usefulness; rather, the whole system of thought that relies on such exclusions is called profoundly into question. Derrida would say that the system is thereby *deconstructed* — that is, shown to be without genuine foundation; in his view what he does is not destruction, because he is merely revealing the contradictions and confusions that are already there. It is easy enough to see that structuralism is such a system — Greimas's paired actants noted earlier (Subject/Object, Sender/Receiver, Helper/Opponent) illustrate that clearly enough — but Derrida goes further: he argues that all of Western thought, going back at least to Plato, is built upon such oppositions. Therefore, to call such oppositions (and the law of non-contradiction they represent) into question is "probably the most daring way of making the beginnings of a step outside of philosophy" (254). But it is only the beginnings of such a step, for to get "outside philosophy" is nearly impossible.

Why is it so hard? Because the only language we have with which to argue about philosophy is the language we have inherited from philosophy — just as the only way we know to think about nature and culture involves making that very distinction. Even in saying that nature and culture do not form a binary opposition, we employ that opposition; we are still talking about nature and culture, and not about something else. If we try to talk about the world in such a way that we avoid the polarity, our readers may not know what we are talking about — they will not recognize that we are challenging their worldview because we will not be using the language which not only expresses but in large part constitutes that worldview. Our language is older than we are; it precedes us with meanings and directions that we cannot alter simply by wishing to; we cannot invent it anew for our own use. As Derrida points out, "We have no language — no syntax and no lexicon — which is alien to this [philosophical] history; we cannot utter a single deconstructive proposition which has not already slipped into the form, the logic, and the implicit postulations of precisely what it seeks to contest" (250). In short, the deconstructors' own discourse is just as subject to deconstruction as anyone else's; they cannot turn these weapons on others without also turning them on themselves.

When Derrida says that he himself cannot escape the paradoxes and problems he finds in Lévi-Strauss's work (and elsewhere in the Western intellectual tradition), he nevertheless distinguishes himself from Lévi-Strauss. He does so by giving up the *hope* of such escape. In the discussion following the first delivery of "Structure, Sign, and Play," someone asked Derrida where he was going with his argument. Derrida replied, "I was wondering myself if I know where I am going. So I would answer you by saying, first, that I am trying, precisely, to put myself at a point so that I do not know any longer where I am going" (267). For Derrida, to know where you are going is to believe that you have a *center*, a "point of presence, a fixed origin," the function of which is "to orient, balance, and organize" your thought, or your structure (247). To paraphrase T. S. Eliot, the center is the still point of the turning world of discourse. Derrida points out that different thinkers in the Western tradition have located the center in different places: in the *archē* (origin or source), the *telos* (end or goal), "transcendentality, consciousness, . . . God, man, and so forth" (249). (The law of non-contradiction is one such center.) What all of these proposed centers have in common is their function: they provide an end point for language, for signification; they are present to provide a ground for language, to give it stability. Another name Derrida gives to the center is the *transcendental signified*, because it stands outside language and yet is supposed to justify and anchor it.

But there is a contradiction in this, says Derrida. Whatever our center is, it must of necessity take its place in the universe of signs. If we wish to explain and justify our claims — claims that can be made only linguistically, through signification — we can do so only by employing *other signifiers;* and we can justify and explain those signifiers only by the use of yet more signifiers. ("What do you read, my lord?" Polonius asks Hamlet; "Words, words, words," the Prince replies.) It is impossible, says Derrida, to get out of the chain of signification; words cannot provide secure foundations for other words; thus there cannot be a transcendental signified. Signification, then, is an endless chain. From this it follows, Derrida argues, *not* that there is and can be no center — which is what he is frequently accused of saying — but that any center we choose is always conditional: it arises in the history of signification; it is not a given from beyond language. In the discussion referred to earlier, Derrida says, "I didn't say that there was no center, that we could get along without the center. I believe that the center is a function, not a being — a reality, but a function. And this function is absolutely indispensable" (271). That is, he does not *reify* the center — claim that it has some objective reality outside of discourse — but on the other hand he knows that we cannot communicate with others without some sense of a shared ground. That shared ground, however, must always be understood to be provisional. Derrida calls this interrogation of the center *decentering* — again, it is a revelatory act of criticism, merely showing what is the case. Decentering is, in fact, the only legitimate philosophical alternative to silence.

For Derrida, the refusal to acknowledge the provisionality of our centers is perhaps the dominant tendency of Western thought about language, and perhaps of Western thought in general; that refusal, and the center-oriented philosophies built upon it, Derrida calls *logocentrism*. (We will soon see why he chooses that term.) Much of his work is dedicated to an examination of the causes and effects of logocentrism. Why do we want a stable center? What consequences does the assumption that there is such a center entail for our discourse? An illuminating analysis of logocentrism — perhaps Derrida's most forceful analysis of it — can be found in his book entitled *Dissemination*, where he deconstructs a passage from Plato's *Phaedrus*, a passage that in Derrida's view is something like the original statement of logocentrism.

In the *Phaedrus* (274c-276b), Socrates recounts a myth describing an encounter between the Egyptian King Thamus and the god Theuth (also known as Thoth). Theuth reveals his "arts" to Thamus, "saying that they ought to be passed on to the Egyptians in general." But when Theuth presents the art of writing, Thamus refuses it: "If men learn this, it will implant forgetfulness in their souls; they will cease to exercise memory because they rely on that which is written, calling things to remembrance no longer from within themselves, but by means of external marks. What you have discovered is a recipe not for memory, but for reminder." Socrates relates this myth approvingly and then suggests that there is "another sort of discourse that is brother to written speech, but of unquestioned legitimacy"; it is perfectly legitimate because it "is written in the soul of the learner." Phaedrus immediately recognizes that Socrates refers to "no dead discourse, but the living speech, the original of which the written discourse may be fairly called a living image." This recognition pleases Socrates, for Phaedrus has understood the problem of writing quite exactly: it is a copy, an imitation, one step away from the real. The spoken word, on the other hand, is fully present in the soul and for this reason is a guarantee of "legitimate" and certain meaning.

Thus Socrates generates a binary opposition — speaking/writing — and, as usual, the purpose of the opposition is to endorse (or "privilege") one pole and demean (or "marginalize") the other. Derrida immediately goes to work on this opposition, pointing out that what the dialogue wants to say and what it actually says are in some conflict: he seeks out an *aporia* — an impasse, an irresolvable contradiction — in the text that undermines the opposition upon which it is built. His analysis is extraordinarily detailed; I will note but three of his conclusions here.

First, Derrida asks us to note that Socrates/Plato attacks writing by reference to a presumably authoritative *myth* — for such an appeal is extremely uncharacteristic of Plato (as many scholars have noted). Christopher Norris makes the point well: "Plato mostly treated myths as an inferior kind of cultural production, useful (the best of them) for teaching simple lessons to ignorant minds, but otherwise totally unsuited for the purposes of genuine enlightenment" (32). Ordinarily, that is, Plato would treat myth as one of the demeaned concepts, like writing, but here he uses it to justify his attack upon writing.

Second, Derrida asks us to note how we experience this passionate denunciation of writing: in a *written* text! Plato

wishes to communicate to us (if he did not invent) Socrates'
attack upon writing, but he can do so only by writing: he
condemns what he does; he does what he condemns. Therefore, the form of the argument is radically at odds with its
message.

These points suggest an anxiety at the very heart of
Socrates' attack, an anxiety that betrays itself even in the very
words Socrates/Plato employs to construct his argument. Derrida — and this is the third point — calls our attention to a
single word, a word that may not appear important to us; but
one of the points Derrida makes in emphasizing it is that our
conventional ideas about which words are important and which
ones are not (which belong to the center and which to the
margin) must also be questioned. The word is *pharmakon*.

Theuth says that he brings "a recipe for memory and
wisdom"; the word translated as "recipe" is *pharmakon*. It is a
word which, Derrida points out, recurs frequently in the *Phaedrus,* though the reader of an English or a French translation
would not know that. For *pharmakon* can mean a variety of
things and hence is translated by a variety of words: "drug,"
"remedy," "cure," "medicine," and "poison." Clearly, the word
may signify precisely opposite meanings. And most of the
potential meanings I have listed appear at one time or another
in the *Phaedrus.* From these simple facts, Derrida draws some
surprising yet compelling conclusions. He argues that it is necessarily the case that, whatever the primary signification of
pharmakon is deemed to be in any given usage, the other possible
significations are always there too, in what Derrida calls *traces.*
Or, to put it another way, no one meaning is or ever can be
fully present: the possibilities flicker in and out of view. Theuth
sees writing as a remedy; Thamus/Socrates/Plato sees it as a
poison. But because language exists historically, gathering and
deploying meaning over time, and no use of a word can be
confined to a single context that eliminates all other contexts
and possible meanings, there is no way to exclude "poison" from
Theuth's "remedy," or "remedy" from Thamus's "poison." Thus

the passage deconstructs itself, reveals itself (upon proper inspection) to contain the seeds of its own refutation.

According to Derrida, differences, which Saussure said enable us to distinguish one signifier from another — "read" from "dead," "walk" from "talk," and so on — are at work even *within* signifiers. There is no signification without difference. Any attempt to arrest this perpetual differentiation, which Derrida calls the *play* of signifiers, in order to achieve linguistic stability, interpretive closure — indeed, any kind of certainty — is logocentrism in action: it claims to have found the *logos,* the Word that justifies language and itself. In Western thinking about language, such attempts have frequently taken the form we see in the *Phaedrus:* the elevation of the spoken word above writing, which Derrida calls *phonocentrism.* The spoken word, says Socrates, is legitimate, being primary and fully present to the listener, whereas writing is secondary and is a token of absence. But he can make this point only by reference to metaphors of writing: the spoken word is "written" or "engraved" on the soul! Therefore, even as Socrates seems to demean writing, he invokes its power; even as he seeks to displace it to the margin, it returns to occupy the center. Socrates says that writing is a secondary form of speaking, but is it not equally legitimate to say that speaking is a secondary form of writing? May we not better understand what it means to be "in language" if we invert the conventional hierarchy — provisionally, of course — and see at the heart of language not the *logos* but *écriture* (writing)?

One final note is vital here. To see language as *écriture* would not, Derrida insists, simply replace one center with another: a provisional center is not — in the sense of the word employed by Derrida — a center at all, because it makes no claims to transcendence, to standing beyond the play of signifiers. And *écriture* is really an anti-center, a refusal to settle down anywhere; according to Derrida, it does not explain to us what language is "really like" — though in attempting to explain it, I have for purposes of clarity fallen back upon such language.

The philosopher Richard Rorty has made this point with particular precision: thinkers like Derrida do not claim "to have discovered the *real* nature of truth or language or literature. Rather, they say that the very notion of discovering the *nature* of such things is part of the intellectual framework which we must abandon" (140). People may want to know where Derrida stands when he criticizes the logocentric tradition, but Rorty says that thinkers like Derrida are content (or try to be content) not to stand *anywhere*, to have *no* answer to that question.

It is for this reason that Derrida introduces his celebrated notion of *play:* since signifiers by their very nature can never settle into stable meaning but rather dance about constantly in a *freeplay* of signification, our only choices are to join the dance or skulk forlornly about the philosophical punchbowl. Those who would insist upon determinate meaning are not only wrong — they are spoilsports.

DECONSTRUCTION IN AMERICA: PAUL DE MAN

Poststructuralist thought in France, as opposed to that in America, is by no means dominated by Derrida. Many other figures, such as Jacques Lacan (see the chapter entitled "Psychological Criticism" in this volume), Julia Kristeva, Jean-François Lyotard, and Gilles Deleuze — not to mention Michel Foucault, to whose work we will come shortly — possess an equal if not a greater authority. Some of these thinkers have become influential in this country, but they have in a sense ridden the coattails of Derrida; that is, American interest in Derrida's thought has provoked an interest in similar thinking. One may choose to attribute this state of affairs to the intrinsic merits of Derrida's work, but another more mundane consideration plays a role here. By 1972 Derrida had begun to divide his time between Paris's Ecole Normale Supérieure and American universities; eventually he established a semi-permanent relationship with Yale, where his work was encouraged, publicized, imitated, and extended by a number of gifted critics, most notably Geoffrey Hartman, J. Hillis Miller, and Paul de Man. (Harold Bloom is often said to be a member of this "Yale Group," but the fact that his work has often appeared with theirs should not obscure the fact that he has disagreed — and still disagrees — vehemently with their most fundamental premises about language.)

Of these Yale critics, the most important is the late Paul de Man — he more than the others developed a critical style that, while clearly indebted to Derrida, stakes out its own distinctive territory. The salient features of de Man's most influential work involve an almost obsessive attention to figurative language — he draws heavily upon Kenneth Burke's identification of the four "master tropes" (metaphor, metonymy, synecdoche, and irony) — and an insistence upon the necessity of rehabilitating the idea of *rhetoric*.

These two concerns are in fact one concern: in one of his most important essays, "Semiology and Rhetoric" (1973), de Man defines rhetoric as "the study of tropes and figures" (6). This is not cavalier; even the solid and scholarly *Princeton Encyclopedia of Poetry and Poetics* endorses such a definition: "From ancient times to the present, rhetoric in the broad sense has meant the art of persuasion, in the narrow sense *the studied ornament of speech*, or eloquence" (emphasis added). Now, why is de Man so interested in tropes and figures? Because they are the features of discourse that most directly "foreground" the differences (in Derrida's sense) by which language works: they mark the points at which we can see most clearly the *aporias* or impasses of meaning that the logocentric tradition has been at pains to neglect. Thus they reveal with special clarity the self-deconstructing nature of language.

This does not mean that tropical or figurative language is intrinsically different from any other kind of language: *all* language deconstructs itself, but some language does it openly. Indeed, de Man seems almost morally offended when he finds a passage that seeks to cover up its own *aporias*. (A good deal of "Semiology and Rhetoric" is devoted to a stern analysis of a passage from Proust that hides its figurativeness by an impassioned assertion of the power of metaphor to make something — in this case, the summer — fully present.) For de Man, the "best" kind of language is obviously self-deconstructing, presumably because it attests to the truth about itself, and truth is better than lies. Thus, in a famous essay called "The Rhetoric of Temporality" (1969), de Man makes the powerful (and very influential) argument that allegory should be preferred over symbolism because it calls attention to its own constructedness and artificiality, whereas symbols try to palm themselves off as natural phenomena that arise organically and make meaning fully present in language.

De Man (following Burke) likes to distinguish rhetoric from grammar: the very idea of grammar suggests that language is explicable in terms of rules, definable patterns, stable structures. (We should remember that the structuralists often spoke in terms of the "grammar" of cultural phenomena.) Grammar is therefore intrinsically logocentric, and as such cannot describe how language really works. De Man provides an uncharacteristically comic illustration of this point by invoking a scene from the TV sitcom "All in the Family": Edith Bunker asks Archie whether he wants his bowling shoes laced over or under; Archie answers, "What's the difference?"; Edith patiently explains what the difference is; Archie sputters furiously at her stupidity. De Man's point: grammar cannot make the distinction between someone who really wants to know what the difference between the two styles of lacing is and someone who is saying (through what we significantly call a "rhetorical" question) that there is no meaningful difference. "It is impossible to decide by grammatical or other linguistic devices which of the two meanings (which [in any given case] can be entirely incompatible) prevails" ("Semiology and Rhetoric" 10). In other words, language cannot provide determinant meaning to language; meanings are generated not by the structures of language (not by grammar) but within multifarious and continually changing historical situations. This is the realm of rhetoric: "rhetoric radically suspends logic and opens up vertiginous possibilities of referential aberration." To learn to live with the absolute undecidability and instability of rhetoric and to live without the comforting structures of grammar is a difficult task but one that de Man thinks is incumbent upon us. In making such arguments, he clearly draws upon the enthusiastic and hortatory nihilism of Nietzsche, who is clearly a predecessor even more important for de Man than Derrida.

MICHEL FOUCAULT

Michel Foucault (who died in 1984) has been variously described as a philosopher, a historian, and a sociologist — or as the incarnate negation of all philosophy, history, and sociology. (He earned degrees in philosophy, psychology, and what the University of Paris calls "Psycho-Pathologie.") What he does is not deconstruction, though very occasionally (as in a much-anthologized but rather uncharacteristic essay called "What Is an Author?") he employs some of Derrida's terminology. Nevertheless, he is frequently associated, in this country at least, with that movement and with Derrida, and it is clear why that association has taken hold.

If Derrida takes apart language to reveal its inner contradictions and *aporias,* Foucault performs a similar operation upon cultural institutions. Foucault looks at the insane asylum, for instance, in his early book *Madness and Civilization* (published in French in 1961), and notes that in the Middle Ages no such things existed: madmen then walked the streets like anyone else. Why, then, were asylums built? Was it merely that our *ideas* about madness changed? Or did our very *perceptions* of madness change so that it was necessary to generate social institutions (with accompanying physical manifestations, like

buildings) that articulated and responded to those new perceptions? Or did the institutions themselves, once produced,
change our perceptions — that is, did they make certain perceptions impossible while fostering and encouraging others? If
so, then how did the institutions get started in the first place?

This method of investigation, which resembles Derrida's
"interrogation of the center," Foucault calls *archaeology*, for it is
a search for origins — origins not so much of ideas as of institutions and structures of perception. All of these can be inves-
tigated and taken apart — which Foucault does, with a sometimes astonishing intelligence and rigor.

This was Foucault's method in the early 1960s — *Madness
and Civilization* was followed, for instance, by *The Birth of the
Clinic* (1963), an "archaeology of medical perception" that ana-
lyzes the institution we call the hospital. But then he began to
consider that discourse itself, especially philosophical and artistic
discourse, is a social institution; and it was this subject that he
began to investigate in the late 1960s, most notably in *The Order
of Things*. Among literary critics, this has been Foucault's most
influential book — perhaps because it is the one that most clearly
shares Derrida's concerns, as the book's French title *(Les Mots et
les Choses)* may indicate — though he quickly moved beyond, if
he did not repudiate, many of the positions it takes.

The book's subtitle is *An Archaeology of the Human Sciences*,
and it is concerned with the question of how we organize and
give structure to our knowledge. "Such an analysis does not
belong to the history of ideas," Foucault says in the book's
preface; "it is rather an inquiry whose aim is to rediscover on
what basis knowledge and theory became possible; within what
space of order knowledge was constituted; on the basis of what
historical *a priori* . . . ideas could appear, sciences be established,
experience be reflected in philosophies, rationalities be formed,
only, perhaps, to dissolve and vanish soon afterwards" (xxi-xxii).
The conclusions that Foucault draws from this investigation
are far beyond the scope of this essay; I will mention only one
of his ruling concepts here.

Foucault divides the history of Europe since medieval times into three large periods — the Renaissance, the Classical Age, and Modernity — and suggests that each of them was dominated not by an idea but by a principle (or set of principles, or structure) around which all the major ideas of the time could be arranged and organized, and by which they could be justified. He calls this principle or structure the *episteme*. Again, I can give only the broadest sketch of what he argues, without explaining his terms. Briefly, the *episteme* of the Renaissance he identifies with the notion of *resemblance,* that of the Classical period with *representation,* and that of Modernity with *Man* (which he sees as the most significant invention of Modernity).

Foucault would later abandon the term *episteme* and with a Nietzschean emphasis would speak of each age's "power/knowledge regime." (He would also abandon the convenient tripartite division of European history.) He would turn aside from the study of institutions and of discourse to attempt to discover and critique the structures that underlie our most elemental drives. (This emphasis produced first *Discipline and Punish,* then the unfinished, multi-volume *History of Sexuality.*) He would characterize these changes as a move from archaeology (a more specific and particular analysis) to *genealogy* (an investigation of what lies behind all institutions and structures) — a characterization that in my view indicates his increasing allegiance to the Nietzschean view of power.

However, both the early and the late Foucault are appealing to literary critics and theorists who admire the analytical rigor of Derridean deconstruction while regretting Derrida's relative neglect of history and culture. And by the mid-1980s there were many such critics, as the next section (and John Cox's essay in this volume entitled "The New Historicism") will show.

TOWARD A CHRISTIAN RESPONSE

Before we embark on a Christian response to deconstruction, we had best consider what, at this moment, is out there to respond to. For deconstruction is not in 1990 what it was in 1980. Then it seemed a juggernaut bearing down upon literary study, willing and fully able to crush us all under its massive wheels; now it appears to be little more than another rejected, or outgrown, approach to literary study. Insofar as this is an accurate depiction of the current state of deconstruction, how did this state of affairs come about?

One significant stage in the history of deconstruction occurred in the mid-1980s, when the very critics who only a few years before had been decried as a threat to literary study — even to the whole humanistic enterprise of university education — got elected to major offices in the Modern Language Association: Cornell's Jonathan Culler joined the Executive Council, while J. Hillis Miller was elected president of the MLA in 1986. Clearly this would not have happened if the MLA's members had thought deconstruction could eventuate in the dismantling of the solid edifice of academic literary study. It is one thing to endorse a radical view of interpretation, quite another to deconstruct yourself out of a job. Even the most bitter opponents of deconstruction began to acknowledge that the Derrideans put on their tweed sportcoats one arm at a time, just like the rest of us.

In fact, by 1986, deconstruction for many critics had come to seem in some ways innocuous: capable of suggesting new ways of reading that could aid in the production of articles and books, and hence in the acquisition of tenured posts, but otherwise looking like academic Business as Usual. Deconstruction's seeming innocuousness was worrisome for others: for many teacher-critics, especially younger professors who had attended college in the sixties and retained some of the political concerns of that period, this apparent apoliticality of deconstruction grew increasingly troublesome. If deconstruction proved to be politically quiescent, then perhaps it had to be left behind.

And indeed this appeared to be the case. For if all claims, all predicates, can be deconstructed, then how can one say with security that the rich oppress the poor, or that sexism and racism should be resisted? Some advocates of deconstruction, notably Christopher Norris, have argued in response that deconstruction is a vital tool in the dismantling of oppressive social and linguistic structures. But since politics necessarily involves not only the eradication of unjust structures and practices but also the erection of new structures and practices that will foster justice, how can one avoid the deconstruction of the new order? A deconstructionist who preserves certain claims and predicates from deconstruction is not a deconstructionist at all but merely a critical analyst of other people's ideas. There is no reason why a follower of Derrida may not express political commitment in action, but whether he can do so in language, given his commitment to the "freeplay" of signification, is quite another matter.

Might it even be the case that, however radical deconstruction may appear to be, it is in fact unable to offer resistance to the political status quo? A case in point is the presidential address that J. Hillis Miller made to the MLA in 1986. In that address Miller claims that there is, or should be, a natural alliance between the political-academic left and deconstruction — but at the same time (almost in the same sentence), he warns that even the most fundamental claims of Marx, for instance, are just as subject to deconstruction as any other claims. Elsewhere in the address Miller sounds like a conventional liberal humanist, indistinguishable from those (like M. H. Abrams and Walter Jackson Bate) who have excoriated deconstructionists: "Truth does not need the protection of any sort of censorship. It will flourish best in an atmosphere of free debate, in teaching and in writing. Any foreclosure of that debate poses a mortal danger to the university" (290). Can *these* statements be deconstructed? Miller — unless he wants to say that his articulated beliefs alone are immune to the "freeplay" of signifiers — cannot say otherwise than "Yes." But where does that leave his argument? Clearly this attempt to bridge the gap between deconstruction and the increasing political awareness of the academy is doomed to failure, unsatisfactory as it must be to both camps.[1]

Here then is the first point at which Christianity must address deconstruction. Living Christianity must seek to serve (in the words of my college's motto) Christ and his kingdom, and must seek to foster (in Nicholas Wolsterstorff's formulation) *shalom*, the peace that grows out of justice. About such actions deconstruction as such, being a thesis about language, can say nothing.[2] But necessary to the practice of Christianity is not only action but also proclamation *(kerygma)*. We are called not only to act upon the world but also to speak to and about its conditions — and to speak with authority and security, rooted in the (written!) biblical witness. And since literature and criticism constantly address the personal and social issues to which the Bible calls our attention, then Christians who study or write literature should be particularly concerned with the preservation of the *kerygma*.

However, if the nature of language is such that meaningful proclamation is impossible — or that its (moral and spiritual) center is subject to deconstructive interrogation, which amounts

---

1. The debate between deconstructionists and politically minded critics reached its height in *l'affaire de Man* — literary theory's version of *l'affaire Dreyfus*. Not long after the death of Paul de Man, it was revealed that as a young man in his native Belgium, he had written articles in support of the Nazi regime. At first de Man's friends and colleagues denied that the articles really supported Nazism at all, but that defense was clearly untenable. Then they began to argue that de Man's deconstructive criticism marked a decided turn away from the repressive regime he had earlier supported. Marxist critics of de Man and deconstruction, on the other hand, argued that deconstruction actually lends itself quite readily to the endorsement of fascist or otherwise repressive politics. The debate continues.

2. This is not strictly true: the deconstructionist could argue that our actions are based on the understanding of our world that we acquire and disseminate through language, and insofar they have and can have no solid basis. But in practice deconstructionists have been willing to make this claim only about other people's beliefs, not their own, and to that extent they have (on this issue) ceased to do deconstruction.

to the same thing, since the point of the Christian *kerygma* is that it is unconditionally and unprovisionally binding — then it doesn't matter what our moral imperatives are. If language can't carry the load, it can't carry the load, no matter how much good it would do us if it were so capable. It is this aspect of deconstruction — its status as a claim about the way that language really works — which has most concerned and threatened Christians, and which we should explore now.

But does deconstruction make a claim about the nature of language? Richard Rorty, we recall, says no: to reiterate his point, thinkers like Derrida "say that the very notion of discovering the *nature* of such things is part of the intellectual framework which we must abandon" (140). But why must we abandon it? What reasons can Derrida give us for abandoning it? As soon as deconstructors get involved in the business of providing reasons, they are perforce in the business of making claims and thus are subject to their own critique. To say that such claims are made only provisionally — employing a temporary and heuristic center — only postpones the dilemma. For why should one accept *this* provisional claim rather than *that* one, or either in preference to a *third* one — unless, of course, the claims are not provisional or contextual at all but rather seek to describe discourse, language in use, as it really is? This is not a question which, to my knowledge, Derrida has directly addressed. Rorty has addressed it by invoking the tradition of philosophical pragmatism (in which he includes not only William James and John Dewey but also Nietzsche) and arguing that we should *use* language (whether philosophical or literary) to help us get what we want. But that merely raises another question: What happens when we disagree with one another about what we want? Will we not inevitably find ourselves making claims and counterclaims, arguing with one another as we have always done?

In one sense, this dilemma only goes to prove what Derrida said back in "Structure, Sign, and Play": that it is terribly difficult to extricate oneself from the philosophical tradition that relies on claims and counterclaims, support and contravention, for its very existence. But it also calls into question the deconstructive insistence that we *should attempt* so to extricate ourselves. Again, what would be the advantage in rejecting the quest to make language speak truly and faithfully, abandoning ourselves instead to the freeplay of signifiers? Ultimately, deconstruction can provide only one answer to this question, and this is it: "Those who hold to the bankrupt concepts of truth and fidelity in language merely fool themselves. We who know how it really is cannot achieve truth and accuracy any more than anyone else can, but we have learned not to want such things and thus are freed from the burden of delusion and the fruitless questing it generates." This answer takes any number of forms, but it is recurrent in apologias for deconstruction. A typical example comes from Vincent Leitch:

> We must sometimes unmask the ministry of meaning, the cure [Leitch refers to Derrida's exposure of *pharmakon*] of history, and the prophecy of truth. We must face, perhaps only fleetingly, utter discontinuity and difference.
>
> Here is what we now know. We are a community of bemused acolytes to Metaphor. We are celebrants of Misreading and inheritors of an indecipherable Scripture. . . . We write the history we make, the selves we are, and the criticism we publish. . . . Mediums of metaphor and madness, we are not responsible, except perhaps for our will to power over texts and for our presumption in writing.
>
> Carnivalesque, our criticism should be entertaining and colorful: we need haunted houses, rollercoaster rides, distended balloons, seductive come-ons, and promising gambles. (267)

In statements such as this, the genealogy of deconstruction is writ large: it is no more than the application of Nietzschean existentialism — with its cult of power deriving from the recognition of utter autonomy — to language. This point of origin is perfectly evident in de Man, relatively obscured in Derrida; but it is at the root of all deconstructive criticism. This is no place to refute Nietzsche; that has been done well enough elsewhere. But it is proper here to suggest that insofar as deconstruction involves the exertion of power over texts, writers, and other interpreters — and the Nietzschean view of belief and action virtually demands that — the Christian can join with the Marxist and the liberal humanist to denounce it as ethically reprehensible.

And indeed there is a strong sense in which deconstruction is, like the philosophy of Nietzsche, little or nothing more than an assertion of power. Robert Scholes, in his books on contemporary theory, has been skeptical about some of the claims of deconstruction, but he has endorsed them insofar as they can help us and our students "unlock textual power and turn it to [our] own uses" (20) — to disarm the text and turn its own weapons upon it. In *Ecce Homo* Nietzsche speaks of "how to philosophize with a hammer," and this is precisely what Scholes and the deconstructionists are counseling. The decisive blow of the hammer is the assertion of the arbitrariness and undecidability of all language — but it is just that, an assertion, a claim to power that refuses to acknowledge the need for rational persuasion and argumentation. No one has exposed this feature of deconstruction as an institutional movement better than Frederick Crews:

> In the human studies today, it is widely assumed that the positions declared by structuralism and poststructuralism are permanently valuable discoveries that require no further interrogation. Thus one frequently comes upon statements of th[is] type: "Deconstruction has shown us that we can never exit from the play of signifiers"; "Lacan demonstrates that the unconscious is structured like a language"; "After Althusser, we all understand that the most ideological stance is the one that tries to fix limits beyond which ideology does not apply"; "There can be no turning back to naive pre-Foucauldian distinctions between truth and power." Such servility constitutes an ironic counterpart of positivism — a heaping up, not of factual nuggets, but of movement slogans that are treated as fact. (172)

Crews' exposure of the bald assertions that underlie deconstruction is shrewd, but it raises another question: Why seek after such textual power? The answer lies in the military metaphor that I used earlier in reference to Scholes: the text (or the author, or a previous critic) is an enemy, well-armed and fierce, with whom I am in a kill-or-be-killed relationship. I must exert my power over the text or else it will exert its power over me. Thus the assertions of deconstruction (like those of Nietzsche) derive chiefly if not wholly from fear — fear of one's personal autonomy being infringed upon by an external force, the text.

But there is something seriously wrong with a system of criticism that transforms an experience as potentially joyful and exhilarating as reading into an especially bitter form of warfare. It is particularly regrettable in that it does not allow the reader to see the textual encounter as a potentially enriching, even ennobling thing; it makes no provision for the possibility that what a text may exercise over us is not necessarily sheer power but rather a legitimate *authority*, like that which Kent recognized in Lear, or which distinguished Jesus from the (far more power-ful) scribes. It further denies us the ability to distinguish between those texts that enrich and those that demean or insult. If every text always deconstructs itself before our very eyes, then we can never learn anything from it; we can only use it for our pleasure, diminish it into a plaything, force it into our already-fixed world of understanding and discourse. Deconstruction makes a prison-house not only of language but also of person-hood; it is the ultimate Romantic solipsism. It asks us to leave behind a world of linguistic meaning and value, claiming (but not supporting the claim) that that world is delusive. And what it offers us in return, its practitioners insist, is "freeplay," a "carnivalesque" game.

But any game has rules, fixed and explicit rules, and deconstruction is no exception. And in this game every text breaks apart in the same way, cracks and crumbles along the same fault lines. As Terry Eagleton says (using another metaphor), "Deconstruction is a power-game . . . [in which] victory is achieved by *kenosis* or self-emptying: the winner is the one who has managed to get rid of all his cards and sit with empty hands" (147). Perhaps the best way to respond to deconstruction is not to argue that more conventional uses of language aren't games but to argue that they are *better* games than any deconstruction can offer. In short, however different it may seem the first few times you try it, deconstruction in the long run is *boring*.

To argue in this way — to accept the game-like character of language — is not to acquiesce in linguistic meaninglessness. It is simply to acknowledge what everyone knows already: that our languages did not suddenly fall from the sky one day, fully formed and complete; that they have developed and still develop over time, changing their character as they respond to the needs of the societies which employ them. Deconstructionists often seem to imagine that if language lacks an absolute rational justification — if the dream of seventeenth- and eighteenth-century linguists to unite *res* and *verba*, things and words, remains unfulfilled — then the only alternative is the eternal play of eternally undecidable differences. In other words, as Eagleton (e.g., 144) and others have suggested, deconstruction typically opposes itself to an old-fashioned scientism or logical positivism that hardly anyone believes in anymore. *Of course* words have histories; *of course* meanings are created through habitual usage and general agreement. Each element of any language may be arbitrary at its origin — but we are not at its origin; we are in the middle of a long and complex history of generated meaning and value. Deconstruction claims to situate our language (and our centers) in history; in point of fact, it ignores history and thereby becomes just another version of the formalism it claims to repudiate.

Some Christians have found deconstruction appealing because they see it as bringing interpretive liberation; but orthodox Christian theology has always insisted that freedom, for creatures, is possible only within structures of constraint. Thus the Apostle Paul says that we can only be either children of God or slaves to sin — that is, that we are always under benevolent authority or naked power; and Augustine, at the end of the *City of God*, says that the saints in Heaven will be truly free because they will be *unable* to sin. Likewise, the historicity of language is not a burden to be cast off in order that we may have something better; it is the very condition of meaning and communication between people. We can talk to one another insofar as we share a language that has a history of meanings. This does not mean that we must accept everything that language gives us; we may and should seek to change it for the better, to — in Eliot's words — "purify the dialect of the tribe." We do so in order to proclaim *shalom*, to bear better witness to the kingdom of God, to learn and teach that which is essential, to praise that which persists. To accept deconstruction is to give over this mission and to be left with only the command to play — for that is what it is, a command. And the outcome of the game and the means by which that outcome is reached are already determined. One recalls the marvelous scene from *Great Expectations* in which Miss Havisham sets Pip and Estella before her, gives them a pack of cards, and insists that they play. And she watches over them with a stern countenance that reminds me of a number of literary critics I have known.

WORKS CITED

(Titles with an asterisk are recommended as introductions.)

Crews, Frederick. *Skeptical Engagements.* New York: Oxford University Press, 1986.

de Man, Paul. "Semiology and Rhetoric." In *Allegories of Reading,* 3-19. New Haven: Yale University Press, 1979.

Derrida, Jacques. *Dissemination.* Trans. Barbara Johnson. Chicago: University of Chicago Press, 1981.

———. "Structure, Sign, and Play in the Discourse of the Human Sciences." In *The Languages of Criticism and the Sciences of Man:*

The Structuralist Controversy, ed. Richard Macksey and Eugenio Donato, 247-72. Baltimore: Johns Hopkins University Press, 1970.

*Eagleton, Terry. *Literary Theory: An Introduction.* Minneapolis: University of Minnesota Press, 1983.

Foucault, Michel. *The Order of Things: An Archaeology of the Human Sciences.* No translator given. New York: Random House, 1970.

Leitch, Vincent B. *Deconstructive Criticism: An Advanced Introduction.* New York: Columbia University Press, 1983.

Lentricchia, Frank. *After the New Criticism.* Chicago: University of Chicago Press, 1980.

Macksey, Richard, and Eugenio Donato, eds. *The Languages of Criticism and the Sciences of Man: The Structuralist Controversy.* Baltimore: Johns Hopkins University Press, 1970.

Miller, J. Hillis. "Presidential Address 1986: The Triumph of Theory, the Resistance to Reading, and the Question of the Material Base." *PMLA* 102.3 (May 1987): 281-91.

*Norris, Christopher. *Derrida.* Cambridge: Harvard University Press, 1987.

Rorty, Richard. "Nineteenth-Century Idealism and Twentieth-Century Textualism." In *Consequences of Pragmatism: Essays, 1972-1980,* 139-59. Minneapolis: University of Minnesota Press, 1982.

*Scholes, Robert. *Textual Power: Literary Theory and the Teaching of English.* New Haven: Yale University Press, 1985.

TOWARD A CHRISTIAN VIEW
OF LANGUAGE

William J. Vande Kopple

EARLY IN THIS CENTURY, FERDINAND DE SAUSSURE CLAIMED that "in the lives of individuals and societies, language is a factor of greater importance than any other" (7). More recently, other scholars have made similar assertions: Michael Holquist has claimed that language is "emerging as the central preoccupation of our time" (xvii); Paul Ricoeur has described language as the area "where all philosophical investigations cut across one another" (3). If such claims are largely true — as I think they are — then it is vitally important for Christians to clarify their views of language. In working toward such clarification here, I treat language as a gift, organizing my treatment under five main headings: (1) the giver of the gift, (2) the recipients of the gift, (3) some aspects of the nature of the gift, (4) the primary effects of the gift on its recipients, and (5) the responsibilities associated with using the gift.

THE GIVER OF THE GIFT

Central to a Christian view, I think, is the belief that the giver of language is God. This belief clashes with the views of many, some of whom follow Johann Gottfried von Herder in "maintaining that language would be more logical if it were from God" (Waterman 15).

Many modern linguists hold that early human beings were the originators of language. Some theorists argue that in developing more complex civilizations and cultures, early humans discovered the appeals and advantages of language (see Whitehead 93). These theorists assert that language originated from such things as cries in work, signals in hunts, and shouts in dances. Other thinkers connect the origin of language to the evolution of the organs with which we hear and speak (Fromkin and Rodman 415). Susanne Langer focuses on the "tremendous specialization of the central nervous system which culminates in the forebrain, and above all the cortices of the cerebral hemispheres" (*Mind* 2: 265). Alfred North Whitehead adds that the cognitive abilities resulting from such specialization had to be "sustained throughout scores of thousands of years" (91) in order to lead to language. Finally, some scholars say that humans developed language only after enjoying "a convergence of a number of evolutionary developments" (Fromkin and Rodman 419).

But I believe that a theory of the origin of language is fundamentally flawed if it posits some being or force other than God as the ultimate source of language. Do I mean to suggest that God could not have used certain kinds of developmental processes in the act of creating humans and endowing them with language? To answer affirmatively would be to take a limited view of God's creative power. No one knows what precise process or processes God used to create Adam and Eve. However he did it, the point I stress here is that it was he — not any other being or force — who endowed them with the general capacity for language, who either gave them the original language to speak or enabled them to develop it, who instilled in them the desire to communicate with him and with each other by means of their language, and who gave them the important work of naming the things of his creation. Beyond this, he gave to their children the capability to acquire and use the language they heard spoken around them.

Probably all modern Christians should consider more deeply the implications of God's being the giver of language. Many Christians seem to feel little awe in the face of the transcendent, perhaps because our lifestyles are so frenetic or because we regard God as our best friend. Too often we forget that God is the Creator and we are his creatures. When we recall this, we can better understand how awesome it is that God endowed us with language at all, that he deigns to reveal aspects of his will to us in the language of Scripture, and that he is pleased when we express ourselves to him in language. Such facts should help us see worship more clearly as a process of God's speaking to us and of our listening and responding to him.

I find it particularly inspiring that we interact with God in language that is essentially the same as that which we use in ordinary contexts. Not everyone accepts this view. John Wilson, for example, argues "that religious language . . . [is] in effect a form of technical vocabulary constituting a separate and different 'language-game' from ordinary speech, and subject to its own independent set of rules" (cited in Prickett 220). What Wilson is arguing for is not what others would consider a matter of stylistic variation — whether, for instance, it is more appropriate to pray in a more formal style as opposed to a more casual one (see Joos). Instead, Wilson is defining religious language as different from the language we use every day. He strips from words in religious language the associations they gather in our work and poetry.

Since I find no compelling evidence for this position and have difficulty imagining what an "independent set of rules" for religious language would be like, I continue to maintain that the language we use in religious contexts is essentially the same as that which we use in ordinary contexts. This position need not diminish one's view of language. Indeed, this position can be taken as further evidence of what we experience in the Incarnation — namely, the intimate and pervasive way in which God himself is with us.

THE RECIPIENTS OF THE GIFT

To the assertion that God gave language to human beings, I add that he gave this capacity only to us. Recently this claim has been disputed with various degrees of forcefulness by several researchers, among them David Premack, Francine Patterson, Beatrice and R. A. Gardner, and Duane Rumbaugh and Sue Savage-Rumbaugh.

Perhaps the best way to see what this dispute centers on is to consider what normal children four or five years old can do with language. They can associate symbols with concepts, even though in most cases the relationship between the symbols and the concepts is arbitrary. They can recall and use an amazingly large number of such symbols, and they can combine and recombine symbols into a great number of different sentences and cohesive sequences of sentences. As they do this, they act not as if they were selecting combinations from a memorized corpus but as if they were generating them with a system of rules. In addition, children can talk of things that are not present at the time of the conversation or of things that do not exist or happen in the real world.

Researchers such as those previously named asked whether an animal could be taught to use a communication system similar to the system that children use. Most of the researchers worked with chimpanzees, trying to teach them to learn systems such as American Sign Language (ASL), and most of them eventually made some impressive claims — among them, that their subjects could learn to use arbitrary symbols, could combine these symbols into strings, and could extend their abilities to cope linguistically with new phenomena. For instance, Francine Patterson claimed that her subject, Koko, had learned to use signs corresponding to the words *gentle, boring,* and *damn* and understood the concepts associated with these signs. And one of the Gardners' chimpanzees, after seeing a swan and having no sign for it, is supposed to have combined the sign for water with the one for bird.

The claim that stimulated the most debate was the one that

these animals could combine symbols into strings. If this were true, said Herbert Terrace, we would have evidence that these primates are capable of learning a system that is similar to language. Terrace granted that the chimps could acquire and use symbols. Evidence for this existed, although many researchers maintained that there is only a faint resemblance between a chimpanzee's use of symbols and ours, pointing out that chimps "learn to utilize those symbols in situations in which trainers will accept no alternative type of response" (Sebeok and Umiker-Sebeok 91). However, Terrace noted that none of the researchers had established that the primates combined symbols by rule. He argued that the strings of symbols that the chimps had produced could have been the products of chance or imitation.

With this in mind, Terrace began a multi-year project in which he tried to teach ASL to a chimp he named Nim Chimpsky. His main question was whether Nim could combine symbols by rule. Ultimately Terrace made some interesting discoveries, none of which would have been true of children acquiring their first language. The mean length of Nim's strings of symbols never grew much beyond one and one-half signs. If the strings appeared longer than that, the reason was that they were highly redundant. Further, as Nim grew older, more of his strings were complete imitations of strings his trainers had used. In addition, few of Nim's strings were spontaneous — most of them were replies to trainers — and many of them were obviously prompted by trainers.

With this evidence Terrace concluded that primates do not combine symbols productively by rule. They may appear to do so, but they are usually motivated either to gain rewards or to avoid unpleasant situations, and they will produce strings by chance, by giving a rotely learned sequence, or by responding to cues or prompts that trainers give, a response labeled the "clever Hans effect" (see Sebeok and Umiker-Sebeok).

Terrace's project is the most extensive one of its kind that I know of. Yet he demonstrated only that one member of one animal species failed to learn one system of communication.

Can members of other species — dolphins or whales, for instance — learn a system of communication similar to language?

Despite the fact that Terrace's findings were highly specific and therefore not broadly representative, I say no. As Noam Chomsky notes, it would be "something of a biological miracle" if animals had the capacity for language and all the advantages that language would bring them but had to wait for human beings to teach them how to use it ("Human Language" 433). Nicholas Wolterstorff claims that it is impossible for animals to develop language. In "Why Animals Don't Speak," he explores the human capability to perform speech actions such as assertion. He notes that "to perform a speech action is to acquire a certain *normative standing* in one's society" (471). That standing is constituted in part by the exercise of various rights and responsibilities. Speaking, then, alters the moral relationship between people and is possible only in a "community of moral agents" (474). Thus language is not a value-free system of structures and structural differences; it is a gift that lies at the heart of our moral lives. Humans can be right or wrong, innocent or guilty; they can be answerable for what they say. Animals cannot be; therefore, they cannot speak. W. H. Auden makes the point eloquently in "Their Lonely Betters": "Words are for those with promises to keep."

SOME ASPECTS OF THE NATURE OF THE GIFT

Many specific aspects of the nature of language can inspire Christians' awe for and joy in God's creating and sustaining power. Here I focus on three aspects: innateness, intricacy, and creativity.

Innateness

Innateness is related to the question of how children develop language. Many scholars respond to this question by arguing that language development is a matter of imitation or response to stimuli. Others argue that language development is a matter of a gradually specified genetic program, a matter of triggering some innate ability, something probably dependent on what Noam Chomsky calls a language acquisition device (see *Syntactic Structures* and *Aspects of the Theory of Syntax*). Still others take a middle position, stressing the interaction of children's innate ability to develop language with their verbal environments (see Oksaar).

Although I lean toward the position which says that language development is innate, I cannot embrace it fully. Studies of children who have been deprived of most linguistic stimulation during what linguists call the critical period for language development, which many view as extending from birth to the onset of puberty (see Lenneberg), clearly show the tragedy of such deprivation. Such children usually develop only the resilient properties of language (for example, how to form major parts of clauses such as the noun phrase) and not the fragile properties (such as how properly to structure questions and negative sentences).

These facts notwithstanding, I think that the case for the innateness of language development has an important place in a Christian view of language. Why? First, it helps combat the influence of behaviorism. Although behaviorism is no longer the dominant theory in psychology, its influence on much of our thought and practice remains pervasive. Second, the case for innateness fortifies the emphasis on language as God's gift to us. Language is not something that we learn by ourselves, some faster than others because they are faster learners. Rather, it is something we develop because of an innate and God-given ability to do so, and children who are exposed to roughly the same amount and kind of language will develop language skills at about the same rate.

In addition, it is important to note that a number of factors strongly support the innateness position.

First, babies seem disposed to attend to speech. Ingenious

experiments have shown that they respond to the sound of voices more intensely than to other sounds. And when only three weeks old, they will respond to shifts between such significant sounds in English as those beginning with *pa* and *ba* (Eimas, "Linguistic Processing").

Second, regardless of where in the world they live, children start producing speech at about the same age and appear to go through similar stages as they progress toward fluency in a language.

Third, even deaf children usually begin to develop language, cooing and babbling as hearing babies do, but stop after months of hearing neither their own nor others' voices.

Fourth, children with IQs so low that they cannot tie their shoes can produce and comprehend sentences. It is difficult to argue that imitation or reinforced responses can lead to success in one task and not in the other, especially since the task of producing and grasping language seems much more difficult than that of tying shoes.

Fifth, young linguistic geniuses — children from normal environments who at the age of two can already read and write well — are better examples of extremely sensitive and rapidly developing innate linguistic abilities than they are examples of excellent responses to stimuli.

Sixth, even young children can recognize ungrammatical language for what it is (see de Villiers and de Villiers). When they hear an ungrammatical string of words, even a string they have not heard scorned by others, they say, "You can't say that." They reject the phrase or sentence on the basis of what appears to be a rule system that has been activated and specified.

A final argument for innateness falls under the heading "deficiency of the stimulus." According to this argument, children do not hear enough language in general or enough well-formed language in particular to account for the linguistic knowledge and abilities they have by the age of four or five.

None of these arguments is impervious to attack, but together they make a strong case for the innate basis for language development. And such a basis is most compatible with a view of God as the one who gives us language.

Intricacy

Here *intricacy* refers to the amazingly complex system of structures and processes in the brain on which our language abilities depend. One way to get a better idea about this system is to consider brain lateralization and specialization, the hypothesis that the two hemispheres of the human cerebral cortex are specialized in different ways. Not everyone accepts this hypothesis, but the evidence for specialization is becoming overwhelming. Earlier, researchers talked about differences between the hemispheres in terms of the *kinds* of things the hemispheres processed. They said, for example, that music is processed by the right hemisphere, while language is processed by the left. Now, however, it is clear that the two hemispheres are essentially distinguished by the kinds of processing they do. For most people, the left hemisphere does analytic kinds of processing, while the right does more holistic kinds of processing. This does not invalidate the earlier pairing of music primarily with the right hemisphere and language primarily with the left. Rather, it explains why these pairings were made.

I used the word *primarily* in the preceding paragraph because control over language is even more intricately distributed within the brain than I have indicated thus far. In some ways, for example, the right hemisphere helps the left hemisphere control language. According to Jeannine Heny, the right hemisphere "helps us understand whether or not an utterance is a question, and whether or not the speaker is angry" (171). The right hemisphere seems to be largely responsible for helping us relate texts to audiences and situations (172).

We can push this discussion further by considering what can go wrong with language. The nearly incredible nature of some aphasics' impairments testifies to the complexity of the

processes controlling healthy speech. Some aphasics can understand commands only if responding to them requires moving
their whole body. Other aphasics have great difficulty naming
things unless those things have affected several of their senses
(see also Langer, *Mind* 2:347-48).

At this point, the mind-body problem comes to the foreground. Although behaviorists tie language use (and other mental activity) to brain functions, others question the reduction of
mental activity to physical occurrences in the brain. I agree with
William Hasker when he says that language and other "'higher'
mental functions, while they are manifested in brain-processes,
have their origin in the mind and cannot be produced by
physical manipulation of the brain" (307). I find this view to
be more compatible with the traditional Christian view of the
nature of human beings made in the image of God.

Creativity

In writing about animals' communication systems, I noted that
children of four or five can create a great number of well-formed
sentences and texts. I now add that, even though all humans
have a finite number of words to work with, they can produce
an infinite number of well-formed sentences and cohesive sequences of sentences.

The word *infinite* might make some readers balk. If you
have trouble accepting my claim, you should try to write the
longest possible sentence in English. You will soon discover that
there is no longest sentence; it is always possible to embed more
elements in a sentence, no matter how lengthy it is (see Chomsky,
Syntactic Structures). If there is no longest sentence, that means
we can produce an infinite number of sentences. And if that is
true, we can produce an infinite number of texts. The added
wonder is that we can produce sentences and texts both about the
actual world and about any world we can imagine.

I never claim that this kind of creativity is identical to

God's. But I do believe that our finite ability is a reflection of the acts of creation of an infinite God (cf. Prickett 191).

THE PRIMARY EFFECTS OF THE GIFT ON ITS RECIPIENTS

Symbols and Concepts

What are human beings like as a result of having language? A good place to start answering this question is with the relationship between thought and language. If all thought depends on language, we could say that the main effect of language on us is that it enables us to think. Many people do believe that all thought depends on language. For example, Ferdinand de Saussure asserts that "no ideas are established in advance, and nothing is distinct, before the introduction of linguistic structure" (110).

There is no decisive evidence on either side of this issue. However, there are reported cases of children who were isolated for such extensive periods that they developed no language at all or only the merest traces of language and yet, when they were discovered, they showed that they could do certain kinds of thinking (such as discriminating one space from another). Further, it is difficult to believe that a physicist imagining four-dimensional geometry and an artist blocking out an abstract painting are totally dependent on language as they go through these processes. But aren't these processes thinking? It seems so. In each case a person is conscious of and can intentionally affect a mental activity.

Having stated this, however, I add that probably most forms of thought tend "toward symbolic and, ultimately, linguistic expression" (Black 78) and that linguistic expression empowers thought in a most significant way. The best way to discover this is to imagine what we would be like without language.

Language is essentially a system of symbols. I use the word

symbol even though some scholars consider it inappropriate for the meaning-bearing units (morphemes) of language. Saussure argues against calling morphemes "symbols" because symbols are "never entirely arbitrary" (68); he uses the word *signs*. Paul Ricoeur agrees, contending that true symbols are "plurivocal"; they call to mind a second meaning through a first (16).

While I agree that the relationship between the sound of most morphemes and the concepts they are linked to is arbitrary, and although I recognize that symbols can be plurivocal, I resist calling morphemes "signs." I agree with Susanne Langer that "a sign is anything that announces the existence or the imminence of some event, the presence of a thing or a person, or a change in the state of affairs" ("Language and Thought" 412). On the other hand, as Langer notes, "a symbol differs from a sign in that it does not announce the presence of the object, the being, condition, or whatnot, which is its meaning, but merely *brings this thing to mind*" (412). Thus I see language as symbolic; it depends on elements that bring other things to mind.

What, then, is the major effect that this symbolic capacity has on us? It enables us to form and hold concepts in our minds, such as the concepts of doggishness, emptiness, and justice. Language allows us to abstract from the tumult of the world's stimuli. We are not mere receivers of stimuli but interpreters of the world, and we frequently use language to express these interpretations. Therefore, although I believe that not all thought is linguistically based, I think that most of the more significant forms of thought are.

Concepts have many important characteristics. For one thing, they are abstract; we do not need concrete stimuli to bring them to mind. Second, they are relatively stable; we can consider essentially the same concept on many different occasions. And third, they can be organized into patterns. We distinguish concepts, group them, and weave them together, producing systems of concepts and individual concepts of greater and greater complexity (see Whitehead 93). As we relate one concept to others, we remember them all better.

If, then, the primary effect of language on us is that it makes us conceptual beings, and if concepts have the characteristics just listed, then language has several wonderful subsidiary effects on us.

First, to a large extent conceptual thinking allows us to be conscious of a self and to distinguish the self from "the other." The self holds concepts in mind and performs mental operations on them. And among these concepts is the one called a self-concept. According to Owen Barfield, "a subjective — or *self* — consciousness is inseparable . . . from rational discursive thought operating on abstract ideas" (204). Or, in Walker Percy's words, concepts about the self help mark "man's ordainment to being and the knowing of it" (136).

Second, once a self is conscious of its own existence, it is driven to expression. This is probably true at least in part because the self wants to make an object of itself for others (Bakhtin, *Speech Genres* 110), thereby seeking to verify its existence from an outside source. In this light we can see more clearly why humans are terrified of not being responded to. But the self is probably also driven to expression in order to make sense of its life and environment. What it can express, it can conceive, and if others accept its expressions, the self has some validation of its conceptions.

Third, since we can call concepts to mind at different times, we can enjoy the effects of fully articulated memory, not just the vague impressions that we have sensed things before. In the words of Alfred North Whitehead, "An articulated memory is the gift of language, considered as an expression from oneself in the past to oneself in the present" (92). Closely related is the claim that with memory comes awareness of time. According to Susanne Langer, "Time is the new dimension which verbalizing and its mental consequence, symbolic thinking, have imposed on the human ambient" (*Mind* 2:333).

Once we can hold concepts in mind and can see relationships among them, it is natural for us to try to discover more concepts and more connections between them. On one level, such discovering should help us feel more secure about ourselves and our environment. We know more and remember more about ourselves and our environment. Discovery is pleasurable, since it reinforces the basic way in which we respond to the world. The pleasure in discovery is so strong that it leads us to invent other worlds in our imaginations and communicate about them to others.

In addition, conceptual thinking allows us to be agents with intentions, not just beings to whom things happen. With conceptions, we can focus on what we will act on, hold the steps involved in an action in sequence, think of things that might be necessary for or might affect our action, and judge on the basis of similar actions in the past how likely it is that our projected action will succeed.

Finally, I believe that because of conceptual thinking we can experience finely articulated emotions. With conceptual ability, we articulate our emotions to ourselves and make fine distinctions among them. Once we do so, we will have a more poignant experience of those emotions. Without conceptual ability we would experience only vague and vaguely similar sensations.

The best evidence that our ability to conceptualize has so many significant effects on us comes from those who try to explain what they were like when they were without language. This evidence is not ideal, since these people either had a language to use before losing it or were developing language before that process was interrupted. Still, the evidence is striking.

Some of the evidence comes from those who were once aphasic and were later able to describe the state of their consciousness when they could not speak. C. Scott Moss records how difficult it was after his stroke to keep an abstraction in mind and "how completely and totally fixed I was on the 'here and now'" (10).

Helen Keller describes her experience at the water pump — when she learned the nature of symbolism — as a miracle, a being "lifted from nothingness to human life" (*My Religion* 21). Her claims are remarkable:

> Before my teacher came to me, I did not know that I am. I lived in a world that was a no-world. I cannot hope to describe adequately that unconscious, yet conscious time of nothingness. I did not know that I knew aught, or that I lived or acted or desired. I had neither will nor intellect. I was carried along to objects and acts by a certain blind natural impetus. I had a mind which caused me to feel anger, satisfaction, desire. These two facts led those about me to suppose that I willed and thought. I can remember all this, not because I knew that it was so, but because I have tactual memory. It enables me to remember that I never contracted my forehead in the act of thinking. I never viewed anything beforehand or chose it. I also recall tactually the fact that never in a start of the body or a heart-beat did I feel that I loved or cared for anything. My inner life, then, was a blank without past, present, or future, without hope or anticipation, without wonder or joy or faith. (*The World I Live In* 113-14)

In this and other passages, Keller testifies to many of the effects of conceptualization that I have just posited.

Keller's "I did not know that I am" can remind one of God's great "I am." In large measure I understand the meaning of God and his Christ as Logos in terms something like this: "In the beginning was the great symbol or concept." Christ was the invisible through the visible; his presence on earth had significance beyond what was physically apparent. Moreover, it was God and his Christ who during creation made the distinctions significant for the cosmos, who brought order and meaning out of chaos.

Concepts: Grounded, Stable, Communicable?

All that I have written about language as a symbolic system rests on several assumptions. One is that we have some reason for associating a symbol with a concept. We assume that our symbol-concept combinations are grounded somehow, that they have a foundation. Another assumption is that as we move from one time and place to another, we will not capriciously start to pair familiar symbols with new concepts. We assume that our symbol-concept combinations are relatively stable. Yet another assumption is that when we communicate a symbol-concept combination to others, we and they will have the same or almost the same concept in mind. We assume that our symbol-concept combinations are communicable.

The key assumption is the first one. If we can be confident that symbol-concepts are grounded, we can be confident that they are stable and communicable.

Probably the most common traditional way to talk about the grounding of symbol-concept combinations is in terms of correspondence theory. This theory begins with the claim that reality, which is divisible into natural essences or kinds of things, exists prior to language. This theory also holds that these natural essences impinge on language in such a way that they are paired with morphemes (meaning-bearing linguistic units) that are fitting and appropriate for them. According to Bob Morgan, "Language is grasped as an innocent medium through which pre-linguistic meanings pass" (450). Positing all these things, correspondence theorists see language as grounded in reality (Thiher 97). And many Christians who have espoused correspondence theory stress that both reality and language are products of God's mind.

Although many aspects of this view are appealing, other aspects are difficult to accept. If one believes in a natural correspondence between things in the world, symbols in a language, and concepts in the mind, it is difficult to explain changes in the meanings of words as well as the dropping and adding of words within a language. Beyond this, correspondence theorists often equate language in general with their own language in particular. Once they discover that other languages dissect reality differently from the way their own language does, it is difficult for them to talk about reality impinging on language.

In fact, they usually start to worry about rebutting the claim that language controls the way we see the world or creates reality for us.

If people believe that morphemes do not stand in a natural, fitting correspondence to things in the world, they can find many alternate ways to explain how morphemes garner their meaning. Some say that morphemes mean what an individual chooses to have them mean. Others say that morphemes mean what one's social and professional groups say they mean (see Gergen 267). Still others say that morphemes mean what one's culture establishes that they mean (see Prickett 30).

The claim about how words derive their meaning which has received the most attention recently is the one made by Jacques Derrida. Derrida's claim extends ideas that go back to John Locke but that are usually associated with Ferdinand de Saussure. What I label a linguistic symbol Saussure calls a sign; it is "the combination of a concept and a sound pattern" (67), the combination of a signifier and signified or a signal and signification. Saussure stresses that the "link between signal and signification is arbitrary" (67). This means that there is no natural or necessary reason for a sound to be paired with a concept, that the pairing is conventional.

This seems harmless enough. One can easily imagine a case for grounding symbol-concept combinations in convention. Members of a group can successfully use words grounded in convention provided that they continually work at clarifying what their words refer to, explore why they use language to refer to certain aspects of reality and not to others, and realize that other people may use language to refer to other aspects of reality. To say that two different groups use language to refer to different aspects of reality is not to say that one or the other linguistic system is wrong, that a group of people can know nothing other than what its language refers to, or that there is no reality to be referred to at all.

But as Clarence Walhout points out, Saussure's definition of the sign has led others to formulate a radically skeptical epistemology (355). How? By extending the implications of Saussure's points. After asserting that a sound pattern is arbitrarily related to a concept, Saussure asks how signs obtain their meaning. His answer is startling: signs are defined "not positively, in terms of their content, but negatively by contrast with other items in the same system" (115); in no way do they result from "imposition from the outside world" (111). Therefore, "to *explain a word is to relate it to other words*" (188). Signs derive their meaning "only by their opposition to and difference from other signs" (Thiher 71).

From these notions Jacques Derrida develops his own viewpoint: that words differ from and defer to each other ad infinitum. To this view he attaches the word *différence* (see "Différence" and *Of Grammatology*). According to this view, since "significations can never come to rest in an absolute presence, their specification is deferred from substitute sign to substitute sign in a movement without end" (Abrams, "How to Do Things with Texts" 572). Accordingly, what we experience as we consider texts is "an interminable free-play of indeterminable meanings" (Abrams, "The Deconstructive Angel" 432). As Allen Thiher notes, "Derrida's view of meaning as *différence* . . . constitutes perhaps the most radical attack on a classical view of representation: There is no locus for meaning, only movement, dynamics, play" (92).

Many people react to Derrida's ideas with incredulity. And they soon realize that these vexing ideas rest on the issue of whether or not we can ground morphemes outside the linguistic system.

Observations on Grounding

A number of commentators have pointed out some of the logical problems with Derrida's ideas. John Lyons writes, "If there were no correspondence at all between the structure of language and the structure of the perceptual world, there could be no sense in the suggestion that language imposes a particular categorization upon the world" (234). And about Derrida's claim that the meanings of texts are indeterminate, Wendell Harris notes, "If I write that all texts are indeterminate, either my text cannot have the determinate meaning that all texts are indeterminate or it has a determinate meaning and is thus false" (119; see also Gunn 49).

To such comments I add a few observations. The first is that it is unfortunate that Saussure's words about the arbitrariness of the sign have inhibited scholars from exploring the relations between sound and sense in language. Before Saussure's insistence that onomatopoeia is of little significance in language (175), some scholars explored the relationships between the sounds of morphemes and their meanings and thought they discovered non-arbitrary connections. For example, Albert Tolman examined sounds he thought had special expressive force and suggested that the motions required to produce them were similar to those associated with their meanings (170). Today such suggestions make linguists suspicious. Perhaps suspicion is justified, but it is possible that in shunning this area of research we have overlooked interesting things — such as the discoveries of Dwight Bolinger. He shows how some sounds, often called phonesthemes, are associated with clearly defined areas of meaning. The sound symbolized by *sn*, for instance, is related to the nose or to smell; it appears in *sniff, sniffle, snivel, snore, snout, snort, snoot, snot,* and *snuff* (197).

Bolinger's point is not that such sounds are related to particular areas of meaning in all languages. His point is that once a particular sound becomes associated with a particular area of meaning, speakers begin to treat the sound in a non-arbitrary way. As evidence for such a general process, Bolinger cites "the well-nigh universal use of *n* in negatives, attracting into its meaning-system words not originally negative, from Spanish *nada* to English *nuts*" (196). In the specific case of the sound symbolized by *sn*, speakers begin to change the meanings of words beginning with *sn* so that they become more closely associated with the nose. At the same time, speakers will tend to use the sound symbolized by *sn* in words they invent to convey meanings related to the nose.

No one knows to what extent such processes operate in English and other languages. My point is that ever since Saussure, linguists have not done enough of the kind of work that would address such issues.

My second observation is that Derrida and others ignore the extent to which the world affects language. As Robert Scholes writes, "In every language there are words for certain things not because language has 'chosen' arbitrarily to create those words but because the things were sufficiently *there* to force language to accommodate them" (97). Support for this assertion abounds. When the American colonists needed to find names for the new plants and animals that they encountered, they asked the natives what they called these things and then approximated the natives' words in their own language. When a technology is invented, language must incorporate new words that name aspects of the technology. Also, when certain things disappear from the world, the words for them often disappear from languages, usually without noticeably affecting the meanings of closely related words. None of this evidence suggests that the world impinges on language to the degree that correspondence theorists say. But it does suggest that the world affects language more than Saussure and Derrida admit in their writing.

If Saussure had recognized more of the effects of the world on language, his definition of the sign probably would have been different. His definition unites two terms — the signifier and the signified. Other definitions of linguistic signs or symbols include a term indicating what the signs connect to in the world. C. K. Ogden and I. A. Richards call it the *referent;* Charles Sanders Peirce calls it the *object*. As Robert Scholes points out, Saussure's definition "ignores the referent entirely" (96). With these points in mind, I agree with Clarence Walhout: Saussure and his followers have failed to recognize that people can use symbols arising from conventions and yet have a great degree of agreement about what the concepts associated with the symbols point to in the world (355). That a concept is arbitrarily associated with a sound does not mean that it is arbitrarily associated with an aspect of reality.

My third observation is that Derrida and similar thinkers appear to view language as having only ideational or referential meaning. That many people see language in this way is evidenced by the prevalence of the conduit metaphor, at least in English (see Reddy). In the terms of this metaphor, "The speaker puts ideas (objects) into words (containers) and sends them (along a conduit) to a hearer who takes the idea/objects out of the word/containers" (Lakoff and Johnson 10). As a result, we have many expressions such as "It's hard to put this idea into words" and "It's difficult to get this thought across to you."

However, language conveys more than referential meaning. It also conveys interpersonal meaning, meaning that is a form of action. This never surprises those who know how children develop language. M. A. K. Halliday writes that the functions which children use language to fulfill appear in roughly this order: the instrumental (getting things done), the regulatory (controlling others' behavior), the interactional (interacting with others), the personal (forming a sense of the self), the heuristic (learning about the world), the imaginative (creating an environment for the self), and — finally — the representational (communicating about the world) (3-8).

The first few of these functions are closer to action than to ideation. Yet many people do not realize that children develop these functions and that these functions are essentially maintained in adulthood: adults do not abandon language as action. Actions provide many ways in which to ground the meaning of language — in agents, objects, goals, necessary conditions, facilitating conditions, immediate effects, and delayed effects. Those who view language as both ideation and action are unlikely to see it as being closed off from the world in a shimmering net of differences.

This last point leads to my fourth observation. Derrida and similar thinkers appear to privilege writing over speech. In fact, as M. H. Abrams points out, Derrida's initial and critical strategy is to overturn the traditional view that speech preceded writing. Derrida focuses on "marks-on-blanks" ("The Deconstructive Angel" 428). In so doing, Abrams notes, "Derrida puts out of play, before the game even begins, every source of norms, controls, or indicators which, in the ordinary use and experience of language, set a limit to what we can mean and what we can be understood to mean" (429).

How should we respond to Derrida's strategy and to the vision that it encourages? Abrams suggests that there is only one adequate response: to say to Derrida what William Blake said to the angel in *The Marriage of Heaven and Hell:* "All that we saw was owing to your metaphysics" ("The Deconstructive Angel" 437). That is, we can see language not as marks on blanks but as the symbolic interaction of people depending on "tacit consensual regularities" (Abrams, "How to Do Things with Texts" 587).

The four observations recorded here certainly do not answer all of the questions about precisely how language is grounded. However, they do suggest the kinds of explorations that might someday provide more answers — explorations of how people in communities build up the "tacit consensual regularities" that Abrams refers to and how they use these consensual regularities successfully to perform various kinds of actions.

OUR MAJOR RESPONSIBILITIES IN USING LANGUAGE

In building a framework within which we can develop positions on responsible uses of language, it is most helpful to use a model or grammar for English. The main things I ask of such a model are these: (1) that it focus on language as it is used in the world, not as it is contrived in a linguist's study; (2) that it therefore focus on texts and utterances, not on isolated sentences; and (3) that it seek to explain why people use particular linguistic structures in particular situations.

I find functional grammars that meet these criteria most useful. Such grammars have been developed by the Prague linguistic circle (see Daneš), by T. Givón in America, and by M. A. K. Halliday and others associated with the London school.

One of Halliday's major claims is that "language is as it is because of what it has to do" (26) — that is, language develops its structure because of the functions it fulfills. As previously noted, Halliday holds that language exists to fulfill several macro-functions or to convey several kinds of meaning.

One kind of meaning, according to Halliday, is the ideational. This is "concerned with the expression of experience, including both the processes within and beyond the self — the phenomena of the external world and those of consciousness — and the logical relations deducible from them" (91). In a clause, ideational meaning is conveyed by elements of transitivity, which indicate what kind of process is being represented as well as the participants in and the circumstances of that process. For example, in the sentence "However, Jacques might abandon the project," ideational meaning is carried by "Jacques," "abandon," and "project."

Another kind of meaning is the interpersonal, Halliday points out. It is a form of action having to do with "personal participation; it expresses the speaker's role in the speech situation, his personal commitment and his interaction with others" (91). In a clause, interpersonal meaning is conveyed by elements of mood, which show what role speakers take on and what role they cast their hearers in. In "However, Jacques might abandon the project," the fact that "Jacques" appears before "might" indicates that this sentence is a declarative sentence within the indicative mood. Interpersonal meaning is also conveyed by elements of modality, which show how speakers judge the truth of their ideational material. In the sample sentence used, "might" is an element of modality.

A third kind of meaning is the textual. It is, says Halliday, "concerned with the creation of text; it expresses the structure of information, and the relation of each part of the discourse to the whole and to the setting" (91). In a clause, textual meaning is conveyed by conjunctive adverbs ("However" in the sample sentence), among other elements.

Halliday's central point is that "a linguistic structure — of which the clause is the best example — serves as a means for the integrated expression of all the functionally distinct components of meaning in language" (34). Since textual meaning functions to enable us to convey ideational and interpersonal meaning, I will proceed on the assumption that clauses and texts are simultaneously ideation and action. With most clauses and texts, we reflect on the world and act in context.

Of course, expressions such as "No wonder!" convey little ideation. And we regard other expressions primarily as actions. When a clerk in a courtroom says, "Court is now in session," we interpret that sentence as an action (that of opening the court session), not as an expression of ideational meaning that we did not know and wanted to learn (see Austin and Searle on such points). But we must not forget that the clerk could not be successful in this act if he or she did not express certain appropriate ideational material; he or she could not open court by saying, "School is now in session."

We regard other utterances primarily as expressions of ideation. We treat most of what we hear in lectures this way. Yet when people lecture to us, they act upon us; they seek to affect our view of reality.

Viewing language as both ideation and action is instructive in many ways. For example, it can help us understand the nature of language in worship. Many of the things we say to God would be pointless if they were only ideational — God does not need us to inform him of things. But as kinds of actions (with the appropriate ideation) they are pleasing to him. In addition, different kinds of literary theorists may be distinguishable on the basis of which kind of meaning they privilege.

It is worth considering what a criticism based on a view of language as both ideation and action would be like.

My main concern here, however, is with our responsibilities in using language. And on the basis of ideational and interpersonal meaning, I identify two fundamental responsibilities.

Where ideational meaning is concerned, I hold that our basic responsibility is to convey to others the clearest, fullest, and most accurate view of reality that we can. Where interpersonal meaning is concerned, I hold that our basic responsibility is to love others, to build them up into Christ. Of course, not all clauses and texts can provide the clearest, fullest, and most accurate view of reality. Nor with all of them can we build up others into Christ as much as possible. We must first determine to what degree a clause or text can fulfill one or the other responsibility and then judge how close it comes to attaining that degree.

I separate these responsibilities primarily for heuristic purposes. In natural discourse they usually cannot be separated. Therefore, the more we convey a clear, full, and accurate view of the world to others, the more we support others in Christ. And this works both ways: the more we support others in Christ, the more we will be helping them toward a clear, full, and accurate view of reality.

Still, as I have noted, with some clauses and texts, one kind of meaning comes to the fore. As it becomes easier to think of one kind of meaning as being dominant in a clause or text, it also becomes easier to identify concerns that are subsidiary to those just mentioned but that are important in judging that clause or text. If ideational meaning comes to the fore, we must also be concerned with how efficient the language is, what kind of values the speaker or writer functions with, and what sorts of claims and appeals the listener or reader must value in order to find the text acceptable. If interpersonal meaning comes to the fore, we must also be concerned with the intention of the speaker or writer, with what the speaker or writer must do to ensure that the verbal action is interpreted properly, and with the context of the action.

At this point, two controversial issues arise. The first is related to ideational meaning and views of the world. Many people assume that their view of reality is already as clear, full, and accurate as possible. They do not ask themselves why they make certain distinctions, and they refuse to believe that other people could make different distinctions. We all know of the trouble this has caused within Christian denominations. Of course, powerful pressures work on all of us to establish our view of the world as the reigning one.

But when we resist objectively assessing or altering our view of the world, we set ourselves up as the ultimate reality; we move close to the essence of pride. We certainly risk overlooking certain aspects of reality, overemphasizing other aspects, and being inconsistent or wrong in connecting certain aspects to one another. One of our strengths as language-users — that we are interpreters of reality — can become a problem. Thus, as Philip Holtrop urges, we must keep a covenant with each other, supporting each other, encouraging each other to express views of reality, listening to each other, making sure we understand each other, and correcting each other (12).

In this area we can learn from M. M. Bakhtin. He argues that the world is dominated by what he calls heteroglossia, that we inevitably encounter different dialects, languages, ideologies, and worldviews (*The Dialogic Imagination* 428). And to a great extent, he notes, we learn about ourselves and the world through dialogic interaction with those who speak differently than we do. Therefore, as James Fowler points out in describing a mature kind of faith, it is wise to maintain "vulnerability to the strange truths of those who are 'other'" (198).

Bakhtin is very helpful in clarifying how we learn about ourselves and the world. He is less helpful when it comes to deciding which view of the world is clearest, fullest, and most accurate. Although we must be open to change and to other points of view, there is a point at which we must commit ourselves to the view that we regard as the clearest, fullest, and most accurate. How to maintain both commitment and openness is one of the ongoing challenges in the responsible use of language.

The second controversial issue concerns interpersonal meaning and truth values. The truth value of information is the main concern of many writers who focus on language and ethics. According to them, what is true is ethical, and what is false is unethical. Yet when it comes to clauses and texts in which action dominates ideation, I would argue against making truth value the ultimate concern.

When it comes to linguistic expressions that are primarily actions, the effects of those actions should be our ultimate concern. If people resist this notion, I ask them how they judge Rahab for saying what she did to those seeking the Jewish spies. Borrowing from Augustine, I ask them what they would say to someone who shows every sign of wanting to murder me and who asks them whether I am hiding in the closet I have just made a frantic dash to.

People come up with all kinds of responses to these questions. Some would respond to my would-be murderer by saying nothing, others by trying to divert his or her attention, others by telling the truth and trusting God to save me miraculously. I argue that we should worry more about potentially devastating effects than about false information.

I do not advocate uttering falsehoods whenever we please for no good reason. I do advocate uttering falsehoods in situations in which true information would clearly have harmful effects. Of course, the situations we face are rarely as extreme as the hypothetical one of my would-be murderer. And we need to do more work on how harmful the effects of a linguistic action have to be in order to justify conveying false information. But this work will probably best be done within the framework just outlined.

FUTURE WORK

Much of what is touched on here should be developed in the future. We have much work to do in developing a clear, full, and accurate view of reality. We must debate the nature and validity of different ways of knowing reality as well as the matter of whether or not we can ever, in this life, reach closure about a view of reality.

Several matters not touched on here should also be closely examined. First, we should re-examine the matter of whether there is a distinct kind of language called the poetic. If there is, is it particularly suitable for describing religious experience? Second, we should examine the relationship between language and gender. To what extent are "genderlects" manipulative, and to what extent are they rooted in nature or in social and cultural experience? Third, we should examine how groups with power use and misuse language. Can they use language in such a way that those whom they oppress come to believe that their oppression is grounded in the nature of the world? Fourth, we should spend more time on metaphor. Is all language essentially metaphoric? How do metaphors help us see new meanings? Do both terms of a metaphor change in meaning as the metaphor is used (see Berggren)? Finally, Giles Gunn claims that there are "fields of experience that we can never subjugate to the forms of our speech, that we can never subsume within the conventions of language, that we can never domesticate or control through symbolic intervention" (192). If such "fields of experience" exist, how important are they to us? Work in areas such as these will probably be of considerable significance to us as we continue to examine language and clarify our views of it.

WORKS CITED

(Titles with an asterisk are recommended as introductions.)

Abrams, M. H. "The Deconstructive Angel." *Critical Inquiry* 3 (1977): 425-38.

——. "How to Do Things with Texts." *Partisan Review* 46 (1979): 566-88.

*Austin, J. L. *How to Do Things with Words.* Oxford: Oxford University Press, 1962.

Bakhtin, M. M. *The Dialogic Imagination.* Trans. Caryl Emerson and Michael Holquist. Ed. Michael Holquist. Austin: University of Texas Press, 1981.

——. *Speech Genres and Other Late Essays.* Trans. Vern W. McGee. Ed. Caryl Emerson and Michael Holquist. Austin: University of Texas Press, 1986.

Barfield, Owen. *Poetic Diction: A Study in Meaning.* 3rd ed. Middletown, Conn.: Wesleyan University Press, 1973.

Berggren, Douglas. "The Use and Abuse of Metaphor." *Review of Metaphysics* 16 (1962): 237-58.

Black, Max. "From *The Labyrinth of Language.*" In *Reclaiming the Imagination,* ed. Ann E. Berthoff, 72-83. Upper Montclair, N.J.: Boynton/Cook Publishers, 1984.

Bolinger, Dwight. "Word Affinities." In *Forms of English: Accent, Morpheme, Order,* ed. Isamu Abe and Tetsuya Kanekiyo, 191-202. Cambridge: Harvard University Press, 1965.

Chomsky, Noam. *Aspects of the Theory of Syntax.* Cambridge: MIT Press, 1965.

——. "Human Language and Other Semiotic Systems." In *Speaking of Apes: A Critical Anthology of Two-Way Communication with Man,* ed. T. A. Sebeok and J. Umiker-Sebeok, 429-40. New York: Plenum Press, 1980.

*——. *Syntactic Structures.* The Hague: Mouton, 1957.

Daneš, Frantisek, ed. *Papers on Functional Sentence Perspective.* The Hague: Mouton, 1974.

Derrida, Jacques. "Différence." In *Margins of Philosophy,* trans. Alan Bass, 3-27. Chicago: University of Chicago Press, 1982.

——. *Of Grammatology.* Trans. Gayatri Spivak. Baltimore: Johns Hopkins University Press, 1976.

de Villiers, Peter A., and Jill G. de Villiers. "Early Judgments of Semantic and Syntactic Acceptability by Children." *Journal of Psycholinguistic Research* 1 (1972): 299-310.

Eimas, P. D. "Linguistic Processing of Speech by Young Infants." In *Language Perspectives: Acquisition, Retardation, and Intervention,* ed. R. L. Schiefelbusch and L. L. Lloyd, 55-73. Baltimore: University Park Press, 1974.

————. "Speech Perception in Early Infancy." In *Infant Perception: From Sensation to Cognition,* vol. 2, ed. L. B. Cohen and P. Salapatek, 193-231. New York: Academic Press, 1975.

Fowler, James W. *Stages of Faith.* San Francisco: Harper & Row, 1981.

*Fromkin, Victoria, and Robert Rodman. *An Introduction to Language.* 4th ed. New York: Holt, Rinehart & Winston, 1988.

Gardner, Beatrice T., and R. Allen Gardner. "Teaching Sign Language to a Chimpanzee." *Science* 165 (1969): 664-72.

Gergen, Kenneth J. "The Social Constructionist Movement in Modern Psychology." *American Psychologist* 40 (1985): 266-75.

*Givón, T. *Syntax: A Functional-Typological Introduction.* Vol. 1. Amsterdam: John Benjamins Publishing Company, 1984.

Gunn, Giles. *The Culture of Criticism and the Criticism of Culture.* New York: Oxford University Press, 1987.

*Halliday, M. A. K. *Explorations in the Functions of Language.* New York: Elsevier, 1973.

Harris, Wendell V. "Toward an Ecological Criticism: Contextual versus Unconditional Literary Theory." *College English* 48 (1986): 116-31.

Hasker, William. "Brains, Persons, and Eternal Life." *Christian Scholar's Review* 12 (1983): 294-309.

*Heny, Jeannine. "Brain and Language." In *Language: Introductory Readings,* 4th ed., ed. V. P. Clark, P. A. Eschholz, and A. F. Rosa, 159-82. New York: St. Martin's Press, 1985.

Holquist, Michael. Introduction to *Speech Genres and Other Late Essays* by M. M. Bakhtin. Trans. Vern W. McGee. Ed. Caryl Emerson and Michael Holquist. Austin: University of Texas Press, 1986.

Holtrop, Philip C. "A Strange Language: Toward a Biblical Conception of Truth and a New Mood for Doing Reformed Theology." *The Reformed Journal* 27.2 (1977): 9-13.

Joos, Martin. *The Five Clocks.* New York: Harcourt, Brace & World, 1967.

Keller, Helen. *My Religion.* New York: Swedenborg Foundation, 1927.

————. *The World I Live In.* New York: Century Company, 1908.

*Lakoff, G., and M. Johnson. *Metaphors We Live By.* Chicago: University of Chicago Press, 1980.

*Langer, Susanne K. "Language and Thought." In *Exploring Language,* 4th ed., ed. Gary Goshgarian, 411-17. Boston: Little, Brown, 1986.

————. *Mind: An Essay on Human Feeling.* 3 vols. Baltimore: Johns Hopkins University Press, 1967-1982.

Lenneberg, Eric H. *Biological Foundations of Language.* New York: Wiley, 1967.

Lyons, John. "Towards a 'Notional' Theory of the Parts of Speech." *Journal of Linguistics* 2 (1966): 209-36.

Morgan, Bob. "Three Dreams of Language; Or, No Longer Immured in the Bastille of the Humanist Word." *College English* 49 (1987): 449-58.

Moss, C. Scott. *Recovery with Aphasia.* Urbana: University of Illinois Press, 1972.

Oksaar, Els. *Language Acquisition in the Early Years.* New York: St. Martin's Press, 1982.

Patterson, Francine. "Conversations with a Gorilla." *National Geographic,* Oct. 1978, pp. 438-65.

Percy, Walker. "Metaphor as Mistake." In *Reclaiming the Imagination,* ed. Ann E. Berthoff, 132-44. Upper Montclair, N.J.: Boynton/Cook Publishers, 1984.

Premack, David. "The Education of Sarah: A Chimp Learns the Language." *Psychology Today,* Sept. 1970, pp. 54-58.

Prickett, Stephen. *Words and "The Word": Language, Poetics and Biblical Interpretation.* Cambridge: Cambridge University Press, 1986.

Reddy, Michael J. "The Conduit Metaphor — A Case of Frame Conflict in Our Language about Language." In *Metaphor and Thought,* ed. Andrew Ortony, 284-324. Cambridge: Cambridge University Press, 1979.

Ricoeur, Paul. *Freud and Philosophy.* New Haven: Yale University Press, 1970.

*Saussure, Ferdinand de. *Course in General Linguistics.* Trans. Roy Albert Sechehaye with the collaboration of Albert Riedlinger. La Salle, Ill.: Open Court, 1986.

Savage-Rumbaugh, Susan, D. M. Rumbaugh, and S. Boysen. "Linguistically Mediated Tool Use and Exchange by Chimpanzees *(Pan troglodytes)." Behavioral and Brain Sciences* 1 (1978): 539-54.

*Scholes, Robert. *Textual Power.* New Haven: Yale University Press, 1985.

Searle, John. *Speech Acts.* Cambridge: Cambridge University Press, 1970.

Sebeok, Thomas A., and Jean Umiker-Sebeok. "Performing Animals: Secrets of the Trade." *Psychology Today,* Nov. 1979, pp. 78-82, 91.

*Terrace, Herbert S. *Nim: A Chimpanzee Who Learned Sign Language.* New York: Pocket Books, 1979.

Thiher, Allen. *Words in Reflection: Modern Language Theory and Postmodern Fiction.* Chicago: University of Chicago Press, 1984.

Tolman, Albert H. "The Symbolic Value of Sounds." In *The Views about Hamlet and Other Essays,* 143-72. Cambridge: Riverside Press, 1906.

Walhout, Clarence. "Ives, Crane, Marin, and 'The Mind behind the Maker.'" *Christian Scholar's Review* 16 (1987): 355-72.

Waterman, John T. *Perspectives in Linguistics.* Chicago: University of Chicago Press, 1963.

Whitehead, Alfred North. "Expression." In *Reclaiming the Imagination,* ed. Ann E. Berthoff, 84-96. Upper Montclair, N.J.: Boynton/Cook Publishers, 1984.

Wolterstorff, Nicholas. "Why Animals Don't Speak." *Faith and Philosophy* 4 (1987): 463-85.

FEMINIST LITERARY CRITICISM:
A CHORUS OF ETHICAL VOICES

Susan Van Zanten Gallagher

During the past twenty years, feminist literary criticism has evolved from a small fringe movement to an influential community of thought. Although we can find several nineteenth- and twentieth-century precedents, this way of talking about literature first gained prominence in the early 1970s in conjunction with the social ferment of the Women's Movement. One of the inspirations for both political and literary feminism was Kate Millett's *Sexual Politics* (1969), which analyzed how Western institutions, including literary institutions, manipulated power in order to establish male dominance and female subordination. From these overtly political beginnings, feminist literary scholarship emerged.

A simple definition of feminist literary criticism is almost impossible. One obstacle arises in some of the early feminists' suspicion of theory as an instrument of the patriarchal system. A common theme throughout feminist criticism is the need to beware of placing too much importance on theory and not enough importance on life and experience. However, few feminist critics reject theory altogether, and a second and greater obstacle to defining feminist criticism stems from the bewildering array of approaches that such critics employ. Feminist literary criticism draws on a variety of other disciplines and theories including structuralism, poststructuralism, Freudian and Lacanian psychology, linguistics, and Marxism.

Unlike many critical approaches, such as New Criticism or reader-response criticism, feminist criticism does not consist of a particular technique by which to interpret texts. Its distinctive element is belief in certain principles rather than technique. Feminist criticism is committed criticism. It does not simply explore a hypothesis; it attempts to improve society. Feminist critics share a common belief about right and wrong which informs their work as literary critics. Most simply put, feminist critics believe that women have been unjustly marginalized and victimized by the structures of society, that this situation needs to be remedied, and that one way to do so is through literary criticism.

Feminist critics follow their ethical imperatives in a variety of ways. Although we cannot attempt to survey all the different extant approaches to feminist criticism, we can identify four of the most significant schools: (1) images-of-women criticism, (2) gynocriticism, (3) deconstructive feminism, and (4) feminist social constructionism. Each approach uses different methods, but all share a common commitment to better the lives of women.

IMAGES-OF-WOMEN CRITICISM

One way that feminist critics attempt to combat the oppression of women is by examining the way women have been portrayed in literary texts. This thematic analysis of the "images of women" was one of the first forms of feminist criticism, and it still continues today in a number of variations. Critics usually analyze the images of women primarily in the traditional works of the canon and in works by male authors.

Examining these images often reveals that women have been stereotyped, dehumanized, and treated as objects in many works of literature. Using the insight of Simone de Beauvoir that marginalized groups are often oppressed by being characterized as deviant or "Other," feminist critics demonstrate that many works of literature depict male experience as the norm and female experience as subordinate. This approach was first popularized in the witty exposure of "phallic criticism" in Mary Ellmann's *Thinking about Women* (1968) and Millett's scathing critique in *Sexual Politics* of "the virility cult" of D. H. Lawrence, Henry Miller, and Norman Mailer.

Some of this initial criticism was very simplistic and thesis-driven, failing to view a work in its full complexity or to note irony or point of view. Consequently, more sophisticated readings often followed an initial critique. Nonetheless, looking at how women are depicted in literature created a new sensitivity to aspects of a text that previously had often been overlooked. Rather than judging a text purely by formalist criteria, feminist critics began judging its depiction of women characters "by standards of authenticity" (Holly 41). They asked pointed questions: Is this character realistic or just a stereotype? Is she reflective and critical? Is she a moral agent, capable of self-determination? When we compare the rendering of a female character to what we know about women from our own consciousness and experiences, we can determine if a character is an authentic person or just an object, an "Other" used to say something about male experience. While such criteria seem appropriate for realistic works, they may not be as suitable for other genres of literature.

During the early 1970s the images-of-women approach dominated college courses in women's studies, and the textbook entitled *Images of Women in Fiction: Feminist Perspectives* (1972) went through several editions. The constant victimization of women uncovered in these studies often made students and professors depressed and angry, but the recognition of this inequity also resulted in a call for works depicting positive role models for women. Subsequently, one of the most noticeable results of images-of-women criticism has been an outpouring of works with strong female characters by authors such as Alice Walker, Margaret Atwood, Toni Morrison, Erica Jong, and Adrienne Rich.

Among the practitioners of images-of-women criticism are those who focus on the significant absence or the overlooked significance of women in texts written by men. Women's absences are important, as Judith Fetterley points out, not only because female readers lack characters with which to identify, but also because specifically male experience is often held up as definitive human experience. Beginning with the critical commonplace that novels depicting the archetypal American experience portray the protagonist struggling for natural freedom against the constricting, civilizing forces embodied by women, Fetterley asks how a female reader is to respond. She concludes, "In such fictions the female reader is co-opted into participation in an experience from which she is explicitly excluded; she is asked to identify with a selfhood that defines itself in opposition to her; she is required to identify against herself" (xii).

Other thematic studies uncover the function of female characters who have been ignored by male critics. For example, Annette Kolodny points out that male critics have often read captivity narratives as male mythology about the frontier, but they ignore "the fact that women, too, required imaginative constructs through which to accommodate themselves to the often harsh realities of the western wilderness" (161). Kolodny examines the potentially symbolic significations of a woman's presence in such stories to uncover that overlooked female mythology. Still other studies suggest that women characters are not always rendered as dehumanized and oppressed but instead are sometimes shown as powerful and feared. Nina Auerbach's analysis of Victorian literature in *Communities of Women* (1978) identifies a complex mythology of strong and sustaining women. The research of both Auerbach and Kolodny turns up the complexity and value of female characters who have been previously overlooked.

The images-of-women approach to criticism reveals its ethical commitment primarily in its concerns about the effects of reading. Adherents of this approach ask a variety of questions. What kind of effects do certain works produce? Does a work show female readers that they are fully human, or does it imply that women are primarily sexual and subsidiary objects to men? Do such works encourage men to view women in a sexist manner or as authentic human beings who need to be treated with dignity? Do our critical practices demonstrate that female characters should not be overlooked and that they often contribute important ideas to a work?

Given these concerns for the effects of reading on both men and women, feminist critics do not hesitate to be prescriptive, asking us to reject as great or at least reconsider the worth of a text that oppresses women by stereotyping them. Feminist critics also openly ask for new, more positive kinds of literature. By looking at how women are depicted in literary works, such critics attempt "not simply to interpret the world but to change it by changing the consciousness of those who read and their relation to what they read" (Fetterley viii). The images-of-women approach to criticism thus battles the oppression enacted by the text as well as the oppression encouraged by the reading of such works.

GYNOCRITICISM

Perhaps the most extensive and influential kind of feminist criticism is gynocriticism, the study of literature written by women. This term was coined by Elaine Showalter, who explains, "Gynocriticism begins at the point when we free ourselves from the linear absolutes of male literary history, stop trying to fit women between the lines of the male tradition, and focus instead on the newly visible world of female culture" ("Toward a Feminist Poetic" 131). Again breaking with the formalist attention to the text, the gynocritic examines the female author's life, the historical and social conditions in which she writes (or does not write), and the distinctive content and style of her work.

Several books published in the late 1970s initiated the discussion of a distinct female literary tradition. Patricia Meyer Spacks' *The Female Imagination* (1975) attempts to identify the transhistorical components of the female imagination. Sandra Gilbert and Susan Gubar take a similar approach in their influential study entitled *The Madwoman in the Attic* (1979). They point out that in the nineteenth century artistic creativity was considered to be a male quality. Accordingly, women writers faced a tremendous "anxiety of authorship," and their writing contains a hidden subtext embodying their rage against patriarchal oppression. Gilbert and Gubar note that these texts employ similar themes and images of confinement and escape, disease and health, fragmentation and wholeness.

Other pioneer studies examine the history of the female tradition. Ellen Moers' *Literary Women* (1976) looks at the way in which women authors created literary networks: reading and commenting on female predecessors, developing friendships and correspondences, providing models and influences. An even closer examination of the literary history of the female tradition appears in Elaine Showalter's *A Literature of Their Own* (1977), which chronicles an extensive literary female subculture with its own patterns of relationships, themes, and images.

Along with identifying a female literary tradition, gynocritics are concerned with defining the distinctive characteristics of women's writing. Do women write different kinds of texts than men? To what can we attribute these differences, if they exist? Showalter identifies four different theories of difference: biological, linguistic, psychological, and cultural. Biological theorists believe that women's bodies give rise to certain kinds of language or patterns of imagery. Linguistic theorists examine how men and women use language differently or argue that women should reject the male-constructed language system to employ their own kind of language. Many psychological theorists employ Nancy Chodorow's theories about female identity as relationally defined and analyze how this affects women's texts. Cultural theorists, who include Showalter, see women's texts as originating in their unique cultural experiences ("Feminist Criticism in the Wilderness" 250-67).

Perhaps the greatest impact of gynocriticism has been its effect on the literary canon. Feminist critics have uncovered the work of numerous lost women writers, such as Kate Chopin, Rebecca Harding Davis, Charlotte Perkins Gilman, Zora Neale Hurston, Aphra Behn, Dorothy Wordsworth, Dorothy Richardson, and Rebecca West. Feminist Press in the United States and Virago Press in Great Britain are now publishing works by women that had long been out of print. Perhaps the most visible and significant contribution of gynocriticism is the newly revised content of many of the standard anthologies, such as the venerable *Norton Anthology of English Literature* and *Norton Anthology of American Literature*. Both collections now feature more women writers.

The gynocritics have demonstrated that the scarcity of women in the traditional canon cannot always be attributed to the lack of available writing by women or to the inferiority of their work. Feminist criticism has contributed to a new awareness of the economic, social, political, and ideological factors that enter into canon constructions. Some feminists believe that white males deliberately neglect women writers in order to protect their own patriarchal power. But even without such conspiratorial theories, we can see that the interested nature of critical activity means that the canon may be constructed with standards that omit women.

For example, the criteria applied by the New Critics of the forties and fifties — who valued ambiguity, complexity, paradox, and tension — may not be appropriate ways to judge all kinds of literature. Yet these critical standards provided the means by which works were positioned in the canon. If we value literature that accurately and effectively depicts women's feelings and experiences, we may elevate genres such as journals, autobiographical novels, and confessional poetry over public essays, philosophical novels, and epic verse. Paying closer attention to the appropriateness of critical standards and reading works with more historical awareness, gynocritics have convincingly demonstrated the excellence of many women authors who were previously ignored or misunderstood.

The value of gynocriticism notwithstanding, its narrow approach could create a women's literary ghetto. Consequently, many feminist critics have become increasingly concerned to incorporate women writers *into* the canon rather than have them exist in their own separate but equal realm. If we believe that literature written by women has inherent value, we will be concerned to have all students, both male and female, encounter female texts. While the gynocritics have overcome the neglect of women's texts by paying concentrated attention to them, the final step must be to incorporate such texts into all studies of literature.

Gynocriticism attempts to battle oppression by exposing and combatting the neglect of women authors. Its mission is to reform various aspects of the institutionalization of literature: the concept of the canon, the criteria by which we judge texts, and the works and authors we anthologize, teach, and analyze. Freeing the suppressed literary productions of women and working to change the vision of the literary establishment are the practical ways in which gynocritics attempt to put their ethical commitments to work in their academic practices.

THE POSTSTRUCTURALIST FEMINIST CRITIQUE

The radical transformation of ideas about the nature of a text prompted by critics such as Roland Barthes, Michel Foucault, and Jacques Derrida had a major impact on feminist criticism in the 1980s, causing a reassessment and critique of much previous scholarship. Rather than viewing a work of literature as a written expression of the author's experiences and ideas, and so reflecting or representing reality, poststructuralist critics think of texts as "signifying systems which inscribe ideology and are actually constitutive of reality" (Greene and Kahn 25). Poststructuralists also reject the authority of the author, given current psychological insight into the fragmentation of the self and linguistic insight into the unreliability of language. These new views of the text result in new kinds of feminist criticism.

No longer believing in the authority of the text or the author, poststructuralists see both the images-of-women critics and gynocritics as naively participating in the patriarchal systems which have oppressed them in the first place. Studying the way women have been portrayed in or omitted from texts assumes that literature is representational, without any reality of its own. Gynocriticism does not question the mimetic quality of literature and may perpetuate the idea that women are "Other," separate from men.

Beginning with the view that a text constructs reality rather than reflects it, poststructuralist feminists have developed a number of critical strategies. The two most influential approaches are those of deconstruction and social construction. While the images-of-women approach and gynocriticism have been primarily American developments, deconstructive feminism arose in France, and social constructionism is prominent among British scholars.

Deconstructive Feminism

Deconstructive feminism takes a more philosophical approach than pragmatic American criticism. Beginning with the structuralist theory that all systems of thought are made up of binary oppositions, such critics argue that the male/female opposition is one of the most pervasive and harmful ideologies. Other forms of feminist criticism have accepted this dichotomy and merely attempt to shift our focus from the dominant male to the neglected female. Conversely, the deconstructive feminists, perhaps best represented by the French critic Julia Kristeva, argue that we must not merely reverse the hierarchy but rather eliminate the opposition between male and female.

The close union between deconstruction and feminism arises in their similar dismantling of hierarchical oppositions. Deconstructionists argue that Western culture, philosophy, and language are all based on binary oppositions, which must be exposed and undermined. Derrida explains that all these systems are "phallogocentric," maintained by recourse to both the Logos, the word, and the phallus as a source of power. Many feminists view the deconstructive project of dismantling Western metaphysics as essentially a feminist project. Any disruption of the closure of binary oppositions assists the feminine cause. As articulated by critics such as Kristeva, the feminine is not so much a biological, psychological, or cultural essence as it is a philosophical position. The feminine is any position or group that is marginalized by patriarchal order, such as non-Caucasian races, the working class, the avant-garde. Deconstructive criticism is feminist criticism.

The American practitioners of deconstructive criticism are known for their focus on the endless play of signifiers in a text, their exposure and celebration of the irreducible plurality inherent in language. Some deconstructive feminists follow this approach, dismantling the authority of the author by refusing to read the text in light of authorial intentions and demonstrating how the text itself deconstructs its author's intentions. However, the more typical deconstructive feminist concentrates not as much on the act of reading as on the act of writing, advocating a new kind of language that undoes representation and points to the gaps and slippage inherent in all language.

Working from the theories of Derrida and the psychologist Jacques Lacan, who identifies the symbolic order of language with the Father, some feminist critics associate logical language with oppressive masculinity. Representation, logical discourse, and symbolic language all participate in the phallogocentric system and so participate in the marginalization of women. In her analysis in *Desire in Language: A Semiotic Approach to Literature and Art* (1980), Kristeva distinguishes between the *symbolic* — the reality of structure and order — and the *semiotic*, the pre-symbolic reality informed by our basic biological rhythms of anal and oral activity. The logical contradictions, gaps, and disruptions that we so often find in symbolic language come from these semiotic pressures.

Kristeva's answer to phallogocentrism is avante-garde writing, which revels in open-ended textuality, double or multiple voices, broken syntax, and repetitive or cumulative structures. Such texts, according to Kristeva, tap the pre-linguistic energy of the semiotic rather than the symbolic order identified with the Father. While some French critics such as Luce Irigaray and Helene Cixous associate the open-ended textuality of such writing exclusively with female biology, Kristeva insists that just as any marginal position is feminine, so any kind of subversive writing technique represents a rebellion against the rule of the Father or oppressive patriarchy. Not surprisingly, Kristeva values highly the work of modernist writers such as Mallarmé and Joyce, and deconstructive feminist readings are most successful with avante-garde texts.

The ethical basis for such criticism may not be immediately obvious. At its best, deconstructive feminism works to expose the ways that cultural and social authorities impose their definition of truth upon us and, in so doing, marginalize and oppress women and their perspectives. Yet deconstructive feminism is also commonly criticized as idealistic and impractical. What difference does Joyce's semiotic style make to the thousands of enslaved Third World women or physically abused Western women? Toril Moi explains the political implications of deconstruction: "Since Kristeva sees . . . conventional meaning as the structure that sustains the whole of the symbolic order — that is, all human social and cultural institutions — the fragmentation of symbolic language in modernist poetry comes for her to parallel and prefigure a total *social* revolution" (11). However, this explanation of Kristeva's perspective should not obscure the limitations of her approach. Because she limits her approach to establishing parallels and is unable to connect the content of a text to the historical and political world, her analysis is ultimately unsatisfactory. Even if we were willing to agree that all logical and representational language belongs to a patriarchal system (which many feminists and other scholars are not), poststructuralist feminists cannot show that subverting logical language in texts could possibly change the oppressive structures of social and cultural institutions.

Feminist Social Constructionism

While deconstructive critics focus on language in an attempt to deconstruct the male/female dichotomy, other poststructuralist feminists examine the ways in which this dichotomy has been encoded in our systems of signification. Such an understanding leads to new insights about texts written by both women and men. By examining texts in their historical contexts, we can begin to understand how concepts of gender have been socially constructed in different times and places, and we may thus learn more about how social or cultural institutions can be reformed to eliminate oppression.

Given a text understood in a poststructuralist light, we now have two alternatives. We can focus on its indeterminate nature, or we can, in Wendell V. Harris's words, "while accepting the principle that language partly creates reality, investigate how the individual *parole* can nevertheless be formulated by the speaker/author in such a way as to be adequately interpreted by the auditor/reader" (117). The social constructionists argue that when we discover meaning in texts, we are able to do so because our community establishes certain principles that we agree to follow to arrive at meaning. By understanding how meaning is generated in a text through these social constructions, we may come to understand our society better.

Feminist critics use the principles of social constructionism to relate the development of particular textual strategies to particular historical situations and conditions rather than to identify universal themes and strategies of women writers, as did the early gynocritics. For example, in *Woman's Fiction: A Guide to Novels by and about Women in America, 1820-1870* (1978), Nina Baym shows how the popular domestic fiction of the nineteenth century depicted issues of particular concern to women of that time. Baym's approach to gynocriticism attempts to locate women's texts in relationship to specific sociocultural situations.

This more pragmatic approach allows us to see the connection between literary texts and historical reality. Texts do not merely reflect reality in a mimetic fashion, but neither are they divorced from it completely, as many poststructuralists imply. Rather, texts represent particular social practices, particular ways of making sense of the world through narrative, metaphor, and symbol. As Gayle Greene and Coppelia Kahn explain, "In their creations of fictions, writers call upon the same signifying codes that pervade social interactions, re-presenting in fiction the rituals and symbols that make up social practice" (4). Studying the meaning and structure of literary texts and exposing their inappropriate practices can thus help us recognize and fight other practices that are embodied in political structures and social organizations. Feminist critics pay special attention to how ideologies of gender have been constructed and propagated, particularly the ideology of the inequality of the sexes.

Texts allow us not only to analyze the way our culture attempts to impose meaning and make sense of the world but also to see how socially constructed ideas are perpetuated. As Greene and Kahn point out, "Since each invocation of a code is also its reinforcement or reinscription, literature does more than transmit ideology: it actually creates it. . . . To invoke the conventional narrative resolution of marriage or death, for example, as most nineteenth-century novelists did, was to sanction them, make them prescriptive as well as descriptive, to perpetuate them as the working myths of the culture" (5). As transmitters of ideology, texts participate in historical reality.

Criticism that examines the social construction of the meaning of gender is applicable to all styles of writing, both realistic and experimental. Each style merely represents a different way in which texts are coded. Like the images-of-women criticism, social constructionism is concerned with the effect on readers of certain patterns of plot and imagery. In Greene and Kahn's example, the traditional resolution of nineteenth-century novels becomes prescriptive of certain ways that women must live in order to fulfill their "proper" role. The perpetuation of cultural myths may work to oppress women and condition them to play socially acceptable gender roles.

While gynocriticism focuses on women's texts and experiences, social constructionism examines the broader issues of gender — both female and male. Accordingly, these types of feminist critics ask "larger" questions. How is gender encoded in a text? What prescriptions about maleness or femaleness does a text promulgate? How does understanding gender in a text help us better understand our culture and our society? Examining these issues may help us to construct ways in which the oppressive aspects of gender, for both women and men, may be overcome.

STRENGTHS AND WEAKNESSES OF FEMINIST CRITICISM

The previous analysis indicates the variety of approaches in feminist criticism and the different kinds of conclusions that feminist critics can draw about a text. Yet all feminist critics share the desire to overcome the unjust neglect of women as readers and writers, and the Christian can sympathize with this basic feminist principle. Although sometimes overstated, the feminist indictment of the literary and critical tradition contains much truth. Christian critics, operating with the biblical understanding of the equal value of male and female persons and perspectives, can applaud the efforts of feminist critics to overcome sexual injustice and to affirm women's contributions to literature.

True, feminist literary criticism undoubtedly has its weaknesses. For one thing, it can easily become too simplistic, ignoring the complexity of a work to concentrate on its female characters or feminine themes. In addition, some feminist critics are too quick to throw out the baby with the bath water, issuing a blanket condemnation of any work that depicts sexism without considering its historical context or other qualities that may in some ways redeem it. And some feminist criticism, primarily some of the earliest criticism, demonstrated intense rage and hostility toward men.

But, despite these failings, feminist criticism has provided many new and helpful ways for us to read texts. It has uncovered and recovered numerous important female literary voices. Because of feminist criticism, women today hear more of their concerns addressed in literature, and men encounter new ideas and learn new perspectives. Feminist criticism has also broadened our view of what literature is. We now have a far better sense of the variety of ways in which human beings have expressed themselves and explored the potentials of God's world in literature. Furthermore, the emphasis that both gynocriticism and social constructionism have placed on the cultural and social contexts of literature has played an important role in the movement away from formalism and the return to a grounding of a text in the historical world. This kind of approach is valuable, for it sees literature as a means of participating in life rather than as an isolated aesthetic object.

Perhaps the greatest strength of feminist criticism,

however, is its insistence that no criticism is neutral, objective, or impersonal. What has been called objective scholarship actually has its own agenda, its own set of priorities and goals. Some Christian critics assume that they can perform an objective "literary" reading and then, as T. S. Eliot once said, *complete* the reading by evaluating the social significance of the work in the light of Christian principles. Such an approach is the logical way to make criticism "Christian" if we assume that the aesthetic and the ethical are discrete categories of thought, as many of the New Critics have insisted. John Crowe Ransom, for instance, argues, "The business of the literary critic is exclusively with an aesthetic criticism. The business of the moralist will naturally, and properly, be with something else" (884). Ransom claims that the meaning of a poem lies in a different realm than that of the ethical.

The feminist critics of the 1970s were some of the first to break with this kind of formal approach. By incorporating ethical commitment into the critical act, feminist criticism goes against the longstanding assertion of New Criticism that criticism is objective and neutral. One of the most basic feminist contentions, according to Toril Moi, is "that no criticism is 'value-free,' that we all speak from a specific position shaped by cultural, social, political and personal factors" (43). So-called objective criticism carries its own set of values, which elevates concepts of beauty and paradox above concepts of right and wrong by claiming that as critics we should only be concerned with the former. Feminist critics, however, consciously acknowledge and purposely apply their values in their criticism and believe that the aesthetic and the ethical can be distinguished but not separated.

If a work's morality is an integral part of its essence, our response and evaluation will include some kind of moral judgment. Feminist critics urge us to be more conscious of the values we apply in our reading; they do not hesitate to suggest that a sexist work is a flawed work, that male critics have often misjudged the writing of women, and that the traditional canon of great works of literature may be biased and incomplete. Also, because they see art as part of life, feminist critics go beyond a close reading of a text to consider other aspects of literary practices, such as the author's life, historical and social influences on the work, and women's responses as readers.

SOME EMBRYONIC IDEAS FOR CHRISTIAN CRITICISM

With its ethical commitment and its emphasis on the influence of belief on criticism, feminist literary criticism has important similarities to the kind of criticism that Christian scholars produce. The various ethical dimensions of feminist literary criticism may provide some models of ways to apply religious beliefs while reading literature. Like feminist critics, the Christian critic regards beliefs about life rather than an interpretive technique as the distinguishing characteristic of literary study. While feminists ground their criticism in the belief that women are unjustly oppressed, Christians ground their criticism in basic beliefs about the nature of God, human beings, and language. Like feminist criticism, Christian criticism must be committed criticism. It should not merely explore a hypothesis; it should attempt to serve God and humanity.

One requirement Christians should make of their criticism is that it promote God's kingdom. In reading and commenting on literary works, Christians should seek to establish a world characterized by the Hebrew concept of *shalom*. Just as feminist criticism wants to change the world to make conditions better for women, so Christian criticism should be driven by a desire to bring about the conditions in which all human beings can live together in what Nicholas Wolterstorff calls "that special mode of flourishing which is shalom: harmony and delight in relation to God and fellows and nature" (222). This larger vision of harmony and right relationship includes but goes beyond the narrower concerns of feminist criticism. A concern to promote *shalom* does not mean that the critic will demand that all texts be overtly moralistic or even model the good. God's kingdom can be promoted by means of negative examples as well as positive, as the stories in the Bible demonstrate. But analysis of literature needs to take into account the ethics of reading and to examine how texts promote social justice, personal growth, appreciation of beauty, and a spirit of delight.

The images-of-women approach of feminist criticism suggests the importance of considering how seeing certain patterns in literary works affects the reader. In applying this approach, Christians should not only be concerned with how Christian characters are depicted in literature, although that kind of study certainly has value. Rather, they should examine the images of humanity that a text includes and inquire whether such images are accurate and useful. If human beings are depicted as depraved, for example, is the depiction useful or merely despairing? Does a work justly depict oppressed groups, or does it simply promulgate racist and sexist attitudes? Applying these ethical concerns to aesthetic evaluations will establish new criteria for what makes a text "good" in the eyes of a Christian. Literary works must not ask a reader to betray her or his nature, which is that of a unique and valuable individual created in God's image. These are the ethics of reading that should concern the Christian critic.

Another aspect of Christian criticism is suggested by gynocriticism. Just as gynocritics pay special attention to overlooked women writers, so we must pay special attention to overlooked Christian writers, especially in contemporary literature. While Christian works of an earlier time were seldom neglected, the declining cultural influence of Christianity in the nineteenth and twentieth centuries has sometimes resulted in the critical disparagement of certain authors, such as Harriet Beecher Stowe, Christina Rossetti, and Isaac Watts. Contemporary Christian writers — for the most part isolated from the structures of institutional power that control success (major research universities, reviewers of *The New York Times*, key editors and publishers) — have even greater difficulty achieving recognition. Surely one of the tasks of Christian criticism must be to assess and proclaim the quality of writing by contemporary Christians.

Similarly, works that contain Christian principles, ideas, and images are increasingly misunderstood by contemporary readers. We have only to look at recent readings of *Paradise Lost* to see how those Christian works that have survived in the traditional canon are now being distorted and de-Christianized. Works with Christian references need the understanding and informed criticism that a Christian critic can bring to them. Most Christian criticism in the last decade takes this kind of approach, for as Christian students go to graduate school, they often write about something with which they are familiar.

But Christian criticism must also go beyond this self-centered concern to consider and promote the value of other kinds of literature that have been neglected or suppressed. The concern for the poor and oppressed that is mandated throughout the Old and New Testament should prompt a concern for those writers and texts that have been unjustly overlooked in traditional criticism. The directive to love your neighbor suggests that Christians need to encounter and champion the other ways of life expressed in texts by women, blacks, Native Americans, and Third World writers. Many of the currently debated issues concerning the canon need careful evaluation in light of Christian beliefs.

Poststructuralism can also suggest possibilities for the Christian critic. While rejecting the poststructuralist destruction of Western metaphysics and contempt for authority, Christians do want to be able to understand how temporal authorities have attempted to impose their conceptions of truth upon others. In order to work effectively for *shalom*, Christians must understand how meaning is often determined by social and cultural situations. Social constructionism may help Christians to understand themselves and their own limited knowledge better and to be able to love their neighbor more effectively.

While this essay certainly has not explored all the implications of feminist literary criticism for Christian criticism, these initial thoughts may indicate future possibilities for reflection and examination. The ethical dimensions of feminist literary criticism provide many admirable examples.

WORKS CITED

Cixous, Helene. "The Laugh of the Medusa." In *New French Feminism: An Anthology,* ed. Elaine Marks and Isabelle de Courtivron, 245-64. Amherst: University of Massachusetts Press, 1980.

Eliot, T. S. "Religion and Literature." In *Religion and Modern Literature: Essays on Theory and Criticism,* ed. G. B. Tennyson and Edward E. Ericson, Jr., 21-45. Grand Rapids: Eerdmans, 1975.

Fetterley, Judith. *The Resisting Reader: A Feminist Approach to American Fiction.* Bloomington: Indiana University Press, 1978.

Greene, Gayle, and Coppelia Kahn. "Feminist Scholarship and the Social Construction of Woman." In *Making a Difference: Feminist Literary Criticism,* ed. Gayle Greene and Coppelia Kahn, 1-36. London: Methuen, 1985.

Harris, Wendell V. "Toward an Ecological Criticism: Contextual versus Unconditioned Literary Theory." *College English* 48 (1986): 116-31.

Holly, Marcia. "Consciousness and Authenticity: Toward a Feminist Aesthetic." In *Feminist Literary Criticism: Explorations in Theory,* ed. Josephine Donovan, 38-47. Lexington: University Press of Kentucky, 1975.

Irigaray, Luce. *This Sex Which Is Not One.* Trans. Catherine Porter and Carolyn Burke. Ithaca: Cornell University Press, 1985.

Kolodny, Annette. "Turning the Lens on 'The Panther Captivity': A Feminist Exercise in Practical Criticism." In *Writing and Sexual Difference,* ed. Elizabeth Abel, 159-75. Chicago: University of Chicago Press, 1982.

Moi, Toril. *Sexual/Textual Politics: Feminist Literary Theory.* London: Methuen, 1985.

Ransom, John Crowe. "Criticism as Pure Speculation." In *Critical Theory Since Plato,* ed. Hazard Adams, 881-90. New York: Harcourt Brace Jovanovich, 1971.

Showalter, Elaine. "Feminist Criticism in the Wilderness." In *The New Feminist Criticism: Essays on Women, Literature, and Theory,* ed. Elaine Showalter, 243-70. New York: Pantheon, 1985.

———. "Toward a Feminist Poetic." In *The New Feminist Criticism: Essays on Women, Literature, and Theory,* ed. Elaine Showalter, 125-43. New York: Pantheon, 1985.

Wolterstorff, Nicholas. "Christianity and Social Justice." *Christian Scholar's Review* 16 (1987): 211-28.

Recommended Introductions to Feminist Literary Criticism

Abel, Elizabeth, ed. *Writing and Sexual Difference.* Chicago: University of Chicago Press, 1982.

Greene, Gayle, and Coppelia Kahn, eds. *Making a Difference: Feminist Literary Criticism.* London: Methuen, 1985.

Moi, Toril. *Sexual/Textual Politics: Feminist Literary Theory.* London: Methuen, 1985.

Ruthven, K. K. *Feminist Literary Studies: An Introduction.* Cambridge: Cambridge University Press, 1984.

Showalter, Elaine, ed. *The New Feminist Criticism: Essays on Women, Literature, and Theory.* New York: Pantheon, 1985.

THE NEW HISTORICISM

John D. Cox

DEFINITIONS AND SOURCES

THE TERM "NEW HISTORICISM" IS COMMONLY USED TO identify a literary critical movement that arose principally in American universities in the 1980s. New Historicism differs from older modes of literary history by focusing on social history rather than on documentary history — that is, by interpreting literature as a cultural product rather than by documenting a literary or biographical record chronologically. New Historicists appeal to social history not simply as a source of illumination for historical references, allusions, and linguistic peculiarities of texts, but also as the site where a symbiotic relationship can be discovered between society and literature. Since this kind of relationship pertains to the present as well as the past, historical understanding inevitably involves the critic's own experience and values. Literature as art is thus much less important than literature as cultural artifact, and criticism as interpretation of the text is less important than the critic as a self-consciously cultural product elucidating how past literary artifacts interact with their social context. Indeed, while New Historicism privileges literary texts as objects of analysis, it need not do so theoretically, since it is potentially a method for examining any historical-cultural manifestation. Steven Mullaney thus begins his discussion of Shakespeare's history plays with a detailed analysis of the sixteenth-century *Wunderkammer*, a German curio cabinet or proto-museum.

New Historicism has been recently canonized in an ongoing series of monographs from the University of California Press, under the general editorship of Stephen Greenblatt. A 1987 advertisement in *The New York Review of Books* gives this description of the series:

> Literary criticism is witnessing, in strikingly original ways, a return to the historical embeddedness of literary production, while the study of history is witnessing innovative explorations of the symbolic constructions of reality. This series highlights the emergence of a powerful new interpretive paradigm with works directed not only to literature but to politics, social practices, religious beliefs, and cultural conflicts.

These are large claims, and they deserve careful examination.

Greenblatt's own book, *Renaissance Self-Fashioning from More to Shakespeare*, is widely regarded as the fountainhead of this particular poststructuralist school and remains its finest and most provocative example to date. Greenblatt first used the term "New Historicism" in his introduction to *The Power of Forms in the English Renaissance*, and it immediately caught on, in contrast to other terms that Greenblatt had tried unsuccessfully to use in describing his method (or so Greenblatt was later to claim in H. Aram Veeser's collection of essays called *The New Historicism*). Herbert Lindenberger's essay is an excellent overview of and accessible theoretical introduction to New Historicism, though Lindenberger takes issue with the term "historicism" and pointedly uses "New History" instead (22, n. 4). Polemical introductions to New Historicism can be found in Jonathan Dollimore (*Radical Tragedy* 5-8), Dollimore and Alan Sinfield (2-17), John Drakakis (1-25), and Greenblatt (*The Power of Forms* 3-6; introduction to *The New Historicism* 1-14). The winter 1986 number of *English Literary Renaissance* is

devoted entirely to essays in the New Historicist mode. Duke
University's journal, *The South Atlantic Quarterly,* has recently
been reconceived and now advertises itself in New Historicist
terms as "characterized by its interest in how social, political,
class and gender issues affect the creating of literature." Edward
Pechter has written a thoughtful critique of New Historicism,
wisely refraining from diatribe or attempted demolition ("nothing I have said undermines the new-historicist enterprise"
[298]), and preferring instead to point out tacit assumptions
and commitments of value: "I am leaving them [New Histori-
cists] naked only in the sense that all interpreters are naked"
(298).

Despite Lindenberger's demurrer, "historicism" is a useful
term for this school. For the New Historicism would not be
possible were it not for the old historicism of Marx, to which
most practitioners of the new school are explicitly indebted.
"Cultural materialism" is an example of that indebtedness, since
this term, which British critics tend to prefer to "New Historicism," is borrowed from Raymond Williams, who adapts it from
Marx. Oliver O'Donovan's critique of generic historicism (58-
75) is therefore illuminating for the New Historicism in particular. Historicism, O'Donovan points out, locates the source
of moral value within human history itself: what we should be
is revealed in the process of our historical becoming. Williams'
assertion (following Marx) that if we have learned anything,
we have learned that we make our own history (13-14) is thus
more than a description of a secular culture's historical self-
awareness: it is in effect an assertion that "the end of history is
for history to become 'conscious of itself.' That is to say, the
emergence of historicist philosophy is itself the end which
history serves" (O'Donovan 68). The implicit triumphalism of
the New Historicism (in the tone of the advertisement cited
previously, for example) is generically related to the triumphalism of nineteenth-century historicism and its affinity with social evolution. To cite a particular critical example, the quasi-
Darwinian historicism that underlay early criticism of medieval

religious drama was insightfully identified by O. B. Hardison (1-34), and a more sophisticated version of this historicism has begun to appear again in the neo-Marxist studies of medieval drama by Walter Cohen and Michael Bristol.

Not all New Historicists are contented bedfellows with neo-Marxism, and neo-Marxists are becoming increasingly sharp in their remarks about New Historicism. Stephen Greenblatt in particular is anxious to distinguish what he does from Marxist criticism, and it is useful to ask what difference he sees. Instead of "cultural materialism," Greenblatt prefers the term "cultural poetics" to describe his enterprise: "Studies in Cultural Poetics" is the subtitle of the series from California, and Greenblatt's introductory essay in Veeser's collection is called "Towards a Poetics of Culture." Behind this distinction between "materialism" and "poetics" can be glimpsed the nineteenth-century distinction between idealist and materialist historicism: for the former, the imagination (the *geistliche* human essence and the origin of poetry) provided access to truth not apprehended by the empirical social sciences that figure so importantly for Marx. While Greenblatt thus uses quasi-Marxist phrases like "the historical embeddedness of literary production," he is not interested in economic determinism as a mechanism for explaining the evolution of literary forms. In this he contrasts strongly with more strictly neo-Marxist critics like Cohen, Dollimore, Bristol, and Fredric Jameson, and his methodology is being attacked as "formalist" and "mannerist" by critics who claim to be more "historical" — that is, more closely aligned with the cultural left (Alan Liu and Carolyn Porter, for example). Reviewing Greenblatt's *Learning to Curse* from a Marxist perspective, Terry Eagleton wittily pillories Greenblatt's fascination with the way the powerful always exploit the powerless: "The claim that human emancipation is a dead duck is offered to us . . . as an eternal verity, along with the Virgin Birth and the Platonic Forms."

Nonetheless, Greenblatt is a historicist, as his own chosen label proclaims, and his trenchant observations about the effects of social class and power are, in effect, well described by O'Donovan:

> We are used . . . to seeing evolutionary moralists sidestep from natural history [i.e., biology] into social anthropology, so that moral values are associated, in the manner most congenial to historicist thought, with human *culture,* a decision which implies a subjective answer, whether rationalist or voluntarist, to the question [whether moral order is inherent or merely perceived] (68).

Greenblatt has learned to think of culture anthropologically as a sign system — hence the phrase "symbolic constructions of reality" in the advertisement for the monograph series. Particularly important here is the influence of Clifford Geertz, whose historicist assumption Greenblatt quotes approvingly in *Renaissance Self-Fashioning:* "There is no such thing as a human nature independent of culture" (3). (Compare a similar metaphysical affirmation — or denial — in Greenblatt's *Shakespearean Negotiations:* "There is no escape from contingency" [3].) Greenblatt's interdisciplinary approach to literature is thus in part a product of the times, for Geertz's influence can be seen not only in anthropology, sociology, and literary criticism but also in history (Stone 14) and even in New Testament studies (Meeks 15, 155-56).

Recognizing New Historicism as part of a broad cultural development is helpful in understanding its premises. Edward Pechter suggests that Greenblatt simply opts for a pessimistic view of the world summarized in the cliché "It's a jungle out there" (301). But Greenblatt's fascination with power relations is consistent with his historicism, for both belong to what O'Donovan describes as a "totalitarianism which allows the critic no ground of rationality unless he is the voice of a 'movement'" (73). Founding a University of California Press series and starting a journal — *Representations* — are unmistakable gestures of academic power, the aim of which is to demonstrate the power of a critical movement. "The critic must describe the future of the culture," says O'Donovan of historicism, "in a way that justifies his concerns; and he must show that he speaks for a constituency sufficiently large or sufficiently determined to make his predictions come true" (73). Even allowing for the rhetoric of advertising, the claim that "a powerful new interpretive paradigm" has emerged is a recognizable historicist claim.

HOW MIGHT CHRISTIANS RESPOND?

To identify the premises of a critical school is not to reject it but to clarify the issues, so that as Christians we can properly qualify those premises and still, in Wallace Stevens' phrase, "learn the speech of the place," which is the language in which we can best be understood.[1] The appropriate model here, as in everything, is God incarnate, for Jesus "learned the speech" of first-century Judaism in Palestine but qualified it in the interest of a mission and ministry that we recognize historically to be distinctively "Christian." Augustine, too, learned the speech of his place — in his case, neo-Platonism:

> If those who are called philosophers, especially the Platonists, have said things which are indeed true and are well accommodated to our faith, they should not be feared; rather, what they have said should be taken from them as from unjust possessors and converted to our use. (*On Christian Doctrine* 75)

We may not regard the results of Augustine's neo-Platonic "language" as entirely benign, but no language is capable of

---

1. The "linguistic turn" in poststructuralist critical theory would appear to assert that we can be understood *only* in "the speech of the place" (a position Stevens himself anticipates). But this is an exaggeration. In common experience, appropriate gestures and a little goodwill can communicate a great deal, even without verbal language, though the scope of such conversation is obviously limited. If one wishes to expand the scope (intellectually and every other way), one must master the language, and that, in effect, is what I am urging we must do with the "language" of critical theory, even if, as Christians, we always speak, as it were, with a strong accent.

immediate transparent impact on all its hearers (especially if they don't know it), and a language of some kind is imperative, at least if one wishes to communicate. Augustine's principle is therefore useful for a Christian response to poststructuralism in general and to New Historicism in particular.

It is important to notice first of all that New Historicism is no more or less un-Christian than the old "New Criticism," in which most current teachers of literature were trained before the late 1970s. Indeed, points made against the New Criticism by New Historicists are often points with which a thoughtful Christian might well feel compelled to agree. The New Critical attempt to read texts as if they were apolitical and ahistorical is itself a tacit political gesture: situating oneself "above" or "outside" history or politics is a concession to the status quo and therefore an implicitly conservative commitment. The political conservatism of the Imagists who were influential in the founding of New Criticism — Eliot and Pound in particular — is symptomatic, as New Historicists frequently point out. By the same token, although Northrop Frye's archetypal criticism seemed quite distinct from New Criticism when it first appeared, in retrospect Frye's attempt to make criticism "scientific" and his insistence that it be apolitical indicate shared assumptions with New Criticism at a deep level.

New Historicism argues not only that critics are inevitably implicated in their criticism but also that artists are implicated in their art. Holding the mirror up to nature can thus be compared to photographing an event for the news: the photographer chooses a subject (thus rejecting others), delimits it, and inevitably influences its outcome. Assisting the victim of an assault one hopes to film is an obvious way to influence the outcome of what one observes, but one just as certainly influences the outcome if one takes the morally dubious course of failing to assist the victim in the interest of filming. In neither case can one claim to be "outside" or "above" the incident; rather, one participates in and contributes to the incident. As Greenblatt points out in his own discussion of the mirror image from *Hamlet*, "Only if we reinvest the mirror image with a sense of *pressure* as well as form can it convey something of its original strangeness and magic" (*Shakespearean Negotiations* 8; my emphasis). New Historicism thus approaches historical artifacts not merely *against a background* of social and political history but as *objects* of a social history that they themselves "represent" — not mimetically but as anthropological or political participants in a culture, like objects in a museum or an ambassador who represents the "pressure" as well as the form of his native country. This kind of representation is what Greenblatt had in mind when he titled the journal he founded.

To approach historical artifacts as cultural symbols is to acknowledge their participation in structures of social privilege or social deprivation, and this approach therefore explains the New Historicist focus on power relations. Spenser's *Faerie Queene*, for example, is not merely an intricate and intriguing set of imaginative literary symbols: its very literary method is itself a symbol of social exclusivity. This is a point, as Michael Murrin suggests, that Spenser himself may have learned from Cicero, who declares that "a poem full of obscure allusions can from its nature only win the approbation of the few" (quoted by Murrin 9). Spenser expresses this opinion in a number of ways in *The Faerie Queene*, and his social purpose is explicit in his prefatory letter to Raleigh: "The general end of all the book is to fashion a *gentleman* or *noble person* in virtuous and gentle discipline" (my emphasis). Spenser aims at the social elite, and he aims to make them better — more virtuous. Since Spenser takes virtue to be the criterion of nobility to begin with, his aim is apparently to make noble persons more noble, or the exclusive more exclusive. This way of understanding Spenser is an example of how New Historicism tends to shift the emphasis from the text alone to the social conditions that gave rise to the text and which the text itself participates in and contributes to. (Compare Greenblatt, *Renaissance Self-Fashioning* 157-92.) *The Faerie Queene* is thus only one sign (or "representation") among many signs of aristocratic culture in late sixteenth-century England, all of which require intensive interpretation, like the *Wunderkammern* discussed by Mullaney. This is why the advertisement for the monograph series refers to "politics, social practices, religious beliefs, and cultural conflicts."

The New Historicist interest in power relations undoubtedly focuses on the grim and sinister aspects of human social life — on exploitation, greed, and destructive self-promotion. But this focus is less innovative from a Christian perspective than it is, perhaps, from the perspective of New Criticism, which emphasizes aesthetic detachment and organic form. For the assumption that human beings devour one another like monsters of the deep is a patristic commonplace borrowed from rabbinic tradition, and it is especially important for Augustine (Markus 72-104). This is in fact a point that Max Weber understood. In opposing the premise that political good follows from political good and evil from evil, Weber points to the early Christians, who "knew full well the world is governed by demons and that he who lets himself in for politics, that is, for power and force as means, contracts with diabolical powers, and for his action it is *not* true that good can follow only from good and evil only from evil, but that often the opposite is true. Anyone who fails to see this is, indeed, a political infant" (123).

Patristic anticipation of some major New Historicist assumptions indicates that the historicist tendency to regard the modern period teleologically as the fruition of history needs to be qualified: on the contrary, New Historicism may be recovering some very old ideas in the Christian tradition. Augustine, for example, understands political life as a collective expression of *libido dominandi* — the desire for power: "The city of this world . . . aims at domination but is itself dominated by that very lust of domination" (*City of God* 5). Hence Augustine's rejection of Cicero's claim that the state should be defined in terms of justice, as it had been since Plato: "Remove justice, then, and what are kingdoms but gangs of criminals on a large scale?" (*City of God* 139). This rhetorical question introduces

Augustine's well-known story of Alexander the Great and the pirate. When Alexander demanded to know the pirate's intention in infesting the sea, "the pirate answered, with uninhibited insolence, 'The same as yours, in infesting the earth! But because I do it with a tiny craft, I'm called a pirate; because you have a mighty navy, you're called an emperor'" (*City of God* 139). Augustine's refusal to define human social and political life in terms of justice is not the only way Christians have thought about society and politics, but it importantly qualifies the New Historicist claim that such a position is inherently denied by Christianity or that it is the newly ripened fruit of modern historical self-consciousness.

Augustine's position, moreover, allows for more than a negative qualification (i.e., that what New Historicism puts forward is not as innovative as it claims). Augustine's pessimistic sense of social and political life emerges from (and is therefore compatible with) an affirmation regarding created order that New Historicism does not make.[2] For the conception of a created order is what historicism fundamentally denies: human nature can be understood only in the context of culture, as Geertz claims, and culture emerges in history. That is why "there is no escape from contingency." Historicism thus implicitly denies the Christian doctrine of creation along with its counterpart, God's redemptive revelation in history, for if history yields its own meaning (or, in other words, if what we know is that we make our own

2. I borrow the phrase "created order" from O'Donovan (*Resurrection and Moral Order* 31-52), as I have borrowed many other things in this essay, not because I regard his book as definitive but because it is the best recent attempt to describe ethics comprehensively from a theological perspective, and the implicit ethical commitment of New Historicism is one of the features that make it compelling to Christians. "Created order" is not to be confused with "natural order": the former necessarily assumes a Creator, while the latter does not. Moreover, the Christian sense of created order affirms that the Creator is also active redemptively in history, and the doctrine is therefore inherently dynamic. At the same time, however, to say that the Creator is active in history clearly affirms more than that we make our own history, as historicists aver.

history), then the created order as God has established and historically redeemed it is at best irrelevant and at worst a cultural fiction designed to perpetuate false consciousness and preserve the structures of social injustice.

THE IMPLICATIONS FOR PRACTICAL CRITICISM

What difference does the Christian affirmation of created order make in practical criticism? For one thing, it need not — indeed, should not — deny the truth of what New Historicism has to offer. Human social and political structures are inevitably fallible because human beings are fallible, and New Historicist insights about power, greed, lust, envy, and conspicuous consumption can be denied only at the risk of denying the truth about ourselves. Indeed, for evangelical Protestants in particular, New Historicism is salutary (as the old historicism — especially Marx's — is also salutary), for they are strikingly naive about the temptations of power and wealth and blind to structures of social injustice, as Billy Graham's coziness with presidents and recent scandals among evangelists have vividly illustrated.

What can be denied, however, is that the truth about human history consists of nothing more than mutual predation. Let us consider an example that illustrates New Historicist assumptions at work in practical literary criticism.

In a brilliant essay on Shakespeare's *Midsummer Night's Dream,* Louis Montrose has pointed out how the structures of gender inequality function in that play to sanction the Elizabethan status quo, which consisted of an unmarried queen on the throne (i.e., with the balance of power in her hands) in a social and political world that presumed male prerogative. In Montrose's reading, Bottom's amour with Titania, the fairy queen, becomes a male sexual fantasy involving subversive violation of Queen Elizabeth's person, with its implicit violation of her power. In support of this reading, Montrose points to a contemporary

dream recounted by Simon Forman, in which Forman accosted
the queen in her nightdress, took her from a weaver who was
kissing her, and then joked bawdily with her himself (32-33).
Montrose's point about Forman's dream is not, of course, that
Shakespeare knew it as a source (despite the striking coincidence
of a weaver making love to the most famous fairy queen of all),
but that it is contemporary evidence of something outside
Shakespeare's play being precisely what Montrose claims
Shakespeare's play to be. In other words, Montrose's essay identifies a striking example of what Greenblatt calls "the circulation
of social energy" (*Shakespearean Negotiations* 1-20).

Montrose is surely right in pointing to exploitative aspects
of male dominance in the late sixteenth century, particularly at
court. The queen herself knew better than anyone how impor-
tunate male courtiers could be with an unmarried queen and
how ruthless and duplicitous she had to be to maintain her
prerogative. Contemporary Erastian idealization of the queen
and her court in fact contained and expressed the real tensions
of power politics.[3] All this can be acknowledged, however,
without acknowledging that Montrose has satisfactorily accounted for *A Midsummer Night's Dream*. His emphasis on the
perversities of power relations (real though those perversities
are) virtually effaces the play's festive focus on marriage, which
is arguably an instituted part of the created order (O'Donovan
69): the duke's wedding is anticipated in the play's opening lines
and celebrated at its close. Moreover, Shakespeare's understanding of marriage as the fruitful union of opposites (however
imperfectly he may have rendered it) is more than idealized
libido: it is a celebration of created order, evident everywhere in
the play's structure and imagery, from the careful alternation of

3. Montrose has explored the relationship between Elizabethan power
and female idealization more insightfully than almost anyone, but it was
initially suggested in Greenblatt's discussion of "Petrarchan politics" (*Renaissance Self-Fashioning* 142-46, 166). Moreover, Greenblatt adapted this phrase
from Orgel's "Platonic politics," found in Orgel's discussion of the Jacobean
court masque (1:49-75).

day and night, city and forest, to the subtle interweaving of the
classical and native dramatic traditions, which is symbolized in
part by the image of Bottom in the arms of Titania. Montrose's
exclusive focus on the court is characteristic of New Historicism
and its fascination with power, as Edward Pechter points out
(296). In Montrose's case this focus has the effect of virtually
eliminating Shakespeare's native dramatic tradition as an object
of critical interest or historical importance. In an argument
much influenced by Montrose, Leonard Tennenhouse goes so
far as to assert that "it was to Sir Philip Sidney's writing [that]
Shakespeare and his contemporaries regularly turned for their
inspiration" (18), even though Sidney himself eschewed the
popular tradition that Shakespeare belonged to.

In sum, while New Historicism is insightful about the
human capacity for defacing the created order, it is not a critical
methodology that has any interest in the claims of the created
order itself. Moreover, it also has no interest in history as the scene
of God's redemptive drama. Greenblatt's understanding of the
Reformers, for example, is informed by his assumption (which is
a fundamentally historicist assumption) that historical movements are essentially power struggles between an old order and a
new one: "Reformers like Tyndale are attempting, in effect, a
seizure of power" (*Renaissance Self-Fashioning* 99). What the
Reformers were attempting to recover anew in the way of God's
redemptive presence in human history is important for Greenblatt only insofar as it becomes a party line with sufficient
consequence to produce political and social conflict. He is right,
of course, to understand the Reformation in a particular political
and social context and to point out in effect that the Reformers
frequently exercised too little charity, uncritically embraced royal
power as a means of opposing the corrupt power of the church,
and often fell prey to self-serving historicist fantasies, as in the
Acts and Monuments of John Foxe. Foxe in fact revived or perpetuated early Christian attempts to understand secular history
eschatologically, as it had been understood, for example, in the
Theodosian settlement that Augustine opposed (Markus 1-21).

Greenblatt's perceptiveness about Tyndale's interest in power may therefore be understood as a case of one historicist recognizing another. But what Greenblatt does not recognize is that Tyndale and More alike — despite their grievous differences — were involved in more than a power struggle: they were both involved in a profound attempt to recover the integrity of the gospel. While Greenblatt brilliantly illuminates the tragedy of their divisive failure, he has little grasp of what they sought to achieve, for whatever else they make of the Reformation, New Historicists have no interest in it as a manifestation of God's redemptive presence in history.

On one level what Montrose and Greenblatt lack as representative New Historicists is charity — the ability to understand human failure in the light of grace. On another level, however, the result might well be called a failure of historical imagination, which is a particularly damaging lapse in a methodology based on historical principles. For the inability to see anything in history but *libido dominandi* is a failure to recognize how much one's own moral insight depends on the acquired understanding of past generations. The refinement of moral vision happens gradually, as in the recognition of slavery as an evil, or the subordination of women. To assess past failure in light of present insight is not therefore wrong, but it is certainly partial and is therefore generically related to the inability to recognize and allow for cultural differences in any context. The implicit ethical triumphalism of New Historicism is still another feature it shares with nineteenth-century historicism, which was inclined to think of contemporary Europe as the finest specimen of evolutionary development, both culturally and historically, and as the means by which the defects of all other cultures ought to be measured.

Recognizing the limitations of New Historicism, however, should not be taken as a denial of the gifts it offers. Following Augustine's advice, we need to accept those gifts, insofar as they are "true and are well accommodated to our faith," and convert them to our use.

Fifty years ago C. S. Lewis remarked that "Spenser was the

instrument of a detestable policy in Ireland, and in his fifth book
[of *The Faerie Queene*] the wickedness he had shared begins to
corrupt his imagination" (*Allegory of Love* 349). This remark is
very much in the spirit of New Historicism, though it does not
go nearly as far as recent New Historicism has made it possible
for us to go. Despite his expressed ambivalence about the court,
Spenser's career follows a recognizable sixteenth-century pattern
of aspiring social and political ambition, and his imagination is
more affected by that pattern than Lewis recognizes. As Greenblatt points out, "Even when he most bitterly criticizes its abuses
or records its brutalities, Spenser loves power and attempts to link
his own art ever more closely with its symbolic and literal embodiment" (*Renaissance Self-Fashioning* 173-74). The same might
well be said of Sidney's *Arcadia*, which Lewis calls "a kind of
touchstone. What a man thinks of it, far more than what he
thinks of Shakespeare or Spenser or Donne, tests the depth of his
sympathy with the sixteenth century" (*English Literature* 339).
Lewis did not fully see what New Historicism sees because Lewis
was himself so deeply indebted to the means of social mobility —
particularly an educational system — first established in the sixteenth century. One can hear his affirmation of that system in his
comment on Sidney's Pamela and Philoclea: "Here are great
ladies; the first fruits of returning civilization and an earnest that
this civilization will rise high and last long" (*English Literature*
338). By the same token, Lewis's phrase "What a man thinks of
it" would no longer be used by any sensitive critic, because the
phrase so clearly conveys a gender arrogance that was an unex-
amined product of Lewis's education.

To understand that both Spenser and one of his best
twentieth-century interpreters had feet of clay should not,
however, be the grounds for dismissing them, either in triumph
or in despair. We may be able to see more clearly than we ever
have the extent to which Spenser's imagination was corrupted
by power (as Lewis put it), but that does not eradicate Spenser's
moral sensitivity in other respects, particularly in his understanding of friendship and psycho-sexual relationships and in
his celebration of the created order. In *Amoretti* his perception

of sexual love as enabled and redeemed by the drama of Christ's death and resurrection is one of the most striking and profound renderings of that relationship in English:

> And that thy love we weighing worthily,
> may likewise love thee for the same again;
> and for thy sake that all like dear didst buy,
> with love may one another entertain.

Spenser's theory of allegory may indeed be tainted by social aspiration, but he uses allegory, as Jonson typically does not, to present a mystery that owes nothing to human power (however much the powerful sought to exploit it for their own ends) and that therefore lies outside the scope of New Historicism. Moreover, Spenser not only presents but also preserves that mystery by means of allegory, so that we understand precisely as St. Paul says we do — "through a glass darkly" (1 Cor. 13:12). Greenblatt's critique of allegory is therefore wide of the mark where Spenser is concerned:

> Allegory may dream of presenting the thing itself — not particular instances of sin or goodness, but Sin and Goodness themselves directly acting in the moral world they also constitute — but its deeper purpose and its actual effect is to acknowledge the darkness, the arbitrariness, and the void that underlie, and paradoxically make possible, all representation of realms of light, order, and presence. Insofar as the project of mimesis is the direct representation of a stable, objective reality, allegory, in attempting and always failing to present Reality, inevitably reveals the impossibility of this project. This impossibility is precisely the foundation upon which all representation, indeed all discourse, is constructed. (*Allegory and Representation* vii-viii)

Our inability to represent Reality precisely is a sign of our human creatureliness that Spenser's allegory preserves. But it does not follow that our inability is a sign of ultimate darkness, arbitrariness, and void: that is more than agnosticism can affirm. By the gift of grace and by the eye of faith, we know the substance of things hoped for, and we possess the evidence of things not seen.

In short, New Historicism enables us to perceive the cultural embeddedness of both historic art and historic criticism: that is its principal gift to the current critical scene. It is indeed a powerful gift, as the monograph advertisement claims, and it has been used brilliantly and insightfully by a number of critics. Paradoxically, it will undoubtedly be used less brilliantly and less insightfully as it gains wider application and becomes the movement Greenblatt hopes to make of it. But that is an inherent human difficulty, originating not in the model itself but in the fallibility of those who use it. Like New Criticism before it, the wider the acceptance the methodology gains, the weaker will be many of its adherents and the less credible its applications. Various defects in the model itself have been pointed out by Pechter as well as here. To summarize: New Historicism's greatest strength (a compelling revitalization of historicism) is also its greatest weakness. If Lewis was on the edge of New Historicism in 1936, he nonetheless avoided its problems because of his rich sense of the moral order outside a historicist construction. We can therefore return to his criticism, just as we return to *The Faerie Queene*, in spite of his obvious failures. For in both we find a continuing sustenance that New Historicism can only approximate because of its inability to find a foothold in the shifting sand of historical contingency.

WORKS CITED

(Titles with an asterisk are recommended as introductions.)

Augustine. *The City of God.* Trans. Henry Bettenson. Harmondsworth, Middlesex: Penguin Books, 1984.

———. *On Christian Doctrine.* Trans. D. W. Robertson, Jr. Indianapolis: Bobbs-Merrill, 1958.

Bristol, Michael. *Carnival and Theater.* New York: Methuen, 1985.

Cohen, Walter. *Drama of a Nation.* Ithaca: Cornell University Press, 1985.

Dollimore, Jonathan. *Radical Tragedy: Religion, Ideology and Power in the Drama of Shakespeare and His Contemporaries.* Chicago: University of Chicago Press, 1984.

*Dollimore, Jonathan, and Alan Sinfield, eds. *Political Shakespeare: New Essays in Cultural Materialism.* Manchester: Manchester University Press, 1984.

*Drakakis, John, ed. *Alternative Shakespeares.* London: Methuen, 1985.

Eagleton, Terry. "The historian as body-snatcher." *TLS*, 18 Jan. 1991, p. 7.

Frye, Northrop. *Anatomy of Criticism.* Princeton: Princeton University Press, 1957.

Geertz, Clifford. *The Interpretation of Cultures.* New York: Basic Books, 1973.

Greenblatt, Stephen, ed. *Allegory and Representation.* Baltimore: Johns Hopkins University Press, 1981.

———. *Learning to Curse: Essays in Early Modern Culture.* New York: Routledge, 1990.

*———. *The Power of Forms in the English Renaissance.* Norman, Okla.: Pilgrim Books, 1982.

*———. *Renaissance Self-Fashioning from More to Shakespeare.* Chicago: University of Chicago Press, 1980.

———. *Representing the English Renaissance.* Berkeley and Los Angeles: University of California Press, 1988.

———. *Shakespearean Negotiations.* Berkeley and Los Angeles: University of California Press, 1988.

Hardison, O. B. *Christian Rite and Christian Drama in the Middle Ages: Essays in the Origin and Early History of Modern Drama.* Baltimore: Johns Hopkins University Press, 1965.

Jameson, Fredric. *The Political Unconscious: Narrative as a Socially Symbolic Act.* Ithaca: Cornell University Press, 1981.

Lewis, C. S. *The Allegory of Love.* London: Oxford University Press, 1936.

———. *English Literature in the Sixteenth Century (Excluding Drama).* Oxford: Clarendon, 1954.

*Lindenberger, Herbert. "Toward a New History in Literary Study." *Profession* 7 (1984): 16-23.

Liu, Alan. "The Power of Formalism: The New Historicism." *ELH* 58 (1989): 721-71.

Markus, R. A. *Saeculum: History and Society in the Theology of St. Augustine.* New Haven: Yale University Press, 1970.

Meeks, Wayne. *The Moral World of the First Christians*. Philadelphia: Westminster Press, 1986.

Montrose, Louis A. "'Shaping Fantasies': Figurations of Gender and Power in Elizabethan Culture." In *Representing the English Renaissance,* ed. Stephen Greenblatt, 31-64. Berkeley and Los Angeles: University of California Press, 1988.

Mullaney, Steven. "Strange Things, Gross Terms, Curious Customs: The Rehearsal of Cultures in the Late Renaissance." In *Representing the English Renaissance,* ed. Stephen Greenblatt, 65-92. Berkeley and Los Angeles: University of California Press, 1988.

Murrin, Michael M. *The Veil of Allegory*. Chicago: University of Chicago Press, 1968.

O'Donovan, Oliver. *Resurrection and Moral Order: An Outline for Evangelical Ethics*. Grand Rapids: Eerdmans, 1986.

Orgel, Stephen, and Roy Strong. *Inigo Jones: The Theatre of the Stuart Court*. 2 vols. Berkeley and Los Angeles: University of California Press, 1973.

Pechter, Edward. "The New Historicism and Its Discontents: Politicizing Renaissance Drama." *PMLA* 102 (1987): 292-303.

Porter, Carolyn. "Are We Being Historical Yet?" *South Atlantic Quarterly* 87 (1988): 743-86.

Stone, Lawrence. "The Revival of Narrative: Reflections on a New Old History." *Past and Present* 85 (1979): 3-24.

Tennenhouse, Leonard. *Power on Display: The Politics of Shakespeare's Genres*. New York: Methuen, 1986.

Veeser, H. Aram. *The New Historicism*. New York: Routledge, Chapman & Hall, 1989.

Weber, Max. *From Max Weber: Essays in Sociology*. Trans. and ed. H. H. Gerth and C. Wright Mills. London: Kegan, Paul, Trench, Trübner, 1948.

Williams, Raymond. *Marxism and Literature*. Oxford: Oxford University Press, 1977.

CRITICAL THEORY

Mark Walhout

Historians of American literary study invariably characterize the period from 1965 to the present, the period after the New Criticism, as the era of Theory. As those who know the history of the profession might have expected, however, the challenge to bring this twenty-five-year era to an end has already been issued.[1] Theory, it is said, has taken us as far as it can, and now we must turn to something else. Some would have us go back to the Great Books; others would have us move on to something new, like Cultural Studies. What is behind this call to forget or surpass critical theory? Many conflicting factors are involved, of course, including everything from humanist nostalgia to radical politics. But significant among them is the stringent, skeptical analysis to which critical theory itself has been subjected in recent years.[2] Theory has been measured against its own pretension and been found wanting, or so we are told. The future of literary study lies

1. On the history and institutional dynamics of American literary study, see Gerald Graff's *Professing Literature*.
2. For an example of a trenchant critique of contemporary theoreticism in the humanities, see Frederick Crews' polemic against the "Grand Academy of Theory" in *Skeptical Engagements*.

elsewhere. If this is indeed the case, then the present volume is destined to be stillborn, another example of Christian scholars belatedly entering a debate the academy at large has already settled. It is only appropriate, therefore, to conclude this book of theory with an examination of the case against theory.

Before we turn to the debate, however, a few preliminary remarks may be in order. First of all, this chapter is addressed primarily to a somewhat narrower audience than are the preceding essays. The other chapters in this volume have been written primarily for readers interested in practical criticism, in the application of contemporary critical theories to the interpretation of literary texts. This chapter, on the other hand, is addressed chiefly to those who are interested in theory for its own sake, though everyone will be affected by the outcome of the debate. The fact of the matter is that this era of Theory has witnessed the creation of a new literary specialization and a new class of critics. Critical theory is now a field of study in its own right, alongside more traditional fields like the Renaissance and Romanticism.[3] Many literary professionals devote their careers exclusively to critical theory, and many more supplement their primary fields with the study of theory. It is this institutional state of affairs, too, that is being called into question by the skeptics — who, paradoxically, tend to be among those responsible for the very phenomenon they seem to be contesting.

Second, a word of caution. For the Christian literary scholar who has not shared in the obsession with theory that has marked the profession for the past two decades, the current skepticism regarding theory may seem a tempting excuse to remain ignorant or scornful of it. But to succumb to this temptation would be a mistake. In the first place, it is important to recognize that the decline of Christian literary criticism in the

3. For an analysis of the literary institution's tendency to diminish the influence of critical theory by turning it into just another "field," see Graff's *Professing Literature.*

profession has coincided with the rise of theory. Christian literary scholars need, therefore, to understand the theoretical turn of the profession in order to break out of their largely self-imposed isolation and re-open the dialogue with their secular colleagues. It makes no difference whether or not the era of Theory is coming to an end, since historical knowledge is essential to an understanding of the present and the future. But there is a second and even more important reason why Christian literary scholars ought to take theory seriously — namely, that an encounter with it can reform and revitalize Christian literary study itself. This, at any rate, is the conviction that lies behind the present volume. Yet it is a conviction that many members of the profession are calling into question as they begin to doubt the value of theory.

AGAINST THEORY

One of the best ways to get at the question of the value of critical theory is through the arguments of the so-called neopragmatists, a group of theorists who, like their philosophical namesakes, challenge established theoretical assumptions on the grounds that they do not reflect actual practice.[4] The best-known advocate of neopragmatism in the field of literary criticism is undoubtedly Stanley Fish, whose notorious *Is There a Text in This Class?* announced two theses that have greatly influenced subsequent thinking about critical theory.

The first thesis concerns the *nature* of criticism, which, according to Fish, is "persuasive" rather than "demonstrative." As critics, he argues,

---

4. The most prominent advocate of neopragmatism in contemporary philosophy is Richard Rorty. One must not make the mistake of identifying him with his literary counterparts too quickly, however. See Rorty's critique of Steven Knapp and Walter Benn Michaels and their reply in *Against Theory*.

> we try to persuade others to our beliefs because if they believe
> what we believe, they will, as a consequence of those beliefs,
> see what we see; and the facts to which we point in order to
> support our interpretations will be as obvious to them as they
> are to us. Indeed, this is the whole of critical activity, an attempt
> on the part of one party to alter the beliefs of another so that
> the evidence cited by the first will be seen *as* evidence by the
> second. In the more familiar model of critical activity (codified
> in the dogma and practices of New Criticism) the procedure is
> exactly the reverse: evidence available apart from any particular
> belief is brought in to judge between competing beliefs, or, as
> we call them in literary studies, interpretations. This is a model
> derived from an analogy to the procedures of logic and scientific
> inquiry, and basically it is a model of demonstration in which
> interpretations are either confirmed or disconfirmed by facts
> that are independently specified. The model I have been arguing
> for, on the other hand, is a model of persuasion in which the
> facts that one cites are available only because an interpretation
> . . . has already been assumed. (365-66)

If Fish's argument is right, then critics who aim for *the* correct
interpretation of a text are fundamentally mistaken about the
nature of criticism. The text is not, as they assume, an independently available fact by which they can judge the adequacy
of their interpretations. Rather, the text is accessible only
through their interpretations of it, which determine what they
see in the text.

Consider the case of Blake's "The Tyger," one of Fish's
main examples from *Is There a Text in This Class?* Is the tyger
of the poem (A) simply the image of a creature that, like the
lamb, reflects one aspect of its Maker's wondrous nature? Or is
it (B) an emblem of evil, so that the poem is really an allegory
of the problem of theodicy? Or is it (C) an analogue of nuclear
holocaust? Or is it (D) an ambiguous symbol that embodies all
of these meanings? The traditional critic, according to Fish,
thinks that one of these interpretations (or some other interpretation) is correct because it fits the facts of the poem better
than the others. For example, the critic who subscribes to in-

terpretation B might point to the poem's weeping stars as evidence that the tyger must, contrary to interpretation A, bring evil upon them. If only interpreter A will set aside his interpretation long enough to see this and other facts about the poem, he will conclude that interpretation B is, after all, the right one. What interpreter B fails to realize, in Fish's view, is that the weeping stars are *themselves* open to interpretation and cannot therefore function as independent evidence. Interpreter A, that is, will not see the stars as weeping because the tyger brings evil upon them; he will see their tears as a sign of wonder rather than of grief. In other words, the two interpreters take the so-called fact of the weeping stars to be two very different things. Thus it is, Fish concludes, that interpreters determine what counts as evidence on the basis of their own prior beliefs; there are no interpretation-free facts. It follows that there is no such thing as *the* correct interpretation of "The Tyger."

Fish's second thesis concerns the *consequences* of his own argument. What are its implications for the practice of literary criticism? "The answer," says Fish, "is none whatsoever":

> That is, it does not follow from what I have been saying that you should go out and do literary criticism in a certain way or refrain from doing it in other ways. The reason for this is that the position I have been presenting is not one that you (or anyone else) could live by. Its thesis is that whatever seems to you to be obvious and inescapable is only so within some institutional or conventional structure, and that means that you can never operate outside some such structure, even if you are persuaded by the thesis. As soon as you descend from your theoretical reasoning about your assumptions, you will once again inhabit them and you will inhabit them without any reservations whatsoever. (370)

One might think that Fish's argument about the nature of criticism would lead to sheer anarchy in practice. After all, if the four readings of "The Tyger" cited above are equally "correct," aren't we admitting that there are no constraints upon interpretation, no way to tell a valid reading of a poem from an invalid one? Not at all, says Fish. In fact, interpretation couldn't occur *without* constraints, for it is the existence of such constraints that constitutes interpretation and distinguishes it from mere caprice. These constraints are defined and upheld by the institution of literary study, which discriminates between valid and invalid readings. Thus the belief that Blake's tyger is a basketball simply doesn't count as an interpretation of the poem, although one can theorize a situation in which it would. It is true, of course, that the constraints the institution places upon interpretation can and do change. For example, interpretation C — that the tyger is an analogue of nuclear holocaust — would not have counted as an interpretation when old-style literary history dominated the profession. But this is very different from the claim that anything goes. Hence Fish's argument cannot be called subversive, skeptical as it is.

Although his argument had radical implications for critical theory, Fish was concerned primarily with the practice of criticism, not critical theory as such. It was left for his fellow neopragmatists Steven Knapp and Walter Benn Michaels to state the case against critical theory in its strongest and most controversial form in their essay "Against Theory." In that deliberately provocative piece, Knapp and Michaels cleverly transferred Fish's skeptical conclusions about *criticism* to *critical theory,* or what they take to be critical theory — namely, "a special project in literary criticism: the attempt to govern the interpretation of particular texts by appealing to an account of interpretation in general" (11). (This definition, they observe, excludes other special projects such as narratology, stylistics, and prosody, which are actually "empirical" rather than "theoretical.") For example, Knapp and Michaels accept Fish's conclusion that the traditional view of the nature of criticism — namely, that it is capable of demonstration — is mistaken; they just go on to argue that theory is supposed to make such demonstration possible, and that theory as such is therefore mistaken. Similarly, they accept Fish's conclusion that his argument has no consequences for critical practice; they just go on to argue that this is equally true of theory as a whole. But there is one major difference between Fish's argument and that of Knapp and Michaels. Whereas Fish denies that his argument has any implications for critical practice, Knapp and Michaels assert that their argument has one all-important implication for critical theory. "If we are right," Knapp and Michaels conclude, "then the whole enterprise of critical theory is mistaken and should be abandoned" (12).

When Knapp and Michaels argue that theory should be abandoned, they mean theory in both its "foundationalist" and its "deconstructive" modes:

> Contemporary theory has taken two forms. Some theorists have sought to ground the reading of literary texts in methods designed to guarantee the objectivity and validity of interpretations. Others, impressed by the inability of such procedures to produce agreement among interpreters, have translated that failure into an alternative mode of theory that denies the possibility of correct interpretation. Our aim here is not to choose between these two alternatives but rather to show that both rest on a single mistake, a mistake that is central to theory per se. (11)

More specifically, foundationalists like E. D. Hirsch try to solve the problems of textual meaning and interpretive belief *methodologically* by grounding meaning in intention and belief in knowledge. Deconstructionists like Paul de Man, on the other hand, conclude from the failure of method that meaning is indeterminate and belief arbitrary. But both sides, according to Knapp and Michaels, are wrong. "In our view," they brazenly declare, "the mistake on which all critical theory rests has been to imagine that these problems are real. In fact, . . . such problems only seem real — and theory itself only seems possible or relevant — when theorists fail to recognize the fundamental inseparability of the elements involved" (12). The meaning of a text cannot be determined by appealing to intention because meaning *just is* expressed intention. Nor can an interpreter's beliefs be justified by appealing to knowledge because knowledge *just is* true belief. In short, since foundationalist arguments are circular, the idea of a theory-governed *method* of interpretation is suspect. But this does not mean, as the deconstructionist thinks, that we can't fix the meaning of our texts or hold our beliefs to be reliable. These acts are part of our critical practice, and interpreters will continue to perform them irrespective of the conflicting dictates of theory.

Consider once again the case of "The Tyger." The foundationalist will argue that there is one correct interpretation of the poem — namely, the one that corresponds to Blake's intention. If Blake meant the poem to be read literally, then interpretation A (or some other literal reading) is correct: the tyger is just a tiger. But if Blake meant us to read the poem figuratively, then interpretation B (or some other figurative reading) is correct: the tyger is a trope of evil. The deconstructionist, on the other hand, will argue that the text of the poem erases any trace of "Blake's" intention, playing the literal and figurative readings off against each other in an undecidable conundrum. As far as Knapp and Michaels are concerned, however, both of these views are false theoretical abstractions from the actual practice of interpreting "The Tyger." In practice, I don't *first* decide what Blake's intention was and *then* determine the meaning of the poem, as if Blake's intention were somehow available apart from its expression in the text. Rather, I decide what Blake's intention was *by* determining the meaning of the text. Nor is it the case, as the deconstructionist would have it, that I can't decide what the poem means. In *theory* I may have no reason to prefer one reading over another, lacking independent knowledge of Blake's intention. But in *practice* I will regard one reading as better than the others, because in practice what counts is not independent knowledge of Blake's intention, which is impossible, but my beliefs about Blake and his poem.

The upshot of all this is that the reader of "The Tyger" is, as far as Knapp and Michaels are concerned, perfectly justified in ignoring critical theory. It is incapable of fulfilling its declared purpose: to govern the way readers interpret the poem. From this it follows, according to Knapp and Michaels, that critical theory has no reason to exist.

Stanley Fish himself, be it noted, is more charitable toward (or more self-interested in) theory than his protégés. He accepts Knapp and Michaels' definition of critical theory and agrees that it does not have the consequences it purports to have, but he is not willing to abandon it altogether. For critical theory is, like interpretation, a valued practice within the institution of literary study. "As a practice," he says, "theory has all the . . . consequences of other practices." It is just that these consequences "are not theoretical consequences; that is, they are not the consequences of a practice that stands in a relationship of precedence and mastery to other practices. . . . So, even though the thesis that theory has no consequences holds only when the consequences are of a certain kind, they are the only consequences that matter, since they are the consequences that would mark theory off as special" ("Consequences" 125). In other words, if the actual consequences of theory are all consequences that result from other practices as well, then theory's claim to be necessary is unfounded. But according to Fish, this need not lead to the disappearance of theory from the institution of literary study. As long as the profession continues to reward theorists, critical theory will continue.

IN SUPPORT OF THEORY

What are we to make of the neopragmatists' bold and challenging attack on critical theory? We can begin by thanking them for charting us a course between the Scylla of foundationalism and the Charybdis of deconstruction, both of which purport to control critical practice but fail to do so in principle. If this is what theory is, who needs it? But is this really what theory is? It may indeed be the case that Knapp and Michaels'

definition of theory as "the attempt to govern the interpretation
of particular texts by appealing to an account of interpretation
in general" is prevalent among theorists themselves. But much
of what goes on in the name of "theory" clearly escapes this
definition. Some theories do purport to govern interpretation,
but not by appealing to an account of interpretation in general.
This category would seem to include ideological theories like
Marxist, psychoanalytic, and feminist theories, but also technical ones like formalist, reader-response, and historicist theories.
On the other hand, some theories do present themselves as
accounts of interpretation in general but don't purport to govern
interpretation. Linguistics and hermeneutics would seem to be
theories of this kind. Knapp and Michaels offer no good reason
to stop calling all of these valuable projects "theory."[5]

The neopragmatists are misleading, therefore, when they
imply that the nature of "theory" in Knapp and Michaels'
narrow sense is the nature of theory as such. By the same token,
they are misleading when they say that theory has no consequences. Clearly all of the theories in the first category just
mentioned have decisive consequences for the practice of criticism; a Marxist reading of "The Tyger," for example, will be
very different from a formalist reading. But it is not just that
Knapp and Michaels' conception of theory is too narrow. It is
also that, in demystifying foundationalist theory (and, by implication, deconstruction), they go to the opposite extreme.
Foundationalists may be wrong to think they can discover *the*
correct interpretation of a text by grounding meaning in intention and belief in knowledge, but Knapp and Michaels are
wrong to collapse these concepts into each other. In this respect,
as W. J. T. Mitchell has observed, "Knapp and Michaels out-
theorize the theorists. Only in theory would anyone want to
deny that there is a difference between meaning and intention;

---

5. Fish offers a defense of Knapp and Michaels' definition of theory
in "Consequences," included in his most recent collection of essays, *Doing
What Comes Naturally.*

in practice, we use the distinction all the time. Only in theory would we want (as Knapp and Michaels do) to collapse the distinction between 'knowledge' and 'true belief' (in practice, to say that I *believe* something to be the case is tantamount to saying that I do not *know* it for a fact)" (9). Mitchell's observation suggests that theorists in turn can out-pragmatize the neopragmatists.

This is exactly what the legal theorist Ronald Dworkin has done in his debate with Fish and Michaels over the problems of interpretive belief and textual meaning. Briefly, Fish argues that a text cannot constrain its interpretation because the text is itself dependent on the interpreter's beliefs. Interpreting, therefore, is really no different from inventing. But this does not lead to subjectivism, according to Fish, since interpreters are themselves constrained by the interpretive rules of their profession. To this argument Dworkin replies, "I cannot imagine a weaker constraint; anything that others could even recognize as an interpretation, no matter how juvenile or silly, by hypothesis passes this test. If Fish has not made interpretation wholly subjective, the difference is not noticeable to the naked eye" (295). In other words, Fish is simply wrong to conclude from the fact that interpretation is always dependent on the interpreter's beliefs that interpreting is really no different from inventing. His problem, according to Dworkin, is his "hidden assumption that interpretation must be homogeneous" (292), that "everything involving interpretation is alike" (294). The fact is, says Dworkin, that interpretation is an "internally structured" and "complex" affair involving "various kinds and levels of belief" (293). Thus a more stable belief can constrain a more variable one; such internal constraints enable us pragmatically to distinguish interpreting from inventing without falling back on the naive claim that texts constrain interpretation independently of belief.

Dworkin's observation provides a necessary correction of my Fishian (not to say "Fishy") account of interpreting "The Tyger." According to Fish's theory, we recall, Blake's weeping stars cannot serve as evidence by which to judge competing readings of the poem, for their meaning also changes from interpretation to interpretation. Dworkin would accept the second half of this claim, but would deny the first half. That is, it may be true that the stars' tears can be interpreted as a sign of wonder or as a sign of grief. Nevertheless, the interpreter's beliefs about the weeping stars are not of the same order as his or her beliefs about the tyger. The weeping stars are, after all, more determinate in meaning than the tyger: they may be weeping out of wonder or out of grief, but either way they are shedding tears — a response that is associated with a limited range of emotions. For this reason, they *can* serve as evidence by which to judge at least some competing interpretations of the poem. The weeping stars, in other words, *do* constrain the interpreter's beliefs about the tyger, which is the cause of their emotion. The tyger must be something that causes wonder or grief; it can't be something that causes hilarity or boredom. Thus Fish is wrong to claim that it is only the institution of literary study, not particular texts, that constrains interpretation, for the more determinate meanings of "The Tyger" restrict our beliefs about the less determinate meanings.

By the same token, Dworkin objects to the neopragmatist identification of meaning and intention, which he calls "the new intentional fallacy." Like their conception of the institutional constraints on interpretation, the neopragmatists' conception of intention turns out to be empty. For Knapp and Michaels, the author intends the text to mean whatever it does mean, so that intention is discovered simply by interpreting the text. As Dworkin points out, however, "The idea of intention, so construed, can play no useful role in interpretation because it is simply a phrase used to report interpretations already established in some other way" (308-9). Dworkin himself, on the other hand, pragmatically offers us a useful conception of intention without falling back on the methodologist's claim that the interpretation of a text must conform to the author's intention. He draws a distinction between "questions which it might be plausible to think we can only answer by attending to the intentions of a particular 'author,' like questions about the sense in which an ambiguous word should be read, and more general interpretive questions [like questions about 'what the characters are really like']. It is plain," he says, "that we can form beliefs about these larger interpretive questions without attributing the pertinent intentions to anyone who meets our quite different tests for counting as the historical author of the text in question" (310). It makes sense, for example, to ask what Blake intended by the *word* "tyger," whereas it makes no sense to ask whether he intended the poetic *character* designated by this word to be like a nuclear holocaust.

In both cases, then — the case of interpretive belief and the case of textual meaning — Dworkin's theoretical point is that interpretation is a much more structured and complex matter than the neopragmatists admit. Surprisingly, it is this insight that makes his theoretical argument more pragmatic than the neopragmatists' anti-theoretical one. Thus we are forced to conclude that the neopragmatists are wrong not only about the nature and consequences of critical theory but also about the specific problems of textual meaning and interpretive belief.

Why, then, should we listen to them? There are two very good reasons for listening carefully to what the neopragmatists have to say. First, they force us to think through the nature and consequences of the most influential new field in the profession. Rightly understood, critical theory is both legitimate and effectual, and the neopragmatists are prompting theorists to reconsider what they do. Second, even when their arguments are bad, the neopragmatists have a knack for locating crucial critical problems, posing them clearly and succinctly. The very failure of the neopragmatists to dissolve the problems of textual meaning and interpretive belief shows how crucial such problems are. Not that the neopragmatists are always wrong. On the contrary, they have made some sound arguments and dispelled some mistaken assumptions. All of this suggests that neopragmatism has, contrary to its stated purpose, made a major contribution to critical theory. For "critical theory" is, in its most general sense, just what critics do when they reflect on their practice.

RETHINKING THEORY AND PRACTICE

If the "Against Theory" debate teaches us anything, it is that our current notions of theory and practice are inadequate. Consider once again the picture of professional literary study painted by Stanley Fish. On one side there is Theory: totally misconceived, utterly ineffectual, a ghost in the machine of criticism — albeit a highly paid one. On the other side is Practice: interpretation in the absence of theoretical guidance and empirical data alike, hermeneutical license restrained only by the rules of the institutional game and the eloquence of professional sophists — business as usual. Of course this is a caricature of Fish's portrait of the profession, which is itself, one hopes, also a caricature. Yet the exaggeration of a good caricature is based on a real tendency in the subject. In the case of contemporary literary study, that tendency is the impending divorce between theory and practice brought about by the use of critical theory to control the interpretation of literature, and by the subsequent reaction against theory.

In order to understand the origins of this regrettable state of affairs, it is important to remember how profoundly contemporary literary study has been affected by the general conditions of modernity. "Today," observed Hans-Georg Gadamer over a decade ago, anticipating the current mood of the literary profession, "practice tends to be defined by a kind of opposition to theory. There is an antidogmatic tone to the word *practice*, a suspicion against the merely theoretic." This suspicion, Gadamer argues, results from the way in which modern science has transformed our notions of theory and practice. On the one hand, theory is now conceived instrumentally: it "is no longer the quintessence of knowledge and of what is worth knowing," but rather "a way of advancing and penetrating into unexplored and unmastered realms." On the other hand, practice is conceived technically: "in starting from the modern notion of science when we talk about practice, we have been forced in the direction of thinking of the application of science" (69-70). The end result of this transformation is "the degeneration of practice into mere technique," the mere application of an already established theory (74). In the case of modern literary study, the practice of interpretation has degenerated into the learned technique of applying a preconceived theory, let us say deconstruction, to a text — any text — in order to produce a predictable deconstructive reading of it.[6]

Thus far Gadamer's position closely resembles that of the neopragmatists. Like them, he is suspicious of the attempt of modern critical theory to dominate interpretive practice. Unlike the neopragmatists, however, Gadamer is unwilling simply to oppose practice to theory.[7] Rather, he seeks an alternative conception of theory that is capable of breaking the circle of modernity. "As far as hermeneutics is concerned," Gadamer ventures, "it is quite to the point to confront the separation of theory from practice entailed in the modern notion of theoretical science and practical-technical application with an idea of knowledge that has taken the opposite path leading from practice toward making it aware of itself theoretically" (130). With this formulation we are back to the definition of theory cited at the end of the previous section: "reflection on practice." As Gadamer explains, this is the Aristotelian, as opposed to the modern scientific, conception of theory as the "cultivation of a natural gift" and "a theoretically heightened awareness of it." In the case of literary study, it follows that "hermeneutics is

---

6. Crews has been attempting to combat this kind of theoreticized reading lately through his book reviews in *The New York Review of Books*.

7. Knapp and Michaels announce their differences with Gadamer in "Against Theory 2: Hermeneutics and Deconstruction."

more than just a method of the sciences. . . . Above all it refers to a natural human capacity" (114). It is the combination of critical theory and natural capacity that constitutes the practice of interpretation, not, as the neopragmatists would have it, merely the institutional conventions of the day.

But what exactly is critical theory according to the Aristotelian account? It is nothing less than a branch of ethics or "practical philosophy"; that is why the practice of interpretation is more than the mere application of a preconceived theory to a text. Gadamer insists that "what separates [practical philosophy] fundamentally from technical expertise is that it expressly asks the question of the good too — for example, about the best way of life or about the best constitution of the state. It does not merely master an ability, like technical expertise, whose task is set by an outside authority. . . . All this holds true for hermeneutics as well" (93). The practice of interpretation, therefore, is not simply the mastery of a technique for the mass production of readings, but requires reflection on its own relation to the good; it is less the application of a theory to the text than the application of what the text teaches to the interpreter's situation. Such application presupposes that the interpreter desires to understand the text rather than to dominate it, which is why Aristotelian ethics recognizes an intellectual virtue proper to the practice of interpretation: *synesis,* "being habitually understanding toward others" (132). This Aristotelian virtue, it is to be feared, has been all but lost in today's theorizing and theoreticized reading of literature, distant as they are from interpretation as a practice.[8]

However, while *synesis* may be an essential precondition of critical theory conceived as a branch of ethics, it is not a substitute for it. Theory is necessary because interpretation aims at the good, not simply at the understanding of particular texts. But theory is, on the Aristotelian model of interpretation, al-

8. For an analytical account of the Aristotelian concept of a practice, see Alasdair MacIntyre's *After Virtue,* especially chapter 14.

ready implicit in the reader's felt responsibility to reflect on the relationship between the particular text he is interpreting, his own situation, and his conception of the good. Given a sense of this responsibility, it is perfectly understandable that a modern reader might, for example, interpret Blake's tyger as an analogue of nuclear holocaust. For the question posed by the poem's speaker, the question of the genesis of such terrible beauty, thereby becomes our question, a new question put to the present by the past. In the nuclear age, Blake's question becomes rhetorical and ironic, for it is no immortal hand but a very mortal one that has split the atom, split theory from practice, and obliterated Hiroshima and Nagasaki. For us, "The Tyger" thus becomes a warning, a reminder that it was once thought that God had reserved certain possibilities of creation unto himself. It is when the theorist begins to meditate on this kind of interpretation that she discovers her true calling: to reflect on critical practice in the light of moral and, indeed, religious belief.

AN AGENDA FOR CHRISTIAN THEORISTS

Where does all of this leave the Christian theorist? What is the task of Christian theory today? In order to address this final question properly, it is necessary to understand the modern history of Christian theory, which can be usefully charted with the help of Nicholas Wolterstorff's model of the development of Christian institutions of higher learning. Wolterstorff traces this development through three stages, the first of which is the stage of evangelism and piety. In this stage, the Christian institution regards itself as a bastion of opposition in a hostile secular society. Part of its educational mission is to judge and, when necessary, to condemn the culture of this secular society. The duty of the Christian critic in this first stage of development, accordingly, is to evaluate his culture's literary texts according to Christian standards, the definition of which is the task of the Christian theorist. Typically this definition involves some conception of doctrinal orthodoxy: a set of dogmas or propositions that literary texts either do or do not imply.

The second stage in the development of the Christian institution, according to Wolterstorff, is the stage of culture. Abandoning its reactionary stance, the institution comes to regard itself as, like its secular counterparts, the heir of the great tradition of Western culture. Its educational mission is to demonstrate the linkages between Western culture and the Christian faith and to enable full participation in the institutions of the society it once condemned. Evangelism and piety are not left behind; rather, they are subsumed in the larger cultural mandate of Stage Two. In keeping with this mandate, the second-stage Christian critic shifts his attention from the task of evaluation to that of interpretation. The important thing now is to understand and appreciate the literary classics of Western culture and to trace their images, themes, and influences to their roots in the Judeo-Christian tradition. The need to evaluate these texts is not forgotten, but the strict test of doctrinal orthodoxy is now regarded as culturally impoverished.

In this stage of development, the Christian theorist's role is dramatically transformed. On the one hand, she is freed from the necessity of defining doctrinal standards of evaluation. On the other hand, the practical critic, busily occupied with explications and empirical studies, has no immediate need of theoretical guidance. So the theorist turns instead to the larger task of developing a Christian aesthetic: a Christian theory of literature that will specify the indebtedness of the metaphysics of literary creation to Christian theology. In this manner doctrinal orthodoxy is salvaged at a time when the application of a dogmatic or propositional test is considered a sign of literary insensitivity. Traditional dogmas and propositions are still important, but their function is now descriptive rather than prescriptive (or proscriptive): they are universal, timeless truths that account for all of literature rather than the specific intellectual context of a limited class of texts. The general aesthetic merit of a text, rather than the orthodoxy of its implied dogmas or propositions, now marks its underlying harmony with Christian doctrine.

The third stage in the evolution of the Christian institution of higher learning is the stage of society — a stage that most Christian institutions, according to Wolterstorff, are just beginning to enter.[9] In this stage the institution returns to its oppositional roots, as it were, without in any way abandoning the cultural heritage it has now claimed as its own. The educational mission of the Stage Three institution is not simply to enable full participation in society, as in Stage Two, but to transform society in order to bring about *shalom*. This mission may well bring the institution into conflict with the secular society and its culture once again, as in Stage One. The difference is that the Christian institution, with all the cultural resources of Stage Two at its disposal, will now regard evangelism and piety as inseparable from the quest for social justice. The Christian critic, too, will participate in this quest, exercising a preferential option for the literature of the oppressed and defending all whose flourishing is enabled or hindered by literary texts. While the third stage of Christian criticism thus involves a return to evaluation, its focus is no longer simply the orthodoxy of the text's stated or implied *doctrines,* but more importantly the nature of the literary *practice* that has produced it — a practice which, because it is a form of action that makes other actions possible, has social consequences that advance or inhibit *shalom.*

What, then, is the task of the Christian theorist in Stage Three? It is, I would propose, to develop *a theory of critical*

9. Wolterstorff's conception of Stage Three emphasizes certain fields and activities within the institution, such as the social sciences and Christian service programs. Properly understood, however, it implies a general transformation of the institution as a whole, including fields and activities that at first glance seem less directly involved in Stage Three — literary study, for example, or the selection of trustees and administrators.

orthopraxis, in which "theory" means not the attempt to dominate practice but rather reflection on practice in the light of belief. The aim of such theorizing is to discover what kind of critical practice advances *shalom.* While it is impossible to know the course such theorizing will take — such foreknowledge would be possible only if theory is master of practice — it surely will recognize the role of the Christian *virtues* in critical orthopraxis. What it means to interpret a text humbly and patiently, what it means to evaluate a literary practice in faith, hope, and charity — these are questions so foreign to this era of Theory that it is difficult to take them seriously. Nevertheless, they are questions that call for serious reflection on the part of the Christian theorist, guided by the practice of the faithful criticism of Stage One and the charitable criticism of Stage Two. In the final analysis, however, the criticism of these earlier stages is not sufficient, for orthodoxy is not a guarantee of orthopraxis any more than doctrine is a warrant of virtue. The Christian theorist, therefore, must work in hope, preparing for the new critical practice of Stage Three, upon which the future of Christian literary study will depend.

WORKS CITED

(Titles with an asterisk are recommended as introductions.)

Crews, Frederick. *Skeptical Engagements.* New York: Oxford University Press, 1986.

de Man, Paul. *Allegories of Reading.* New Haven: Yale University Press, 1979.

Dworkin, Ronald. "My Reply to Stanley Fish (and Walter Benn Michaels): Please Don't Talk About Objectivity Any More." In *The Politics of Interpretation,* rev. ed., ed. W. J. T. Mitchell. Chicago: University of Chicago Press, 1983.

Fish, Stanley. "Consequences." In *Against Theory: Literary Studies and the New Pragmatism*, ed. W. J. T. Mitchell. Chicago: University of Chicago Press, 1985.

————. *Doing What Comes Naturally: Change, Rhetoric and the Practice of Theory in Literary and Legal Studies.* Durham: Duke University Press, 1989.

*————. *Is There a Text in This Class? The Authority of Interpretive Communities.* Cambridge: Harvard University Press, 1980.

Gadamer, Hans-Georg. *Reason in the Age of Science.* Trans. Frederick G. Lawrence. Cambridge: MIT Press, 1981.

*Graff, Gerald. *Professing Literature: An Institutional History.* Chicago: University of Chicago Press, 1987.

*Hirsch, E. D. *The Validity of Interpretation.* New Haven: Yale University Press, 1967.

Knapp, Steven, and Walter Benn Michaels. "Against Theory." In *Against Theory: Literary Studies and the New Pragmatism,* ed. W. J. T. Mitchell. Chicago: University of Chicago Press, 1985.

————. "Against Theory 2: Hermeneutics and Deconstruction." *Critical Inquiry* 14 (Autumn 1987): 49-68.

————. "A Reply to Richard Rorty: What Is Pragmatism?" In *Against Theory: Literary Studies and the New Pragmatism,* ed. W. J. T. Mitchell. Chicago: University of Chicago Press, 1985.

MacIntyre, Alasdair. *After Virtue.* Notre Dame: University of Notre Dame Press, 1981.

Mitchell, W. J. T. "Introduction: Pragmatic Theory." In *Against Theory: Literary Studies and the New Pragmatism,* ed. W. J. T. Mitchell. Chicago: University of Chicago Press, 1985.

Rorty, Richard. "Philosophy without Principles." In *Against Theory: Literary Studies and the New Pragmatism,* ed. W. J. T. Mitchell. Chicago: University of Chicago Press, 1985.

Wolterstorff, Nicholas. "The Mission of the Christian College at the End of the 20th Century." *Reformed Journal,* June 1983, pp. 14-18.

AFTERWORD

Leland Ryken

THE ESSAYS IN THIS BOOK ARE EXAMPLES OF CHRISTIAN literary criticism. We should feel no awkwardness in that label. One of the legacies that reader-centered criticism has bequeathed is the concept of interpretive communities. An interpretive community is simply a group of literary scholars who share a common set of interests, beliefs, and experiences, and who read and discuss literature in terms of that agenda. Every literary critic belongs to one or more interpretive communities. Christian literary critics are such an interpretive community.

The purpose of this afterword is to cast a retrospective look over the essays that make up this volume and in so doing to achieve a twofold purpose — to identify the underlying trends in current literary theory that constitute the context of Christian literary criticism, and to clarify the methodology that Christian critics employ. On the basis of the preceding essays, it is possible to generalize about both topics.

THE LANDSCAPE OF CURRENT LITERARY THEORY

The contributors to this volume have signaled their awareness of the travel guide to current criticism that I am about to sketch. Their signals will be more evident if the context is delineated systematically. My map is intended to be descriptive rather than overtly evaluative. Christian critics, including those who contributed to this volume, do not agree among themselves about how hostile or friendly these trends are to a Christian perspective.

Many of the leading trends on the current critical scene can be traced back to the rise of reader-centered criticism. The chief legacy of this movement has been a new subjectivism in literary study. Critics today feel free to talk about literature in terms of their personal perceptions. They feel no obligation to adhere to a party line or to muster their allegiance to a received interpretation when they discuss works of literature. If anything, there is a tendency toward iconoclasm in literary interpretation.

The new subjectivism has produced a radical pluralism in approaches to literary study. Literary study has rarely been monolithic, but until recently the things that critics did with works of literature fell into a defined range of categories. Literary critics no longer speak a common language, nor is there any clear consensus about what critics should do with works of literature. This radical pluralism has produced a chaotic and bewildering situation in which undergraduate students cannot possibly grasp what is going on behind the scenes, in which young scholars find it difficult to know what direction to take, and in which older scholars undertake their work with the feeling that their approach to literature is hopelessly obsolete. When scholars from other disciplines (such as biblical scholarship) look at the amorphous phenomenon of contemporary literary criticism, they are utterly confused by the rival approaches.

The subjectivism and pluralism of current criticism have produced the isolation of the critic. In a way analogous to what twentieth-century writers have done, many leading critical theorists and analysts of literary texts have cultivated a special-

ized technical vocabulary that isolates their discourse from all
but a handful of trained literary scholars interested in the same
critical approach. There was a time when literary scholars la-
mented that they could not communicate with scholars in other
disciplines. Today they cannot communicate across the chasms
within their own discipline. The isolation of literary study even
from people who teach literature at the college level has become
an identifiable feature of the current scene. For a person to
become a firsthand expert in all the approaches covered in this
book has become a virtual impossibility.

Underlying many of the critical schools today, moreover,
is a prevailing skepticism. Its commonest form is skepticism
about the ability of language and literature to communicate
precise meaning. The most extreme form of this skepticism is,
of course, deconstruction. This influential movement is rooted
in theories that view language as an arbitrary system of signs.
Adherents of this theory typically reduce a text to a series of
contradictions and ambiguities in an attempt to show that it
has no obvious or determinate meaning.

One such critic, Lawrence Lipking, described his classroom strategy in *Profession,* a publication of the Modern Language Association. When Lipking teaches Yeats' "Sailing to
Byzantium," he dismantles the poem into an endless web of
contradictions. By the end of the class session, he has cowed
his students into believing that "we do not command our own
language, and we cannot escape it. Hence the true 'meaning' of
'Sailing to Byzantium' . . . is the impossibility of ever arriving
at a true meaning. . . . Some of [the students] now perceive the
class as . . . an analysis of how the poem does not make sense."
To make this incident more noteworthy, let me add that Lipking is one of the editors of *The Norton Anthology of English
Literature.*

The politicizing of literary study is another current development. By this I mean approaches to literature that use literature and its study to advance a social program. Feminism
and Marxism are the clearest examples. Critics in these tradi-

tions make it clear that their interest in literature is motivated by social and political goals. To use a distinction that C. S. Lewis popularized, these critics are interested in using literature rather than receiving it.

Even criticism that is not as overtly political as this illustrates another feature of the current landscape — the tendency of criticism to be ideologically based. Critics are increasingly willing to show that their criticism is rooted in a philosophy of life. Much of this philosophy is broadly skeptical, and much of it is Marxist. At the very least, critics are currently prone to talk about the presuppositions with which they approach the study of literature and to align themselves with specific interpretive communities. A goal of the present volume has been to uncover the ideological undergirdings of contemporary literary theories.

Rejection of the recent critical past is another salient feature of the current critical landscape. Proponents of critical theories are today rarely content simply to assert their own position. It has become a ritual for writers of critical essays to take time to pay their disrespects to Romantic theories of the imagination, formalist criticism, the humanist tradition, and Northrop Frye. In fact, essays are incomplete if they do not re-enact this ritual slaying. Harold Bloom's Freudian theory of a literary Oedipus complex is truer of contemporary literary theorists than it ever was of writers.

Another trend of the moment is increasing hostility to Christianity. The critical establishment has been alarmingly secular for a long time. But indifference to Christianity is today moving in the direction of hostility. In an article entitled "A Critic against the Christians," Jonathan Culler charges that the problem with literary study in the United States is its "unreflective acceptance of Christianity" and its covert "legitimation" of Christianity. He claims that teachers of literature have "abandoned the historic mission of education," which is "to fight superstition and religious dogmatism." Culler looks back with disgust to an occasion when he actually voted to help fund an

English Institute session on the Hebrew Bible. "Not one of us" on the committee, he now recalls, "thought to argue that celebration of this powerfully racist and sexist text was pernicious and inappropriate."

In his 1986 MLA presidential address, J. Hillis Miller painted a naively optimistic picture of the current state of literary studies, especially the triumph of theory. Even if one agrees with Miller's assessment, I do not see how anyone reading the address can avoid sensing how thoroughly irrelevant Christianity is to Miller's picture of literary study. There is simply no place for Christian criticism in the landscape he paints. There was not a single Christian critic among Miller's heroes. The enthusiasm for theory in current criticism turns out to be far more censoring than it pretends to be. Miller himself ended his address by scolding all who refuse to jump on the deconstruction bandwagon.

There are more subtle forms that the anti-Christian and secular bias can take. One is the sneering review of books that have a Christian bias or display a sympathetic interest in Christianity. Another is the reinterpretation of Christian texts. If a critic finds the Christian element in Milton or T. S. Eliot objectionable, he or she simply ignores it and chooses other aspects of such writers' work for attention. I have seen discussions of Milton's Adam and Eve that dismiss their spiritual relationship to God as inconsequential to a twentieth-century reader and focus solely on their human relationship to each other.

Selectivity of material can also discriminate against Christianity. I remember sitting in a Spenser session at an MLA convention and hearing a leading Spenser scholar tell us, "Don't teach Book 1 of *The Faerie Queene*. There are many reasons to teach books other than Book 1." No doubt there are, if one wishes to divest *The Faerie Queene* of its Christianity. The Jewish author of a recent study of T. S. Eliot's literary theory explicitly admits his "lack of attention to the Christian aspect of Eliot's critical thought" on the grounds that he

(a) considers his "capacity for understanding Eliot as a Christian to be limited" and (b) thinks that the importance of Christianity for Eliot's philosophy of criticism "has been overemphasized" (Shusterman 3).

A final feature of the current critical landscape is the assault on the traditional canon of literary texts that are regarded as most worthy of study. The canon is under attack by critics who are skeptical of the veneration and meaning that generations of readers have attached to what is loosely called the great tradition. Various forces have converged to produce a climate of thinking in which a critic can write, "It can hardly be denied that the canonical tradition . . . is now dying from inward exhaustion and external erosion. . . . There seems no reason to believe that the canonical tradition will continue and no particular reason to regret that it's had its day" (Easthope 161-62). On this issue, as on other specific issues, there is no unanimity among Christian critics as to whether the trend is friend or foe. What is shared, however, is an awareness that the trends I have outlined are important and require a Christian assessment.

TOWARD A CHRISTIAN CRITICISM

Until recently, it was possible for Christian criticism to merge its identity with the critical establishment. Of course this compatibility carried a price tag. The temptation was great to rest content with the establishment's treatment of works of literature and even with its defense of literature. Since there was little overt hostility from established critical procedures, there was no impetus to do anything very radical or distinctive in developing a Christian aesthetic. Today, however, a cozy alliance between Christian criticism and the larger critical establishment is not an option. With no critical establishment on which to piggyback, Christian critics have no alternative but to establish their own identity. With the current critical scene in disarray, Christian critics have every reason to be themselves.

What, then, ought to characterize Christian critics as an interpretive community? As the essays in this book illustrate, there is no single answer to that question. We can, however, identify underlying principles that Christian critics share.

One is the acceptance of Christian doctrine and morality (both ultimately derived from the Bible) as constituting an authoritative framework of beliefs and values. T. S. Eliot stated this very succinctly in an essay entitled "Religion and Literature," which remains the best starting point on this issue: "What I believe to be incumbent upon all Christians is the duty of maintaining consciously certain standards and criteria of criticism over and above those applied by the rest of the world; and that by these criteria and standards everything that we read must be tested" (105).

If we add to this Eliot's comment that "literary criticism should be completed by criticism from a definite ethical and theological standpoint" (97), it is obvious that Christian criticism is based on a principle of integration. To integrate simply means to bring two things together. Christian criticism brings together either literature or literary theory and Christian truth and experience. All of the essays in this book begin by scrutinizing a current critical theory as it is in itself and then proceed to assess its premises and practices according to tenets of the Christian faith.

As Christian critics undertake such assessment, it becomes apparent that a Christian aesthetic must be based on the broad foundation of Christian doctrine as a whole. Contrary to some recent trends in Christian criticism, no single Christian doctrine will suffice as a basis for Christian literary criticism. As the authors of this volume have interacted with contemporary theories, they have evoked a wide range of Christian tenets. Nothing less than the whole grand edifice of Christian doctrine provides the scope and flexibility with which to deal with the multifariousness of literary theory and literature itself.

An aesthetic based on the broad foundation of Christian doctrine will intersect at virtually every turn with critical traditions from Aristotle through the latest critical fashion. Some of the intersections will produce collisions, while others will result in smooth mergers. The doctrine of Scripture or special revelation, for example, is on a collision course with deconstruction and other versions of the "prisonhouse-of-language" philosophy. The very fact that God revealed the most important truth that we can imagine in written and literary form commits Christians to a belief in the ability of language to communicate truth.

A given Christian doctrine might collide with one critical tradition and be compatible with another. The Christian belief that artistry and beauty have value and reflect the nature of God finds itself in conflict with various modern anti-art movements and with the tendency of much reader-response criticism to devalue artistic form and beauty. Conversely, the Christian affirmation of form and artistic craftsmanship as having value because God gave these gifts to humankind fits in very well with some varieties of formalist criticism, though Christian criticism must of course add the theological perspective.

We should note in passing, then, that a genuinely Christian criticism will not be totally distinctive from other criticism. It cannot avoid being influenced by other theories, nor should it attempt to avoid such influence. The assumed premise of some recent Christian critical theory is that if a viewpoint resembles an existing critical tradition, it is less than Christian. But surely it is possible for two critics to hold essentially the same idea about literature from different derivations. It is also possible to agree with part of an aesthetic theory and disagree with another part of it. One can agree, for example, with the prominence that the Romantics gave to the imagination in literary experience without accepting their ideas about the autonomy of the artist, their deification of the creative imagination, and their elevation of artists to the status of super-people.

The doctrines of common grace and natural revelation are

foundational to Christian criticism. Both doctrines assert that all truth is God's truth and that we do not need to inquire into the Christian orthodoxy of writers or critics before we know whether they have spoken the truth. Some Christian critics have been far too quick to regard as automatically unchristian any idea that can be traced to current critical theories. It is true that whenever Christian criticism corresponds in some ways to another literary theory, the possibility arises that it will in some sense be a Christianized version of hermeneutics or humanism or formalism or classicism or whatnot. But, as the essays in this volume demonstrate, there is nothing pernicious about this as long as the theory is genuinely Christian.

To some extent, Christian criticism will adapt itself to current popular trends in literary theory. If the truth about literature is partly derived by empirical means from the discipline of literary study itself, Christian critics will naturally find themselves attracted to one or another critical approach on grounds other than those of Christian doctrine. But once a critic has taken an interest in a critical approach such as feminism or New Historicism, the task of testing its presuppositions and conclusions begins. This methodology underlies most of the essays in the present volume. In general, the authors began with a sympathetic interest in their selected theory and then proceeded to assess its strengths and weaknesses by Christian principles.

But some current trends are too intransigent to the Christian faith to allow for syncretism. In such cases, Christian critics begin their critiques from an oppositional stance. Such a critique may be positive in the sense that a Christian critic may affirm the basic principle of an approach (such as the importance of language in the literary enterprise or the importance of ethical considerations to the critique of literature) and then develop a Christian view of it as an antithesis to prevailing theories.

To interact with current theories as the authors have done in this volume is half of the task of Christian literary theory.

The work that remains to be done is to develop a Christian aesthetic based on principles derived from the Christian critic's own agenda of interests, including Christian doctrine. For purposes of this book, we have allowed contemporary literary theory to set the agenda of topics. Many Christian critics legitimately object to such a procedure because the agenda of concerns in contemporary theory is often not of primary interest for a Christian critic. From this has stemmed the inadequate attention by Christian critics to contemporary theory that Clarence Walhout rightly laments in the introduction to this book. Christian critics feel a tension between their duty to interpret and assess current literary theory and their desire to devote their energies to a Christian aesthetic based on their own beliefs and interests.

The present volume has aimed to correct an imbalance by undertaking a Christian critique of contemporary literary theories. That undertaking should not be mistaken as an attempt to formulate a Christian aesthetic. The approach that has emerged is by the very nature of the case unsystematic and piecemeal. Yet it can legitimately be called an "approach" because the authors have all appealed to a standard of Christian belief as they have assessed various contemporary theories of literature.

Underlying the essays in this book has been the premise that literary criticism is as much a personal matter, as much the product of a personal sense of life and belief, as literature itself is. As Christian scholars, the contributors to this volume have interacted with contemporary literary theories in terms of who they are. They have illustrated what it means that Christian literary critics are an interpretive community in the current critical landscape. That community is linked at many points to other interpretive communities, but in its acceptance of Christian doctrine and morality as an authoritative foundation for belief, its distinctiveness is obvious.

WORKS CITED

Culler, Jonathan. "A Critic against the Christians." *Times Literary Supplement,* 23 Nov. 1984, pp. 1327-28.

Easthope, Anthony. *Poetry as Discourse.* New York: Methuen, 1983.

Eliot, T. S. "Religion and Literature." In *Selected Prose of T. S. Eliot,* ed. Frank Kermode, 97-106. New York: Harcourt Brace Jovanovich, 1975.

Lipking, Lawrence I. "The Practice of Theory." *Profession* 83 (1983): 21-28.

Miller, J. Hillis. "Presidential Address 1986: The Triumph of Theory, the Resistance to Reading, and the Question of the Material Base." *PMLA* 102 (1987): 281-91.

Shusterman, Richard. *T. S. Eliot and the Philosophy of Literary Criticism.* New York: Columbia University Press, 1988.

INDEX OF NAMES